Beyond Branding

BEYOND
branding

how the new values of transparency and integrity are changing the world of brands

edited by
nicholas ind

**KOGAN
PAGE**

London and Sterling, VA

A CarbonNeutral publication
To soak up the carbon dioxide emissions in the production of this book and to help protect our climate, the writers of *Beyond Branding* have planted native trees with Future Forests.

First published in Great Britain and the United States in 2003 by Kogan Page Limited
Paperback edition 2005

120 Pentonville Road
London N1 9JN
United Kingdom
www.kogan-page.co.uk

22883 Quicksilver Drive
Sterling VA 20166–2012
USA

ISBN 0 7494 4399 5

British Library Cataloguing-in-Publication Data

A CIP record for this book is available from the British Library.

Library of Congress Cataloging-in-Publication Data

Beyond branding : how the new values of transparency and integrity are changing the world of brands / edited by Nicholas Ind.
  p. cm.
Includes index.
 ISBN 0-7494-4399-5
 1. Brand name products. 2. Brand choice. 3. Product management. I. Ind. Nicholas.
 HD69.B7B49 2003
 658.8'27--dc22   2003018047

Typeset by Saxon Graphics Ltd, Derby
Printed and bound in Great Britain by Biddles Ltd, King's Lynn, Norfolk

Contents

Contributors

Malcolm Allan (Malcolm@inergy.org) is the founder and a director of three companies: Inergy, which specializes in the creation of intellectual capital through creativity and innovation; Authentic Transformational Leadership, a company that enables individuals and groups to realize their leadership potential and the development of people as the true brand of organizations; and Placebrands, a company that, as its name suggests, enables places to develop their brand.

He has worked in the UK for central and local government, for private sector consultancies PA and VH&A, and set up and run a number of private training and business support companies. His companies have won the IIP UK Best Partner award three times. Malcolm has also won a CISCO/*Inc* Magazine award for innovative use of the Internet for his work on the GlobalPartnership – a Web-based international trade initiative linking business in the UK to the rest of the world.

Simon Anholt (simon@earthspeak.com) is an international strategy consultant who advises governments (including the UK, Croatia and Slovenia) and corporations (including DreamWorks, DuPont and Timberland) on branding, cultural and ethical issues. *The Economist* describes him as 'one of the world's leading consultants to corporations and governments who wish to build global brands'. He is an editor of the *Journal of Brand Management* and a regular contributor to many academic and marketing publications. His best-seller on global advertising, *Another One Bites the Grass*, was published in the United States by John Wiley in 2000, and his latest book, *Brand New Justice*, on how branding can build the economies of emerging markets, was published by Butterworth-Heinemann in 2002.

Julie Anixter (JAnixter@LAGA.com) is an author, speaker, designer and educator committed to positive change for organizations and individuals through design, branding and innovation. She is the strategic director of Lipson Alport Glass & Associates, a brand marketing and design consultancy headquartered in Cincinnati, Ohio, where she leads the company's consulting efforts, working closely with clients on a wide variety of brand and design projects including naming, brand positioning (rBT), new product development (InnovationStream®), strategic brand research and consulting, and Brand Inside:Brand Outside™ (BI:BO), a holistic approach to total brand alignment. She also manages the tompeterscompany!–LAGA Alliance, which brings organizational development and training capabilities to total brand alignment projects.

Her background blends 20 years of corporate brand design and strategy, helping organizations develop and implement brand strategy across all media, as well as the marketing and deployment of new brands. Prior to joining LAGA, Julie served as managing director for the tompeterscompany!, where she worked closely with Tom. She was part of the development team, with Tom, that created the Brand Inside:Brand Outside, WOW!Projects™, Professional Service Firm Thinking and Brand You Consulting and Training Practices that have been used by organizations as diverse as Fidelity, the US Navy and Ian Schrager Hotels.

Prior to joining the tompeterscompany!, Julie served as the director of employee development for Equity Office Properties, and chief learning officer at Anixter Inc. Julie holds a Master's degree from the University of San Francisco, and is completing a second Master's degree in the Institute of Learning Sciences at Northwestern University.

John Caswell (john@grouppartners.net; www.grouppartners.net) is the chairman and founder of Group Partners, an independent business built to deliver expert advice and solutions in an innovative, unique, highly visual and interactive way. John has designed the Progressive Framework Methodology, an approach that allows solutions to be co-created by the client and its advisers through the application of its Business Equation – a system of understanding the 11 laws of contextual logic.

Previously, John ran his own agencies and consultancies, before his company was acquired by WPP in 1996 after the highly successful Euro96 football championships, which his agency was responsible for. During these years his consultancies and agencies created major marketing programmes for IBM, Ford, Benetton, Philips, Microsoft, Xerox, SAP, Oracle, Time Warner, Sony and many other Global 2000 businesses. Prior to this John was responsible for the launch and marketing of the BBC microcomputer during four very formative years with Acorn Computers in Cambridge.

John also sits on many boards as a non-executive, and is on the advisory board of Cazenove, the leading private equity firm, and many steering groups in various market areas across the world.

Thomas Gad (thomas.gad@brandflight.com) has worked on brand development, communication and advertising for some of the best-known companies in the world, including Nokia (including the creation of the famous slogan 'Connecting People'), SAS, Procter & Gamble, Compaq, Microsoft, Telia, SEB and Nordea. He was international creative director at Grey Advertising for 17 years. In June 2002 he founded a new branding and communication advising company, Brandflight, with offices in Stockholm and London.

Thomas has developed a unique four-dimensional method of creating, transforming and maintaining brands, and published this in the book *4-D Branding* (Financial Times/Prentice Hall, London, 2001), with foreword by Sir Richard Branson. His latest book is *Managing Brand Me: How to build your personal brand* (Pearson-Momentum, London, 2002), a book he wrote with his partner Anette Rosencreutz.

Sicco van Gelder (sicco.van.gelder@brand-meta.com) runs a Netherlands-based global branding consultancy called Brand Meta. He is also a co-founder of Placebrands Ltd, a firm dedicated to helping cities, regions and countries define their purpose and achieve their full potential. The other co-founders are Malcolm Allan, Simon Anholt and Niclas Ljungberg, two of whom have also contributed to this book.

Sicco has held senior international research and consultancy positions with leading companies in Asia and Europe. He has lived, worked and travelled across four continents. His exposure to the great diversity of these continents has helped him to develop his understanding of and sensitivity to differing cultural, motivational, economic, social and competitive issues. He is the author of *Global Brand Strategy: Unlocking brand potential across countries, cultures and markets* (Kogan Page, London, 2003). Sicco holds a Master's degree in human geography from the University of Amsterdam.

Nicholas Ind (nind@equilibriumconsulting.com; www.nicholasind.com) is a writer and brand consultant based in Scandinavia. Previously he ran IconMedialab's brand consultancy arm in Sweden. Using Thomas Gad's Brand Me technique, he defines his personal mission as 'to help organizations achieve success by focusing and enhancing the passion and commitment of people in their working lives'.

Before he joined Icon, Nicholas had his own branding consultancy in the UK, was a director of a design group and was an account director in an advertising agency. Nicholas is the author of six books, including *The Corporate Image* (Kogan Page, London, 1990); *Terence Conran: The authorised biography* (Sidgwick & Jackson, London, 1995); *The Corporate Brand* (Macmillan, Basingstoke, 1997) and *Living the Brand* (Kogan Page, London, 2001).

He is a former director of the Design Business Association, a member of the advisory board of *Corporate Reputation Review* and the editorial board of the *Journal of Brand Management* and is an Industrial Fellow at Kingston University. Nicholas has a degree in English and history and a postgraduate degree in business from Strathclyde Business School.

Tim Kitchin (timkitchin@topenworld.com) is a communications consultant based in Kent, England. After graduating in modern languages from Clare College, Cambridge, he trained as an accountant, before entering the world of corporate public relations. He has been a director of several major international PR consultancies, but launched out as an independent consultant in 2001 to focus on multi-stakeholder communications strategy within complex environments. He works closely with management consultancies and communications consultancies on planning and strategy issues, and is a non-executive adviser and equity holder in several emerging technology companies. Tim developed the concept of brand learning, which codified the ways in which corporate brands serve as a catalyst for corporate evolution. He is co-author of *Managing Corporate Reputations* (Kogan Page, London, 2001).

Chris Macrae (wcbn007@easynet.co.uk) is a mathematician and innovation adviser with offices in London and Washington, DC. He maps how companies can transparently value intangibles. Leadership advantage now depends critically on seeing human relationship flows of trust required for living systems to network economic and social win–wins.

Chris's books and research of brands in 30 countries over two decades benchmark how global branding has steadily deteriorated across a broad spectrum of human relationship needs. Chris helped found CBO Association as the premier worldwide think tank enquiring how the power of brand leadership could be reformed to multiply value across cultures and stakeholders. One outcome of this is the meta-disciplinary humanitarian movement of Beyond Branding. Chris has also been encouraged by the European Union Knowledge Angels community and many other human disciplines, including the futures circles of economics journalist Norman Macrae, to open-source the missing governance system of transparency and dynamic valuation. *The Map* is being published by John Wiley, and details of rapid change learnings being made by industry and social syndicates are updated at www.valuetrue.com.

Denzil Meyers (denzil@widgetwonder.com) is a branding and communications strategist, consulting since 1992 as account planner to many top 25 US ad agencies and their Fortune 500 clients. Previously, he worked at ad agencies Chiat/Day, Foote Cone & Belding, and D'Arcy Masius Benton & Bowles.

In 2001, Denzil founded widgetwonder, an internal brand consultancy and facilitators of living brand scripts, corporate storytelling, innovation practice and co-creative skills training.

Denzil is a founding member of the Association for the Advancement of Improv in Business (AAIB). He believes improv experience has the power to transform organizational dynamics, change people's lives and help evolve the emotional intelligence of the human race. He hopes it's not too late.

Denzil's first entrepreneurial adventure was as a writer and producer for radio, which remains his favourite electronic medium. Denzil can also be found twice a week playing percussion with a Brazilian samba band, or occasionally making wine from the fine grapes of Sonoma County, California. He conducts a weekly workshop for creative writers.

Denzil is a graduate of George Washington University in Washington, DC.

Alan Mitchell (ASMitchell@aol.com) is a business writer and author of *The New Bottom Line* (Capstone-Wiley, 2003) and *Right Side Up* (HarperCollins Business, 2000). A founding member of the Buyer-Centric

Commerce Forum (buyercentric.com) and a former editor of *Marketing Magazine*, Alan has been tracking developments in marketing and branding for the last 15 years. Now freelance, Alan has regular columns in a range of specialist magazines such as *Marketing Week*, *New Media Age*, *Brand Strategy*, *Precision Marketing*, *Marketing Business* (the journal of the Chartered Institute of Marketing) and *Finance & Management* (for the Faculty of Finance and Management of the Institute of Chartered Accountants in England and Wales). He also contributes to other publications such as the *Financial Times* and serves on the editorial board of the *Journal of Brand Management*.

John Moore (johnm@roundourhouse.com) is a marketing consultant based in London. After studying philosophy and politics at Oxford, he worked as researcher to Lord Sainsbury before going into advertising. He formed his own consultancy in 1988 and has worked with a range of brands, particularly in the financial services sector. He has also worked with many of the UK's largest independent schools to develop their marketing.

In recent years he has trained in NLP and completed a postgraduate training in humanistic psychotherapy. Other training experiences include firewalking and learning to fly floatplanes into (and, even more helpfully, out of) lakes in British Columbia. Like Denzil Meyers, he is a founder member of the Association for the Advancement of Improv in Business (AAIB). He formed a new consultancy, www.roundourhouse.com, in 2002 to help businesses market with authenticity and integrity.

Ian Ryder (ian.ryder@tesco.net) is Vice-President, Brand and Communications, Europe, Middle East, India and Africa, for Unisys Corporation. Ian was formerly Director, Global Brand Management for Hewlett-Packard Company in Palo Alto, United States and is a graduate of IMD in Lausanne. He has held senior marketing roles in several major technology companies and has provided independent brand strategy advice to many other companies inside and outside the technology industry. International speaker, chairman, author and lecturer on the subjects of brand strategy, reputation and customer management, and a Fellow of the Chartered Institute of Marketing, Ian has pioneered some breakthrough thinking in marketing and the role of such current 'buzz' topics as CRM, CSR and knowledge management.

Ian is a subject specialist reviewer for Harvard Business School Press, sits on the board of the US Brand Masters programme and the UK board of the *Journal of Brand Management*, and is a non-executive adviser to the British Olympic Association. He is a Fellow of the RSA, chairman of the Technology Industry Business Leaders Group for the Marketing Society and chairman of the Conference Board's European Council on Customer Strategy, and he co-developed the Unique Organization Value Proposition (UOVP™) – a new concept in brand management and the subject of a book, *Competing on Value* by Stan Maklan, Simon Knox and Ian Ryder (Financial Times Management, London, 1998).

Jack Yan (jack.yan@jyanet.com) founded Jack Yan & Associates (http://jya.net) in 1987, one of the earliest virtual companies, with bases and representatives in over a dozen countries worldwide. In the late 1990s, he examined how brands and business performance were linked, discovering the best practices of organizations that he now applies to his company's clients. His branding research has included work on the success factors of cross-media brands.

Among his company's interests are business consulting, imaging, software and media, including the fashion magazine brand *Lucire*. He writes on topics ranging from branding and business responsibility to fashion and typography, in numerous publications worldwide and is a regular international speaker.

Jack has a passion for individual freedoms and global harmony, and works with networks focusing on business responsibility and ethics.

He holds two business degrees and a law degree from Victoria University of Wellington. His personal site is at www.jackyan.com.

Preface

In 2002 Jimmy Carter was awarded, finally, the Nobel Peace Prize. At the awarding of the prize, Carter seized the opportunity to articulate his thoughts on the impact of wealth disparity:

> at the beginning of this new millennium I was asked to discuss, here in Oslo, the greatest challenge that the world faces. Among all the possible choices, I decided that the most serious and universal problem is the growing chasm between the richest and poorest people on earth. Citizens of the ten wealthiest countries are now seventy-five times richer than those who live in the ten poorest ones, and the separation is increasing every year, not only between nations but also within them. The results of this disparity are root causes of most of the world's unresolved problems, including starvation, illiteracy, environmental degradation, violent conflict, and unnecessary illnesses that range from Guinea worm to HIV/AIDS.

You might question how this connects to brand and indeed what branding can do about any of these problems. Surely this is an issue for politicians, development economists and aid workers not marketers. Take a traditional view of marketing and you would probably be right. However, it is the view of the writers of this book that, when businesses account for 51 of the largest 100 economic entities in the world, branding not only should have a wider social perspective, but it must do so if it is to have continued relevance. To be clear, the argument is not that business should suddenly become altruistic. That might produce a feeling of well-being, but of itself it is not sustainable. Rather business has to change its mode of thinking because doing the right thing is good for business. Companies have to recognize their accountability not only to shareholders, but to all audiences and to society as a whole. They have to adopt a human perspective so that they benefit people rather than manipulate them. They have to be transparent and open to overcome suspicions of duplicity. These are the sort of attributes we would expect of a nation state and increasingly we expect them of corporations. Business cannot assume a position of dominance without a concomitant assumption of responsibility. By ignoring these factors, we will face more protests from people who feel the threat of overweening corporate power. By accepting them business can have a beneficial influence and help solve (perhaps better than government) some of the most challenging problems in the world, while still being profitable. To get there, companies will have to incorporate into their brands a broader understanding of their audiences and they will have to adopt values that promote a human focus, authenticity, transparency and integrity. Most importantly they will then have to integrate those values into their day-to-day thoughts and actions (always the hard part). And finally they will also have to adopt measuring systems that focus on wins for all stakeholders.

Many organizations are far removed from this ideal. Hence this book, which has grown out of the frustration of a group of people who feel that for too long branding and branders have had a particularly narrow view of the world: one that is short-termist, shareholder focused, narcissistic and communications led. These are tendencies that do little to promote positive relationships and trust – things that are integral to brand building. However, rather than carping from the sidelines, this group resolved to make their voices heard and in the summer of 2002 defined a manifesto. That may sound portentous, but 'The Medinge Manifesto' as it has become known, after the location just south of Stockholm where the group meets each year, is designed both to proclaim a viewpoint and to gel the ideas of the individuals:

Creating true value through transparent relationships

A conspiratorial financial system has severely damaged the reputation of corporate America and global businesses, in what *Fortune* June 2002 called 'Systems Failure'.

Currently, the headlines continue to focus on ways in which organizations have deliberately deceived the outside world about their financial performance. However, the Medinge signatories believe that, even without active dishonesty, established financial measures are profoundly misleading as a way of assessing the value of any business.

These financial measures were designed for an industrial economy and simply do not work in a knowledge economy – in which honest creativity and trusting relationships are the growth hormones for lasting value – enduring over the lifetime of a pensioner; not just the contractual-cycle of a CFO.

In this real economy, around 85% of business value is 'incommensurable'. It cannot be meaningfully measured or managed by accountants. The resulting financial knowledge vacuum is being randomly plugged with context-less snippets of transparency leading to further stakeholder confusion and corporate inertia.

In short, human beings are a primary source of value creation yet their impact, potential and resilience is nowhere accounted for on the typical balance sheet.

This leaves responsible businesses with a huge gap to fill. Accounting protocols fail to model the ways that organizations create value. Although enforcing existing financial rules with greater vigour is a pre-requisite for rebuilding trust, it merely adds scaffolding to a decaying structure.

Our collective challenge, which the Medinge signatories embrace, is to create new standards for managing the health of organizational relationships – assessing the functional, psychological, spiritual, and social benefits they provide. This new system will be built on the solid foundations of human values and mutual honesty.

Our view is that an organization's value stands or falls on its ability to foster positive exchanges of value – between all of its stakeholders.

This central tenet of the Medinge signatories will only become more critical, as the networked economy places organizations under ever closer scrutiny. We believe that this will greatly increase the need for organizations to be open, transparent and honest in their dealings. In a creative world, greater value will result from more open and trusting relationships. By organizing transparent value exchanges, marketing and innovation reassert themselves and organizations can play a truly positive and dynamic role in the community.

For the writers of this book, the manifesto has been the point of accountability and has defined the subject matter. In turn the contributions have enriched the manifesto – adding depth of meaning. Although some of the chapters have overlapping ideas, each contribution aims to work as an individual piece. Thomas Gad focuses on the changing nature of leadership while Jack Yan describes the view from Generation Y. Chris Macrae critiques the current methods of measuring value, and John Moore challenges the lack of authenticity in brands. Alan Mitchell describes brand narcissism, Tim Kitchin, brand sustainability and Ian Ryder, brand anthropology. John Caswell argues for the importance of a system-wide perspective, and Julie Anixter argues for an inside-out one. Denzil Meyers looks at the responsible use of power, and together Sicco van Gelder and Simon Anholt look at socio-economic issues. To keep the challenge up, my role as editor has been to comment and question, but each chapter has also been posted to other commentators, who have aired their views, not least Malcolm Allan, who has been a most effective additional editorial voice.

We do not see the book as the end of our efforts, but rather as the beginning. It is one element of our cause to persuade managers of the importance of engaging with society and helping to solve the real challenges in the world. You too can make a contribution to this. If you would like to join, comment or critique, visit the Web site at www.beyond-branding.com.

1

A brand of enlightenment

Nicholas Ind

> The ideals of human perfectibility and of achievement are authentic anti-
> dotes to the existential anxiety of guilt. What is true for an individual is
> also true for our institutions. This understanding of existential guilt will
> ultimately lead us to measure all institutions – such as a business, the
> family, education, the law, commerce and politics – by the degree to
> which they support the development of human potential.
>
> (Koestenbaum and Block, 2001: 314)

The Age of Enlightenment was a period of unprecedented growth in terms
of freedom, knowledge, toleration and commerce. Its champions, such as
Bentham, Locke and Smith, believed in the idea of human potential and
progress, and changed the way we think about the world. The enlightenment created the modern age, but the pursuit of happiness it espoused
and our sense of well-being are no longer so certain. In the 21st century it
is no longer axiomatic that increased wealth means a better life. What
progress now means is not so clear. Research shows that the correlation
between wealth and happiness begins to disappear once people reach
incomes of above $10,000 GDP per head. Equally there is no absolute corre-
lation between income and life expectancy. For example, African American
men, although many times wealthier than the men of one of the poorest

states in India, Kerala, have a lower chance of reaching old age. As the Nobel prize winning economist Amartya Sen says (2000: 14), 'The usefulness of wealth lies in the things that it allows us to do – the substantive freedoms it helps us to achieve. But this relation is neither exclusive (since there are significant influences on our lives other than wealth) nor uniform (since the impact on our lives varies with other influences).' If wealth and with it consumption can no longer guarantee our happiness, the question remains as to whether it can make our lives richer through enhancing our freedom. And can the much criticized world of brands make a real contribution to this? The challenge here is to rethink the way brands work and to reorient them clearly towards people.

In the era of Adam Smith and Daniel Defoe business became central to the modern world. For the first (and perhaps the last) time it received a positive press. Since then the business world, while of intriguing interest, has come to be seen negatively. Writers such as Thackeray, Dickens, EM Forster and DH Lawrence portrayed the businessman as cold, cynical and manipulative. A character such as Gerald Critch in *Women in Love* typifies the business tycoon of literature. He is efficient and ruthless, driven by a desire to succeed and willing to trample over the interests of his employees. He is a self-centred man in thrall to machines and systems. He believes that his will-power can overcome all obstacles. Yet he is unable to develop true relationships. It is telling that Lawrence, who uses warmth and cold symbolically to express life-giving power and spiritual death, lets Gerald die in the Alpine snow. Gerald is a metaphor for the overweening ambition and pride of every fictional business character from Orson Welles's Citizen Kane to Gordon Gekko in *Wall Street*. It is as if the desire to control and manipulate is inherent in the business psyche and is untempered by any depth of self-knowledge.

The idea of the brand is central to much of the criticism of business. This is because the brand is where the organization most overtly interacts with people and creates the opportunity for manipulation. The writer Naomi Klein's argument in the seminal book *No Logo* is that the overly powerful organization does indeed exploit its customers by restricting competition, charging higher prices and hiding the truth of the means of production. These are valid criticisms and deserve attention. However, before we accept this view completely we should also recognize that brands can increase choice, enhance freedom and provide enjoyment. This suggests there is nothing inherently wrong with the concept of branding itself, but that managers and employees in an organization can act with good or bad intent. To encourage the former and discourage the latter, managers need to understand that it is in their business interests to promote the good. This will never deliver perfection, but it can begin to change the image of the brand at large and put the brand back where it belongs – on the side of the individual. Thus, this book does not aim to refute the negative image of business in general and brands in particular. Nor does it seek to attack business. Rather it recognizes that business can be a force for evil, but it can also be a force for good. Brands can enrich people's lives or manipulate them. Employees can find fulfilment at work or entrapment. The task is to create a culture and system where the focus is more consistently focused on the positive.

WHAT IS A BRAND?

A brand is something that is owned by buyers and other stakeholders.[1] This is an idea that is sometimes difficult to grasp, but it indicates that the power in a relationship between an individual and an organization is not necessarily where we think it is. The argument is this: just as capital is a concept, so is a brand. Although a brand is related to a physical product or service it is itself immaterial. It is a transforming idea that converts the tangible into something of value. The key question is how does it manage this transformation? It does so by delivering something of value. Thus a brand only exists in a buyer's mind and it is the buyer who has the power to begin, sustain or terminate a relationship with it. This fact creates an immediate problem of measuring the value of a brand because the company does not control the life of the brand – the customer does. Brand value is determined by an understanding of likely future performance and predicted cash flows. However, these are defined in large part by an extrapolation of past customer acquisition and loyalty.[2] And as the example of Arthur Andersen demonstrates customer loyalty can disappear in an instant.

However, while buyers have the power, they are also swayed by their own needs and desires. These will be both functionally and emotionally determined and can be met by the acquisition of relevant products. This need is partly to do with the intrinsic value of the product but mostly to do with the transformational quality of the brand concept. We are willing to pay extra to an organization for this because of the perception of added value. This is an issue of trust. We buy Puma shoes, Diesel jeans and Apple computers because we trust the authenticity of these brands. We believe from past experience and from the reputation of these products that they will fulfil our brand needs. This creates a position of vulnerability. We rarely have complete knowledge of a product and its performance, so we have to trust that the product we bought last time will confer the same benefits if we buy it again. If the brand is trustworthy it reduces anxiety and doubt. It makes our decision making easier and safer. As Alan Mitchell, one of the contributors to this book, notes, 'Brand is a specific tool by which we make real markets work: a tool which real people use to navigate their way to real value exchange. The reason why brands have become so important is because they are so good at helping to create efficient exchange.'

We see this exchange and trust-building process at work all the time. For example, imagine a piece of software advertised by an entirely unknown name – we would be much more cautious about buying it than if it comes from a name we know, such as Adobe. There is still no guarantee that it will meet our expectations, but we can be reassured that what we know of the company's reputation means it should perform to certain standards and that if it does not there is recourse to compensation. However, this building of trust is not instantaneous – it takes time. We deconstruct the messages that we receive. We read newspapers, talk to our friends, look in shop windows and observe others. If these messages are consistent we may be willing to try a product. If the experience of use is consistent and the after-sales service is good we may repeat-purchase it and become a brand enthusiast and advocate. We would then expect the performance of the product to be broadly consistent with our last experience – we begin to trust the brand and to become willing to allow the company to try to build a relationship with us. Nonetheless the freedom to choose to accept this relationship or not is ours.

Brands that enhance our sense of well-being and freedom further our sense of self. They can enhance our higher needs for esteem, socialization and self-actualization. These are people-centric brands that help us to obtain value. Brands can also disappoint. They can manipulate our beliefs, they can be meretricious and they can try to limit freedom of choice. These are seller-centric brands that operate from the perspective of the brand builder. That they act in this way may be expedient, but it does not build long-term value for the brand and it undermines the very reason we pay for the reassurance of brands: trust.

EXPEDIENCE, EXAGGERATION AND EXECUTION

Most organizations know that keeping the long-term trust of the customer is central to their success and many companies do deliver. Yet there are also surprising failures and these can have a profound impact on customers, employees and shareholders. There will of course always be mistakes and errors of judgement but in some cases the roots go deeper to the nature of business and its role in society. These factors can be clustered into three broad areas: expedience, exaggeration and execution.

Expedience

'The dominant values in most businesses and public sector organizations are expedience and efficiency. They value what works, often at the expense of what has meaning and what a wider view of social responsibility might entail' (Koestenbaum and Block, 2001: 276). The commonly held view of business – especially in the Anglo-American corporate world – is that it exists to serve the interests of shareholders. Although this viewpoint is debatable and much of the rest of the world adheres to a more balanced view based on stakeholder capitalism, the reality is that the United States alone accounts for 40 per cent of the world's economic activity. The clear accountability for chief executives in the US model is to provide the best possible returns for the owners of the business. Ideally this should be a long-term position. It is always possible to boost short-term performance by expediency – downsizing, re-engineering, accounting procedures – but these often do little for sustainability. As Lou Gerstner, the former CEO of IBM, observes, there is an obsession among security analysts with the next quarter's performance and with revenue. The danger in this is that 'a preoccupation with revenue can also lead to maximizing short-term results at the expense of long-term competitive position' (Gerstner, 2002: 269). This pressure to perform, not only among chief executives but at all levels, and the fixation with short-term numbers are the fundamental source of distortions. The impact of this on a brand varies. Short-term thinkers who are interested in fast returns and their next career move will tend to be expedient in their management of a brand, while managers with a long-term focus will see things in terms of the development of the brand and its relationships with customers. As an illustration of alternative ways of thinking, take the relative positions of two healthcare companies.

As reported in the summer of 2002 (Koerner, 2002), the British drug company GlaxoSmithKline was basking in the success of its new anti-anxiety drug, Paxil. From its approval by the US Food and Drug Administration in April 2001 it had become the number two SSRI (selective serotonin reuptake inhibitors) drug – widely used in the treatment of mental disorders. The disorder it was treating was general anxiety disorder (GAD) – something that US news reports estimated affected more than 10 million people in the United States. GAD, according to the press and television features, 'left sufferers paralysed with irrational fears' (Koerner, 2002). Actually, Paxil had been around since 1993 as an anti-depression drug, but had made little headway against better-known competitors. The solution was to tap into people's social problems and reposition Paxil as an anti-anxiety drug. SmithKline, as it then was, found in *The Diagnostic and Statistical Manual of Mental Disorders* a rare condition known as social anxiety disorder, a debilitating form of shyness. As entries in the *Manual* tend to act as a proof of a disease for the FDA and because the drug already existed, there wasn't the same long process to market as a new drug. As the trade journal *PR News* put it, the goal was now to 'position social anxiety disorder as a severe condition' (Koerner, 2002). To this end SmithKline began a campaign to market the disease. It began with a poster campaign that bore the insignia of a group called The Social Anxiety Disorder Coalition and its three non-profit members. However, this wasn't a grass-roots body but rather something constructed by SmithKline Beecham. The other advantage of a campaign promoting a disease rather than a cure is that companies don't have to detail the side effects of the drugs. In addition to the poster campaign there was a series of TV, radio and press releases claiming that social anxiety disorder affected one in eight people in the United States. Eloquent patients talked about their problems, and members of the medical profession (some paid consultants to SmithKline Beecham) talked up the disease. The consulting firm Decision Resources predicted that the 'anxiety market' would expand to at least $3 billion by 2009.

In another market sector this story might not be so uncomfortable. We might imagine a baking product being repositioned from one type of ingredient usage to another. The idea of promoting disease, especially one that targets vulnerable people, seems less palatable, because unless it is genuine it feels expedient. It is seller-centric.

Contrast this example with Baxter International (Hammonds, 2002). One of Baxter's products was a dialysis filter that was made by a company acquired by Baxter in 2000 called Althin Medical AB. In the summer of 2001 patients in Madrid and Valencia who were undergoing dialysis treatment using equipment that featured the Althin filter died. It wasn't clear as to the source of the problem, but the filters were a common link. Baxter recalled the products in Spain and instituted an investigation, but there was no evidence of product failure. Then similar deaths occurred in Croatia. Baxter announced a global recall and then put together a team of 27 people from different disciplines to try to locate the problem – they found nothing, but then a quality engineer in the Swedish plant noticed a few bubbles on the recalled filters. When the filters leaked they were injected with a solution to locate the problem. The solution was non-toxic, but the toxicologists theorized that it gasified when heated to body temperature, causing a fatal embolism. There were still doubts about this and it didn't explain why the problem had not occurred before. Still, this presented Baxter with a dilemma – how to act appropriately. The company has a series of values – respect, responsiveness, results – that it uses to define its actions. First of all, Harry Kraemer Jr, the Chairman and CEO of Baxter, apologized and then the company shut down Althin, taking a charge to earnings of $189 million. The company notified other rival manufacturers and over the next few months reviewed its procedures to prevent repeats in another area of the business. Additionally Kraemer recommended that his performance bonus be cut by 40 per cent and that top executives take a 20 per cent cut. As Keith Hammonds, writing in *Fast Company*, observes about the dip in the stock, but its rapid recovery:

> The Message to CEOs: Investors like honesty, including public apologies. (Kraemer visited New York to apologize in person to the president of Croatia). So, it turns out, do employees. Kraemer was flooded with emails and phone messages from appreciative workers... To him, there is nothing extraordinary about what Baxter has done. This is simply how organizations and their people should behave.

> (Hammonds, 2002)

The Baxter case demonstrates the willingness of managers to think long-term about the responsibility of the organization to the people who use its products. As Larry Elliot and Richard Schroth note, 'creating the culture with the right orientation requires leadership from the top and work by the entire company. You do not turn it on and off. Your culture is either based on candor or honesty or it is not' (Elliot and Schroth, 2002: 111).

Exaggeration

If we want to sell something like a house or a car to someone we tend to overstate virtues and underplay any failings or limitations. Equally when marketers promote brands there is a tendency to exaggerate. In simple terms the goal is to project an image that taps into people's perceived values and lifestyles. For the individual, the process of considering brands is a cathartic process that helps them define their own identity. However, this is not static – the transformational potential of brands means that a person's sense of identity is forever changing in tune with received messages. There is a sense of illusion here. While the language of brand promotion can overstate, we are willing recipients of the half-truth. As Camus's character Meursault in *L'Étranger* demonstrates, an individual who tells the truth is a rare and difficult person. We allow ourselves to be deceived by the language of marketing because in part it suits us to do so. The existentialist philosopher Peter Koestenbaum points out that we have to accept this untruth and illusion for a sense of well-being. It is simply too uncomfortable to accept the reality of ourselves. The implications of this can be negative. Just as the character J in *Three Men in a Boat* convinced himself he had everything in the medical dictionary from A to Z, apart from housemaid's knee, by simply equating the symptoms he read about with his own feelings, so we have the potential to convince ourselves that we are afflicted by SAD or a similar illness. On the other side we can convince ourselves to do good. A brand can make us better people.

Take the example of Future Forests. This company has a very simple idea: to save the planet by planting one tree at a time. Global warming is a concept that is so large that most people feel they can do little to tackle it, but Future Forests has focused in on people's sense of individual responsibility and targeted its brand accordingly. It enables people (and companies) to understand their individual contribution to global warming through the amount of CO_2, carbon dioxide, they produce (from turning on their TV sets, running their cars, going on holiday etc) and then to understand how they can cut their emissions down, and then compensate for them by paying to have trees planted (which absorb CO_2) or fund climate-friendly technologies like wind power (which balance out CO_2 emissions). So, for example, individuals can choose to 'neutralize' the 1 tonne of CO_2 from driving their car, by planting five trees per year in a long-term forest of their choice with Future Forests (CarbonNeutral driving). This gives customers a positive sense of empowerment. Future Forests argues that forestry is a very efficient way to absorb CO_2 emissions. Avis Europe, which is one of their biggest customers, notes that the involvement in tree planting has led its people to consider the whole issue of environmentalism more carefully. Future Forests' co-founder Sue Welland says:

> Our position on that is that you can't plant your way out of global warming. But if you're trying to engage people, you have to find the thinnest edge, which is something that people really understand and is tangible. People don't understand the language [of global warming] and can't find the attachment points. We got rid of all the nebulous stuff and brought it down to bite size, easily understandable chunks. A tree is a symbol. It's a way into people. It's a gateway experience.[3]

One of the impressive aspects of Future Forests' brand is its belief in transparency. Guided by its brand values, it puts all corporate information it can on its Web site. The language is informative – pointing out the issues and providing the opportunity for the solution. The approach to the media is the same: provide substantive information and keep the organization open to the outside. As a virtual company, Future Forests feels this integrity is vital to building the trust of all its audiences.

Execution

Organizations are not inherently evil. We are the individuals who populate these organizations and we can make good or bad decisions. The way we act is defined at least in part by the broader influence of society (which in turn is influenced by business). If the world accepts and perhaps praises power, unbridled greed and exploitation, then we should not be so surprised if some individuals behave in a limited way. Alternatively if we are serious about individual responsibility, environmentalism and the alleviation of global poverty, then individuals are more likely to think about the broader accountability of their decisions. This is not to argue that every decision a business makes needs to consider global poverty, but awareness of the issue adjusts the mindset of the decision maker. The difficulty for modern organizations is that devolution of decisions and the empowerment of individuals has reduced control. Overall this is a good thing for both business and the individual, but it does create executional problems, especially if employees are not united by a common and positive set of values. Just think about the impact of Nick Leeson's decisions on the long-established Barings Bank brand.

The onus therefore must be on the organization to define clearly its brand values and to encourage individuals to act in accordance with them. Only then will people at all levels make decisions that are not narrowly defined but take into account the full responsibilities of a business. An interesting example of this is the brand Nike. Nike is a challenging brand and part of its power and appeal to customers has been its willingness to support the cause of athletes by running campaigning advertisements and attacking the International Olympic Committee. This is a brand built on irreverence. However, this positive impression has been tempered in recent times by the company's record in managing its employment policies, especially in the developing world. Nike has long manufactured in the Far East but, because it subcontracts work to local factory owners, it disassociated itself from the exploitative conditions of its factories and the use of child labour. It failed to see the connections between its brand, which espouses honesty, competitiveness and teamwork, and the idea of children working in sweatshop conditions. As Nelson Farris of Nike says, 'One of the biggest mistakes we made was to think we don't own the factories, so that's their problem. That's when we recognized we were more powerful than we realized and, as a consequence, people expected more of us. Employees were embarrassed and disenchanted and confused. The media had sweatshops and child labour in every sentence.'[4]

To its credit Nike has moved to independent and open auditing of its global employment record, but the failure to recognize the connectedness of decisions was the primary cause of the criticism of the brand.

FINDING THE SOLUTIONS

The subsequent chapters of this book will explore from the perspective of various authors the problems that brands face, but more importantly they will offer solutions to improving the role and the performance of brands. This book is not just a critique of the world of brands, but rather a set of ideas as to how brands and branding can contribute to progress. The solutions fall into a number of broad categories: self-correction, persuasion and pressure, democracy and transparency, and legislation.

Self-correction

Adam Smith's championing of free markets was his reaction against the power of vested interests in 18th-century Britain: 'people of the same trade seldom meet together, but the conversation ends in a conspiracy against the public, or in some diversion to raise prices'. He believed that freedom equated to a greater degree of fairness for people. However, he was not in favour of free markets in all circumstances. He also recognized that certain aspects of society, including the need to provide well-funded public education, should be legislated for and supported by the state. On the whole we should recognize that free markets are a good thing and that many of the problems that exist for developing nations are not the result of too much freedom, but vestiges of government interference, such as agricultural subsidies in the European Union and trade barriers under one guise or another. One of the great virtues of free markets is their ability for self-correction. Nowhere is this clearer than the influence of buyers on brands. Consumers do not always adjust their buying behaviour because of the positive or negative actions of companies, but their attitudes are swayed by them and businesses are concerned about the impact of public perception on their reputations and brands. This type of failing can simply be because the brand in its pursuit of growth or profitability forgets the primacy of customers. (Research by Gallup (2002) reveals that employees believe that only 66 per cent of company leaders are trying to do what is best for their customers, and even fewer – only 44 per cent – believe corporate leaders are trying to do what is best for their employees.)

This lack of consumer orientation has been obvious in the case of McDonald's. Its first ever quarterly loss of $343.8 million in 2003 was clearly due to its focus on its real estate and franchise revenues and its lack of interest in customers. There has been a failure to generate genuine new products and there has been a record number of complaints (including complaints about the way complaints are handled). *Fortune* magazine reports (Grainger, 2003) that, on the University of Michigan's American Customer Satisfaction Index, McDonald's has ranked at the bottom of the fast food industry since 1994 and that it sits in 2002 below all airlines and also the Internal Revenue Service. The only source of growth has been new outlets. There has been a downward spiral of lack of innovation, disappointed franchisees and disengaged employees, customer complaints, reduced revenues and poorer shareholders – the company lost $20 billion in market capitalization in 2002. McDonald's has now realized, perhaps belatedly, that the customer is the real source of value.

Equally, companies can also forget their broader societal role. Research by Tom Brown and Peter Dacin, who conducted three studies into the nature of corporate associations, found that 'all three studies demonstrate that negative CSR [corporate social responsibility] associations can have a detrimental effect on overall product evaluations, whereas positive CSR associations can enhance the product evaluations' (Brown and Dacin, 1997). Similarly research commissioned by BT and The Future Foundation (1998) into 'The Responsible Organization' concluded that 'our research among consumers confirms the positive impact good corporate citizenship has on corporate reputation and consumer trust'. This is something that Shell realized to its cost over its Brent Spar platform. This North Sea oil platform had reached the end of its useful life and the company decided to sink it. This may or may not have been the best environmental decision, but the dangers of pollution were seized upon by Greenpeace, which campaigned vociferously against the idea. As a result of their actions, Shell, which historically had been seen as a good corporate citizen, found that its status as a socially responsible organization among consumers declined by 10 percentage points.

As Simon Anholt has pointed out in his book *Brand New Justice*, the other key driver towards self-correction is the need for big companies to find new buyers. Many businesses have begun to recognize that the pool of customers in established markets is limited. This has led to a stagnation of demand and the search for new geographical opportunities. Although this can lead to companies seeing developing countries as just another sales outlet and an opportunity for margin enhancement, a more enlightened view is that a market that only consists of perhaps a third of the world's population is not truly global. This is driving brands to focus on sustainable development, not as an act of altruism, but because their long-term growth depends on these new consumers: 'they [big companies] need consumers who are wealthy enough to buy their products, have enough free time to enjoy them, are educated enough to consume advertising messages and evaluate products and brands, and live in countries where there is the liberty to make money and spend it' (Anholt, 2003: 160). As an example of this approach, Anholt cites Hewlett-Packard's e-inclusion programme, which works with companies, NGOs (non-governmental organizations) and governments to improve the facilities, health, education and infrastructure in developing markets.

Persuasion and pressure

One interesting long-term effect of the Brent Spar case was to change Shell's perception of its role in the world. Shell has embraced the idea of sustainability, and its ex-Chairman Mark Moody-Stuart has headed Business Action for Sustainable Development (BASD). One of the key changes has been that some NGOs have moved from a stance of hostility towards business to working with business organizations to encourage change. The power of NGOs has also grown inexorably. For example, in the UK, 48 per cent of the population has worked formally for a voluntary organization in the last year and 74 per cent either formally or informally. Internationally the number of NGOs has grown from 6,000 in 1990 to 40,000 in 2002, and membership of such high-profile NGOs as the World Wide Fund for Nature (World Wildlife Fund in the United States) increased from 570,000 in 1985 to 5,000,000 in 2002. As *The Economist* (1999) says, 'Over the past decade, NGOs and their memberships have grown hugely... Democratisation and technological progress have revolutionised the way citizens can unite to express their disquiet.' This pressure impacts on different audiences in different ways. Shareholders want to see good corporate behaviour because of the risks to the business of unethical behaviour. Governments, under pressure from their electorates, want business organizations to fill the void they have left by retreating from public areas. And employees prefer to work for organizations that are seen to act positively. This is not simply to suggest that businesses should set up corporate social responsibility departments. Rather CSR and the idea of sustainable business need to be incorporated into their operations.

An example of this is the Dutch bank, ABN AMRO, which in consultation with NGOs is redefining existing and developing new policies on lending. It has started a programme of micro-loans to small businesses in developing countries, which provides small loans to individuals and small companies that do not have good access to the banking market. In the case of project finance for mining businesses and for forestry, the company adheres to principles that insist the projects it funds take account of environmental and social issues. This also has value to the bank's clients because they are facing similar sustainability issues. It is equally true that many clients are working with the same NGOs. As Paul Mudde, SVP in charge of sustainable development at the bank, says, 'sustainability is not charity. The essence of sustainability is to integrate economic, social and environmental criteria in the key business processes of the organization. It is based on a triple bottom-line concept of three Ps, which stand for people, planet and profit.' The power of a bank such as ABN AMRO and equally major brand manufacturers and retailers is that by sticking to their own principles of good behaviour they can define the standards that suppliers should adhere to. At the same time a level playing field with competitors is important. This is one of the considerations when ABN AMRO actively seeks cooperation with other institutions on sustainability. All these initiatives spread the principles of good governance and sustainability inexorably into all corners of the business world. When, for example, the Swedish retailer H&M insists on acceptance of unions in suppliers' businesses and their freedom to strike, on clear standards of child labour and sensible standards of health and safety, it not only has a direct impact on over 900 companies in Europe and Asia, it also sets a standard for retailers and suppliers to follow.

The role of the brand here is as a catalyst for changing attitudes and in the case of some people as a spur to action. For example, the Nobel Peace Prize, the leading peace prize brand (there are roughly 300 in the world), has a power that goes beyond the monetary awards it makes. Its value lies in its courage and independence. The Nobel Committee makes its sometimes contentious awards to people and organizations that it believes have furthered the cause of peace. Although it has never formally defined this term it is clearly on the side of human rights, arms control, disarmament and humanitarianism. As Geir Lundestad, the Secretary to the Norwegian Nobel Committee, says, 'The prize has many different functions. It's a loudspeaker for lesser-known laureates. It's a protective mechanism. And sometimes the prize can influence a political situation, such as it did in 1996 when we rewarded Bishop Belo and Jose Ramos-Horta for their struggle for East Timor's right of self-determination.'[5] Lundestad believes that people's expectations of the prize are greater than it can deliver. However, the positive impact of this is that it gives people hope and reminds them of the possibility of the peaceful resolution to problems. It helps to get peace issues on the agenda as it did by awarding the prize to Aung San Suu Kyi in 1991, which led to the UN condemning Burma's military regime. And it acts as an incentive for laureates to achieve more – as was clearly the case with the 2002 laureate, Jimmy Carter. It is the prize as a brand that gives it this transformational quality. It confers moral authority on its winners. If the prize did not enjoy widespread recognition, a reputation for integrity and impact on the emotional needs of people, it would not have this capacity.

More democracy and transparency

'What is the meaning of democracy, freedom, human dignity, standard of living, self realization, fulfillment? Is it a matter of goods, or of people? Of course it is a matter of people' (Schumacher, 1974).

In interactions between people and organizations there has to be a congruency between what is offered and what is delivered. This is the basis of trust. This idea of trust has to be driven by a relatively high degree of transparency. This enables the customer and other audiences to have faith in the delivery of brands. This of course is not an unquestioning relationship. Consumers will still demand certain standards of behaviour from companies and they will ask questions of brands that are seen to fall short of expected standards. As Amartya Sen (2000: 40) notes, 'Transparency guarantees (including the right to disclosure) can thus be an important category of instrumental freedom. These guarantees have a clear instrumental role in preventing corruption, financial irresponsibility and underhand dealings.'

The difficulty as previously noted is that pressures on businesspeople often discourage transparency. There is a tendency to ignore the unpalatable and hide the injurious. A pilot study by the One World Trust (Kovach, Neligan and Burall, 2003) into the behaviour of intergovernmental organizations (IGOs), transnational corporations (TNCs) and international NGOs suggests that it is not only business that fails in this regard. All of these types of organizations fail to provide participation and accountability to stakeholders. Although there is the opportunity to legislate to encourage transparency, it is more valuable to encourage a voluntary openness. Within organizations the biggest driver for greater participation and openness should be that it benefits effectiveness. Research by the communications group at Erasmus University in Rotterdam demonstrates that employee communication is a vital component in organizational identification. This posits that there are three factors in employee communication in terms of their impact on identification: the perceived quality of organizational messages; the perceived quality of the communication channels; the quality of the communication climate. However, of these communication climate appears to be the most important. Cees van Riel (1999) suggests that 'how an organisation communicates is more important than what is communicated. This stresses the importance of "soft" aspects in communication like openness, honesty and participation in decision making, resulting in the necessity for managers to pay serious attention to communication climate, specifically their own role in improving the climate.'

However, the reality of transparency in organizations is somewhat different. The most common situation is one of distrust. Research consistently shows that people do not feel that they fulfil their potential at work and that internal politics prevents effective communication. The employee may have the desire and the potential to become an active participant in the organization, but there are clear barriers to engagement. Manville and Ober (2003) write, 'the entire shape of the modern company reflects a fundamental distrust of its members'.

In their interactions with external audiences, companies also benefit from full disclosure. This recognizes the interdependency argument. A decision made in the interests of one audience such as shareholders or customers will have an impact on all other key audiences. Yet the balkanization of many organizations prevents these linkages being made. Consequently measurement systems tend to monitor parts of interactions rather than the whole. When the impacts on customers, employees, shareholders and other audiences are linked together it tends to encourage behaviour that is designed to deliver benefits for all. In this instance brands do not become narrowly focused and problems like Nike faced over its labour policies can be averted. However, changing this thinking is not easy. While we can argue that organizations should see the full range of their responsibilities – which is much easier if the focus is external – it is far harder in practice. One of the challenges faced by Lou Gerstner in taking over IBM was its inward-lookingness – a focus on internal politics rather than customers. Reflecting the environment that exists in many businesses, Daniel Ellsberg (2002: 53) in writing about his time as an adviser to the Lyndon Johnson government noted the prevailing philosophy as 'do what's good for your boss, the man who hired you; put that above what you think is best for the country, above giving the president or the secretary of defense your best advice if that would embarrass your boss'. Making the customer the focus of the organization and bringing the customer experience inside the business is one of the best antidotes against a narrow focus and myopic thinking. It also stimulates transparency, because if the customer is a partner rather than an audience there is less to hide.

Legislation

'Guidelines, rules and policies do not in themselves make us honest. They only mark the pathway we should follow' (Kraemer, 2002).

In the wake of corporate misdemeanours, especially in the United States, there has been a clamour for new legislation. The value of this would be to encourage a greater degree of transparency and to stimulate increased and better-informed choice. Shareholder influence on good brand behaviour is perhaps somewhat muted. One of the difficulties here is that shareholders do not always have sufficient knowledge to exert pressure. Partly this is a failure on the part of the shareholder to seek out the information, but the larger blame lies with the organization and its failure fully to disclose its activities. Legislation should, as the philosopher Karl Popper (2002: 134–39) argued for democratic institutions, prepare for the worst and hope for the best. Hoping for the best, however, requires us to be active participants. We should not disassociate ourselves as outsiders from the system and from corporations. As Marx pointed out, our responsibility extends to the system and for the institutions within it. As consumers, employees and shareholders we can bemoan the failings of business organizations yet we are still willing participants. If we are to be campaigners for change we have to use our power individually and collectively to encourage it. As Popper also wrote about institutions – they cannot improve themselves; the problem is one to be solved by people. This again hints at the importance of democracy and freedom. As businesses grow in power,[6] so does their accountability. They acquire larger roles that put them at the centre of our social worlds. They can use this power for good by promoting essential freedoms, such as Reebok instituting employee democracy in its factories in China, or for control, such as Microsoft campaigning against freedom of choice for schools in developing markets.[7]

SUMMARY

Popper in his book *The Open Society and its Enemies* argued that the two prevailing theories of the world could be defined in terms of open and closed societies. Closed societies are represented by totalitarian systems and espouse the idea that institutions are everything and the individual nothing. In contrast the open society puts the individual at its centre. It praises intellectual honesty and truth. It also lays down alongside the creed of freedom the point of responsibility: that we must all work to improve the world in which we live. The focus here is to argue for open organizations that encourage a similar freedom for people to choose. To do so businesses have to be transparent and willing to engage in a wider world than the narrow focus of shareholder returns. And they have to enable people to make free and informed choices about the brands that help them define their individuality. If brands opt for the closed world they do not have a long-term future.

REFERENCES

Anholt, Simon (2003) *Brand New Justice: The upside of global branding*, Butterworth-Heinemann, Oxford

Brown, TJ and Dacin, PA (1997) The company and the product: corporate associations and consumer product responses, *Journal of Marketing*, **61** (1), pp 68–84

Economist (1999) Citizens groups: the nongovernmental order, 11 December

Elliot, LA and Schroth, RJ (2002) *How Companies Lie: Why Enron is just the tip of the iceberg*, Nicholas Brealey, London

Ellsberg, Daniel (2002) *Secrets: A memoir of Vietnam and the Pentagon papers*, Viking, New York

Gerstner, Louis V (2002) *Who Says Elephants Can't Dance?*, Harper Business, New York

Grainger, David (2003) Can McDonald's cook again? The great American icon ain't what it used to be, *Fortune*, 30 March

Hammonds, Keith (2002) Harry Kraemer's moment of truth, *Fast Company*, November, pp 93–98

Koerner, Brendan (2002) First you market the disease... then you push the pills to treat it, *Guardian*, 30 July

Koestenbaum, Peter and Block, Peter (2001) *Freedom and Accountability at Work*, Jossey Bass Pfeiffer, San Francisco

Kovach, H, Neligan, C and Burall, S (2003) *Power without Accountability? The global accountability report 2003*, One World Trust

Kraemer Jr, Harry (2002) Values-based leadership is not an oxymoron in corporate America, Speech to Chicago Executives Club by the Chairman and CEO, Baxter International, 15 October

Manville, Brook and Ober, Josiah (2003) Beyond empowerment: building a company of citizens, *Harvard Business Review*, **81** (1), January, p 51

Popper, Karl (2002) *The Open Society and its Enemies*, Routledge, London; first published 1945

Riel, Cees van (1999) *Ten Years of Research, 1988–1998 of the Corporate Communication Centre, Erasmus University Rotterdam*, Special issue on communication research in Belgium and the Netherlands, 27 January

Schumacher, Ernst (1974) *Small is Beautiful: A study of economics as if people mattered*, Abacus Books, London

Sen, Amartya (2000) *Development as Freedom*, Anchor Books, New York

NOTES

1   As Tim Kitchin argues in Chapter 5, a brand is owned by all stakeholders not just by customers.
2   As Alan Mitchell notes in Chapter 3, the very idea of loyalty to an organization is absurd.
3   Interview with author, 2003.
4   Interview with author, 2000.
5   Interview with author, 2003.
6   There are an estimated 60,000 transnational corporations and, of the 100 largest economies in the world, 51 are corporates.
7   In Peru, Microsoft tried to enlist the US Ambassador in Lima to undermine unfavourable legislation that proposed open source software in schools and also contributed money to the Peruvian school system. And while Chief Executive Steve Ballmer stated in March 2002 that Microsoft wants to be a responsible leader, he was also copied in on an e-mail, according to the *International Herald Tribune*, from the then head of worldwide sales that explained that, if a government or educational deal looked doomed, discounts should be used to win the business (in possible contravention of EU law). It said, 'Under NO circumstances lose against Linux.' (Quoted in *Financial Times*, 16 May 2003, p 19.)

2

Whose brand is it anyway?

Denzil Meyers

Brand image, brand identity, brand promise, employer brand, brand equity, brand name, brand vision, brand mission, brand values, brand attributes, brand manners, brand personality, brand relationship, live the brand, brand experience. The list of jargon and buzz words goes on and on...

This book promises to discuss the brave new world 'beyond branding' and explore how the suddenly trendy values of integrity and transparency are changing how brands are judged and how they should be managed by their corporate handlers.

Unfortunately, the appeal of the title reflects what seems to be a widely held view today, that corporations and their brands have historically conducted themselves without integrity and without transparency. This realization should be met with riots and protests, and indeed it has, in Seattle and Davos and other cities where corporate leaders meet. The opposites of the new positive values are manipulation and obfuscation, which are the old values and goals ascribed to corporate brands and marketing in books like Naomi Klein's *No Logo* and Eric Schlosser's *Fast Food Nation*. These books tell the story of a modern-day *The Jungle*, Upton Sinclair's 1906 novel of that era's hidden secrets of exploitation of humanity by industry.

The authors of this book are not out to save brands and branding in their contemporary form. In fact, we think the current system is so broken, so corrupt, so oblivious to real human values that we'd like to encourage corporations to unceremoniously dump their entire framework of consumer manipulation, employee alignment, brand management, and over-reliance on pumping out marketing to drive financial results and start afresh, building a new framework based on sustainable human values and a long-term view of business vitality and relationships.

What branding has been up until now is a symptom, but not the root of the problem. The root is probably deep inside our species' historic struggle to survive, where the short-term thinking and competitive strategies of our primal brains ensured the next generation. (See Chapter 3 for a detailed look at how these strategies manifest themselves in limiting corporate operational and branding behaviour.) But in an era where we have the ability to kill almost everything on the planet with nuclear weapons, where people and communities can exchange information electronically almost instantly with others tens of thousands of miles away, where clean water and breathable air and native plants and animals are endangered by pollution and exploitation, where the activities of multinational corporations connect the lives of people from countries all over the world together through the creation and consumption of products and services, where national economies succeed or fail interdependently, the short-term thinking and competitive strategies of our primal brains seem dangerous and even reckless.

As an alternative, the authors of this book are suggesting a new view of organizational relationships that is based on openness, honesty, transparency, shared-value creation and mutually beneficial exchange. We intend to make the case that these values can drive business performance better than the old values, because the resulting trust and goodwill will serve to multiply value creation in a positive sum equation, as opposed to the zero-sum equation of the dog-eat-dog world from which we hope and pray the world is moving.

As past branding practices followed the perspectives of the industrial era in which they were formed, 'beyond branding' can likewise be a manifestation of new values and a new view of stakeholders and markets. While old brand management and marketing have been the B52 bombers of exploitation and obfuscation, can beyond-brand practices be the messengers of transparency and integrity? For the world, for business, for consumers and employees and other stakeholders, for ourselves and for our children, we hope business and political leaders can see the pressing need for a great leap forward.

But first, a short explanation of our use of brand...

THE POWER OF ASSOCIATION

Over the past 100 or so years, the term 'brand' has undergone radical evolution from commodity, to product, to experience, to relationship, to this book's current usage – the interdependent living system of stakeholders. It's our view that a brand, rather than being an object of exchange, can be viewed as the sum total of relationships among stakeholders, or the medium through which stakeholders interact and exchange with each other. This dynamic is true for all stakeholders, not just for the stakeholder class we call 'consumers'.

I don't think, perhaps contrary to some views, that there is simultaneously a consumer brand, an employer brand, a stockholder brand etc. I think there is one brand identity, which is chosen by all stakeholders and which unifies stakeholders and defines the community. Brand identity is the same for all – choosers and rejecters.

A brand has users – people who choose to engage for the purpose of changing something in their lives. It's true that different stakeholders engage for different needs, but mass stock ownership in developed countries and mass media coverage of business news means that the boundaries between consumer, employee and stockholder are collapsing.

In 1907, Ferdinand de Saussure (1972), called the father of modern linguistics, introduced the idea that words (language) consisted of the *association* of a sound/image (the signifier) with an idea or expectation or experience (the signified). Today, this definition sums up a brand nicely: the association of a sound/image (the name 'American Express', the image of the Green Card) with an idea or expectation or experience (perceived values, a service promise and usage satisfaction). In this example, the American Express brand is neither solely the name and logo, nor the content of expectations and experiences, but the association of the two to each other.

As UK advertising guru Jeremy Bullmore (2001) has said, 'people build brands as birds build nests, from scraps and straws we chance upon'. The applicability to brands is that, while a corporation may own and control the sound/image, it certainly cannot control the content of associations users make. In fact, while corporations spend mightily on advertising, public relations, employee communications, packaging design etc to influence the content of their brand, at the same time competitors, usage experiences, word of mouth and other sources are competing with the sound/image owner to push for potential partners' attention.

Saussure made this case as well – that while the two parts (identity and content) are dependent on each other to create meaning, the association of the two occurs in the minds of users. Further, he asserted that no individual could fully control the introduction or meaning of a new word. Words gained meaning to the extent that users were willing to accept them and found them useful. This shared-value nature of language and meaning applies to brands as well as any other part of language. Brand meaning and value then are seen as the product of agreement among users.

Today, consumers, employees and investors increasingly have access to the same body of information. Company profit statements, news stories about lawsuits being filed by disgruntled employees, and anti-company Web sites are jumbled together with advertisements and promotions. Stakeholders use all of these sources to make decisions of value about a company's promises and how those promises might be delivered. The three classes of target audience are converging rapidly, and people frequently occupy more than one class at the same time.

Still, the brand identity remains a constant for all users. It is not three brands – consumer, employee and capital investor. It is one brand, with three (or more) different demands for value. The difference is between managing three brands from a producer-centric perspective, and managing one brand's value and exchange demands from a multi-stakeholder-centric perspective.

To summarize the stakeholder-led view of brand as an interdependent living system:

▌ Brand identity owners influence, but are not in control of, brand content. Competitors, users and employees all influence and contribute to what a brand means in the marketplace.
▌ Stakeholders/users may associate any content or experience with brand identity, not just marketing. Content channels are converging, and there's nowhere to hide inconsistencies.

▎ Brand identity is the common door into a relationship for all stakeholder classes, which are also converging. Consistent brand identity means that multiple brands such as employer brands are a fiction.

Together, these three points provide a strong argument that brands are ideas that summarize agreement among stakeholders. A brand may be different in content for different types of users and their interests, but its ultimate meaning and value are dependent on users' agreement. Where there is no agreement among stakeholders, there is no brand content.

A simple example is the value of a can of Coca-Cola. If the company prices it at $1.00 to pay employees and stockholders what they demand, but a consumer doesn't agree, what is the value of the can left sitting there on the shelf? It may cost $1.00 to produce a Coca-Cola, but that cost doesn't determine its value.

Or consider the way airlines determine the value of their product: higher prices for business travellers who must be in a certain place by Thursday morning and home on Friday, and lower prices for a leisure trip with a Saturday night stay; higher prices around winter holidays, and lower prices for a young couple shopping for a spontaneous weekend getaway.

Setting the stage

The authors who follow speak about the brand in this way – as a stakeholder-led relationship system governed by freedom of choice (to choose or reject), transparency among users and shared-value creation. Their chapters will introduce new ways to map value creation and demands, interpret the complex interdependent dynamics of this brand relationship system and explore its implications for managing various stakeholder classes.

The remainder of this chapter will discuss a number of fundamental changes occurring in the world marketplace that are driving the popularity of the aforementioned values of integrity and transparency, and which are likely to multiply. The impacts of these changes are creating new vulnerabilities and opportunities for business, especially the world's largest corporations and their well-known brand names.

NEW STANDARDS, NEW STAKEHOLDERS

Early in 2003, the US animal welfare group People for the Ethical Treatment of Animals (PETA) launched a bumper sticker and poster campaign in Kentucky, London, Toronto and Bombay to pressure fast food retailer KFC to improve the lives and deaths of the 700 million chickens the chain serves each year. Among the group's goals were to improve the diets of breeder hens and to require chickens to be gassed before being slaughtered. PETA was hopeful; it had already won several battles with KFC rivals McDonald's, Burger King and Wendy's. The KFC boycott was its first international effort.

KFC responded that the company has strict guidelines for suppliers, enforced by surprise audits, which have been developed by the KFC Animal Welfare Advisory Council. But Ian Duncan, a member of the Council, was quoted in the *New York Times* expressing sympathy with PETA's methods, saying, 'I've been doing research into chicken welfare since 1965 and change has been very, very slow. I used to be against them [PETA] but I can see they are getting things done' (Becker, 2003).

At the same time, KFC competitor McDonald's was being sued in US federal court by eight teenagers who believed eating the chain's fast food had made them obese. Many people laughed when the suit was filed, and it was ultimately thrown out of court. But the presiding judge kept the possibility of future suits open when he said McDonald's might be vulnerable to claims because the company seemed less than honest about the food value, ingredients and fat content of its products. The judge cited McNuggets, which company documents revealed contain more than 30 additives and contain twice the amount of fat of a McDonald's hamburger.

Opinion polls conducted in the aftermath showed that the majority of US citizens thought the children and their parents had clearly gone too far, and were trying to shirk responsibility (*Week* magazine, 2003). But along the way, media pundits made analogies to early lawsuits against tobacco companies, and fast food opponents were able to air some uncomfortable truths about the marketing honesty and production processes of fast food.

Debra Goldman (2002), writing in the US advertising industry news magazine *Adweek*, pointed out two significant observations. First, she noted that tobacco companies' legal vulnerability was not in the idea of the product itself being dangerous, but in the public's growing conviction that the industry had been dishonest in hiding the dangers of smoking and in its marketing. Second, she wondered how McDonald's could dismiss the plaintiffs' charge of being coerced by advertising, while at the same the company spends hundreds of millions of dollars on advertising annually. Isn't it clear that McDonald's also believes its ad spending has some impact on consumer behaviour?

The KFC example provides a glimpse at phenomena much larger than can be solved by corporate social responsibility (CSR) programmes. Corporate behaviour is being attacked by members of core target groups. Concerned citizens increasingly seem willing to associate dissatisfaction about mainstream issues of food safety and human rights with corporate brands. Members of government and the press participate freely, and seem to delight in exposing corporate double standards and hypocritical behaviours.

Corporate transparency and integrity are currently hot topics, owing to a series of well-publicized accounting failures, conflicts of interest among accounting and Wall Street investment firms, and out-of-balance executive pay schemes. The resulting and related larger-context stories involve the worldwide erosion of confidence in multinational (mostly US- and EU-identified) corporations and their brands, and a wave of changing relationship dynamics among corporate stakeholders that promises to impact the way business managers do their jobs and the criteria by which their performance is evaluated.

The brands at the heart of this crisis in corporate confidence are not far away – they're the brands consumers see in the marketplace, the brands offering employment opportunities, the brands hoping to attract capital investors, the brands lobbying legislators for more favourable foreign trade protections and pollution standards. Other dissatisfied stakeholders like non-governmental organizations (NGOs) and activist investor groups are increasingly opting in (uninvited) to relationships with corporations to push for change using open access to media channels and brand awareness among consumer segments as primary weapons.

Yet despite all the hand wringing and attention being given to corporate governance and restoring trust, the marketplace still seems somewhat uncertain about the actual business benefits of this trend. The causal relationships between corporate governance, corporate social responsibility and business performance remain soft and poorly defined. In addition, corporate managers seem unprepared for the changes coming their way. Industrial-era ways of looking at and managing business functions are being challenged, yet new models and methods have not been developed to replace the old.

The authors of this book believe that corporate managers need a new framework that will help them make sense of an environment in which they and their brands will be judged by standards that are more complex, less financially driven and more human than have been used in the past.

We believe these new standards will be more sensitive to multiple and sometimes competing value demands, not just financial growth and profit, and will reflect a growing understanding that corporate brands and performance are a result of dynamic and interdependent relationships among many stakeholder classes. In this view, brands are seen as systems of freely entered relationships among marketplace peers, rather than as objects to control.

The following chapters each look at the brand value scenario from the perspective of stakeholders – employees, consumers, NGOs, investors, developing countries – and their needs in relationship with a brand, rather than from the perspective of what business wants (usually profitability or risk reduction). As co-authors, we share the belief that the world is waking up to place new demands for honesty, transparency and value on business, and that business must respond first of all by learning to listen better to stakeholders, and second by aiming to engage and co-create with stakeholders rather than striving for control and exploiting them.

We see these changes as matters of survival. This is not a book about feel-good corporate social responsibility, more sensitive management styles or tempering business goals with morality. Neither do we seek to make yet another case for blindly investing in intangibles without measurable benefits to business.

Rather, we are aiming to help businesses value, measure and manage business relationships more productively for everyone involved. The world is demanding from businesses a better understanding of how they manifest themselves in the world, yet today businesses seldom measure more than their financials. Businesses that don't change this dynamic will increasingly put themselves at risk and miss valuable opportunities for generating sales, recruiting the best employees, raising capital and avoiding punitive legislation.

PEOPLE AND RELATIONSHIPS, NOT BUSINESS FUNCTIONS

One area where this book would like to challenge traditional business thinking and approaches is in how we define value. Most corporations define and manage the value they create solely by financial measures – profitability and growth – with very little (if any) concern about the wider implications of their business processes. We believe this single-minded view is incomplete, in that it ignores the component relationships among stakeholders and the brand that are the true drivers of corporate value.

True, there is a compelling argument to be made that investors buy shares for financial gain, not for any other reason. But there's growing evidence that this dynamic is changing; that other concerns of investors and the demands of other stakeholders are taking a more active role in determining the value of a business in the world, and that financial performance is increasingly dependent on multiple measures of trust and goodwill among stakeholders.

In early 2003, I interviewed 40 US corporate executives, board members and accounting industry regulators about the forces changing their jobs, their companies and their lives. These interviews provided a concise summary of the evolving environment:

▌ *Demand for corporate transparency, openness and performance*
One result of this demand is new standards in personal accountability for corporate leaders. An overt manifestation is the new Sarbanes–Oxley Act in the United States that requires CEOs and CFOs personally to sign and attest to the accuracy of their companies' financial statements. The Act outlines harsh new penalties for fraud or negligence, including fines and possible imprisonment. The Act has created significant new compliance and internal control requirements for corporations, and especially for executives.

Additionally, many companies are revamping their boards of directors to make them more independent and more accountable to capital investors, other stakeholders and the long-term health of the business. The result is new friction and tensions between management and boards, with boards demanding more information and more over-sight of executive decision making and performance.

Because employees, customers, investors and communities increasingly enjoy open access to each other and to information about the brands and companies they choose, inconsistencies between corporate stated values and behaviours/actions, and inconsistencies in managing expectations across multiple stakeholder classes create unnecessary risks to good brand and business relationships.

▌ *Interdependence of multiple performance-drivers*
The changes in CxO accountability and in CxO relationships with directors are amplifying a recent trend towards performance measurement of all business functions. As corporations have sought to drive superior performance, managers have sought new ways to understand and manage component performance-drivers like customer loyalty and acquisition costs, employee satisfaction and retention, IT integration and implementation, productivity and knowledge management, innovation and speed to market.

The first step is recognizing the link between individual areas and the market. The second step is recognizing how these areas operate interdependently to drive excellence. In one of my interviews, a CIO spoke of 'touching one area, and seeing the ripples manifest across the entire organization'. Even while the connections between independent drivers and bottom-line profit are still tenuous, there's a growing recognition that these areas (and the people within them) must be managed interdependently.

These areas can be understood and managed as groups of people (performance communities, perhaps), not as business functions in their own functional silos.

▌ *Emerging recognition of multiple stakeholder classes and their power*
Increasingly, corporate boards are behaving more like a class of stakeholders for leaders to manage rather than insiders that management can count on to play along. But both CEOs and boards are also starting to recognize that other stakeholders are using public demands for openness and transparency and a new electronic media environment to push their way to centre-stage and be heard.

The media environment is a major factor, and the media can be seen as a stakeholder class in itself. The Internet has made more information from more sources more available to more people. Rather than replacing traditional media, the Internet has combined with phenomena like 24-hour business news and new satellite television stations so that corporations (and governments) are less able to control what is said about them than ever. It's not the volume that's important, but the freedom of information that makes the difference, and the ability for all stakeholders to access the same media sources.

While capital investors used to be a relatively small part of the population, the West's baby-boom has fuelled a corresponding boom in stock ownership. Stock ownership in the West has become a mass phenomenon, and capital investors today are also likely to be a company's potential consumers, strategic partners and employees. The current generation of capital investors demands financial performance, but it's their other demands, such as for environmentally responsible practices or fair labour policies, that increasingly challenge leaders to manage multiple and competing priorities.

Employees have been gaining power as well. The information economy puts a premium on education, and the freedom and skills needed to act and engage other stakeholders. As mentioned, employees have more information about their employers than ever before and in a service economy are the face of the brand. The result is less ability to control and more need for leaders to recruit and engage employees to deliver for customers.

Corporate brand managers are losing not only their ability to control what is said about their brands and where, but even their ability to control and define who is a stakeholder. Socially conscious investors, consumers concerned about the quality and safety of mass-produced and mass-marketed food, and crusading NGOs can be viewed as a new class of self-defining stakeholders who are choosing to engage with the brand. Importantly, these stakeholders may not engage for reasons that are intended by the company, such as to buy the product or service, but for reasons that may be hostile to the assumptions of corporate managers (eg to impact corporate policy and behaviour).

The conclusion is that a single-minded focus on business functions is not enough. Increasingly, business performance is being broken down into its component parts but, instead of a value chain of functions serving the customer, we see a value web of interdependent stakeholder classes. The web's classes each have somewhat different needs, but feed on similar information that often comes not from corporate leaders but from other stakeholders in the marketplace. Trust and goodwill towards leaders and towards the brand come from consistency, keeping promises and openness. And trust and goodwill make the difference between superior and mediocre performance, since these are the drivers of loyalty, productivity and engagement.

SHARED VALUE AND COLLABORATION, NOT CONTROL AND EXPLOITATION

The authors of this book believe that another area business leaders should reconsider is their model for creating value, which in most cases is based on exploitation, ie purposefully inequitable value exchanges with partners.

From the vantage point of the industrial era, this approach made perfect sense: raw materials are procured, value is added by means of processing or packaging or manufacture, costs for employees and equipment are accounted for, and the goods are resold at a profit that is shared among the original investors.

This scenario may look like good business, but today it can also be viewed as a series of win/lose value exchanges. At each step of the process, the company defines success by getting from its partner more than it gives. The greater the win for the business/loss for the partner, the greater the success. It's a model that thrives where competition for raw materials, capital or labour is artificially stifled, where actual or long-term costs are obscured, where transparency is limited and where the strong can overpower the weak. Unfortunately, the model also views customers, employees and strategic partners as subordinates, rather than as equal partners. And of course, customers and partners are also taking a win/lose approach, so that dishonesty and hidden costs exist on both sides. Managers say they want to reap loyalty and respect, yet the opposite is sown.

But today, globalization and a changing political environment are tearing down walls to new business competitors; consumers and employees are enjoying explosive growth in choices of products, careers, where to live and sources of entertainment and information; financial scandals are accelerating calls for increased ethical standards and fiscal transparency. The triumph of the free market has raised stakeholders' expectations to the point where satisfaction and loyalty are falling, and people are ignoring or avoiding advertising in record numbers. Corporate marketing has trained a generation of consumers to demand more, and now those demands are outstripping big business's ability to deliver.

From the vantage point of a business's stakeholders, the industrial-era equation may be read this way: finite raw materials are stripped from the earth, destroying natural habitats and old-growth forests, while a few get very rich and the general populace live depressing Third World lives. Or foodstuffs that are grown in a way that pollutes groundwater, kills the soil and drives family farms out of business are then over-processed (which kills nutritive value), over-packaged (using non-renewable materials and creating unnecessary waste), over-advertised and overpriced. Or the production of chemicals to be used around the world causes disease in a small town, while the evidence is positioned as 'inconclusive' by company public relations managers.

In these scenarios, employees are seen as costs to be contained, and efforts are made to pay and invest as little as possible, including migrating low-skilled jobs to developing countries from developed ones. Some industries recruit specifically from populations who are easily exploited (eg undocumented workers), or invest heavily in new technology that has the stated goal of eliminating employee training completely and keeping hourly wages low (eg the fast food industry).

Next, a company may invest in marketing, seeking to dominate markets and acquire mindshare (military metaphors abound in marketing) by trumpeting loudly the absolutely best aspects of its product or service, exaggerating the benefits versus competition and obfuscating limitations or long-term dangers or hidden costs. Along the way, the corporation may invest further in lobbying government to provide it with special incentives in the form of tax breaks, loopholes or limited liability, under the argument that the growing business provides jobs for voters, even as top executives in the Unites States are compensated at 500 times the salary of the average worker.

Lastly, the company then may legally engage in many forms of fiscal sleight of hand, in the form of pro forma financial statements, unreadable and dense annual reports, conflicted interest relationships with investment banks and accountants, or off-shore incorporation to avoid taxation, all of which allow it to present the best possible appearance of financial health to the marketplace.

How can a corporation adapt to an environment in which this kind of story is being written and read daily? How can traditional marketing compete with this kind of view of a company and its practices? It's obvious that capital investors can't succeed unless the business serves customers well. But what happens when demands for quarterly profits start to conflict with the need for investments in new products or investments in training employees or transparency in environmental impact?

As we see the equation, the industrial-era approach has two main drawbacks. First, by viewing partners exploitatively, by focusing on short-term sales and by validating obfuscation of long-term costs, it creates huge amounts of risk for companies, which later is expressed as lost customers, increased marketing costs, lack of innovation, product liability lawsuits, disengaged and unproductive employees, eroded brand value etc.

Second, it pits stakeholder groups' interests against each other, creating conflict where cooperation would likely provide much more opportunity. The industrial-era framework based on win/loss takes a zero-sum view of value and casts the company in control of value exchange. This zero-sum view neglects to acknowledge the value that consumers bring to a brand (by how it fits into their lives), the ability of employees and customers collaboratively to increase value exchange through excellent service and feedback, or the impact of competitors' brands on perceptions of one's own.

Our alternative view is that openness, transparency and a co-creative approach to managing brands and business operate on a 1+ sum value equation, and that the economies of trust-based collaborative value exchange will outperform competitive zero-sum exploitation. By connecting communities of stakeholders together and helping them recognize their common values, shared goals and perspectives, a new value equation can be calculated, one in which satisfied stakeholders will act as a multiplier of value. The authors on the following pages each explore an aspect of this new value equation. We hope your thinking will be challenged, and that you'll be inspired to explore and experiment yourself.

Please let us know what you discover...

REFERENCES

Becker, Elizabeth (2003) Group says it will begin a boycott against KFC, *New York Times*, 5 January

Bullmore, Jeremy (2001) Posh Spice and Persil: both big brands; both alive; and both belonging to the public, Speech to the British Brands Group, London, 5 December

Goldman, Debra (2002) Commons sense may not be McDonald's ally for long, 'Consumer Republic' column, *Adweek*, 2 December

Saussure, Ferdinand de (1972) *Course in General Linguistics*, tr Roy Harris, Open Court

Week magazine (2003) Best columns, Fast food: you deserve a tort today 14 February (summarizing a column by Adam Cohen in the *New York Times* the previous week)

3

Beyond brand narcissism

Alan Mitchell

You must guard against not only complacency, but also narcissism – the temptation to stare into the mirror when you should be looking out of the window. Our business is not about understanding our brand. It's about understanding people.

(Doug Daft, CEO, Coca-Cola)

In a recent show in London, US comic Michael Moore brought one sketch to a crescendo by taking out a pair of scissors and snipping a loyalty card in two. 'Say after me!' he shouted. 'I am loyal to myself! I am loyal to my community! I am *not* loyal to a corporation!'

'Loyalty' never was a very good word to describe repeat purchase. But the words we choose have a habit of betraying our underlying attitudes and assumptions. Marketers conjured up the word 'loyalty' because in their dreams consumers are, indeed, loyal to their brands.

A human being 'loyal' to a soap powder? Or a bank account? Or an airline? As soon as we stop to think about it, we can see how absurd this notion is. Yet such absurdity is so common nowadays that no one (except a few iconoclastic comedians) blinks an eye. This absurdity is a disease: the endemic disease of brand narcissism.

THE NARCISSISTIC PERSONALITY DISORDER

In Greek legend, Narcissus was the poor creature who was so enraptured by the sight of his own reflection that he pined away, gazing at it until he died. Modern psychiatrists classify narcissism as a clearly identifiable personality disorder. According to the American Psychiatric Association's reference bible DSM IV (*Diagnostic and Statistical Manual of Mental Disorders*), the narcissistically wounded personality tends to display some or all of the following attributes:

∎ a grandiose sense of self-importance;
∎ fantasies of unlimited success, power and brilliance;
∎ a belief that one is superior, special and unique;
∎ a constant seeking for attention and admiration;
∎ a preoccupation with how well one is doing and how favourably one is regarded by others.

A personality disorder? Or a brand manager's job description? You take your pick, because the similarities are striking. After all, 'Look at me! Look at how wonderful and attractive I am!' is the fundamental agenda of advertising, direct marketing, public relations, sponsorship and so on: no brand ever got successful by being a shrinking violet.

Does this similarity matter? Who cares if marketers sometimes use silly words like 'loyalty'? Isn't it a trifle condescending to suppose that marketers and their publics can't cope with a bit of narcissistic preening? We all take it with a pinch of salt anyway, don't we?

Perhaps we do. But that's not the point. 'Look at me!' brand preening is just one, superficial, symptom of a dysfunction that reaches right back into the heart of how we create, distribute and exchange value. The problem with narcissists is that they only understand their relationships with other people in terms of themselves. They are only interested in other people to the extent and degree that these other people provide them with a mirror in which to regard themselves further. They use other people for their own purposes – their own self-glorification. And because they so routinely use people for their own narcissistic ends they want for friends. In fact, precisely because they use other people for their own ends, they have a habit of hurting and disappointing, turning many a friend into an enemy along the way.

Brand narcissism is very similar. It attempts to use people for the purposes of the brand, and in so doing destroys the win–win heart of branding. This explains why, instead of fulfilling their role as the consumer's friend, as trusted beacons of superior value, brands are widely perceived as superficial, exploitative, manipulative and even dehumanizing. It explains why branding, which is commonly hailed as one of the secrets of a business's success, can easily become one of its biggest problems.

There is one important difference between personal and brand narcissism, however. Brand narcissism isn't generated by individuals' psychological make-ups. It is a *systemic* disorder where, as systems thinker Peter Senge (1990: 44) put it, even people with the best intentions 'just find themselves compelled to act in certain ways'.

This chapter analyses the pressures that drive even the best-intentioned marketers and companies to behave narcissistically. These drivers run deep, including the way markets are structured and work, companies' internal operational imperatives, their motivations and incentives, and their go-to-market methodologies. It shows how, by tackling the systemic roots of the disorder, we can open the door to new win–wins and new dimensions of wealth creation.

THE WIN–WIN HEART OF BRANDING

Before we attack the problem – the dark side of the Jekyll and Hyde brand character – let's remind ourselves of the win–wins of branding and why they are so important. No modern economy can prosper without efficiently matching supply to demand and connecting buyers to sellers. If this matching and connecting fails to happen , 'making' simply becomes 'wasting' as firms end up making the wrong things or being unable to sell them. Branding is critical to helping both matching and connecting work:

▐ *Matching*. Brands facilitate efficient, effective matching because branding requires firms to seek to understand what a particular market wants and develop a package of attributes to meet these wants. Clearly, this creates potentially rich win–wins.

▐ *Connecting*. By building their brands as 'value beacons' – clearly defined, easily identified, trustable source of value – sellers help buyers to simplify choice, speed up navigation to desired sources of value, reduce verification costs (will it do what it says on the tin?) and add reassurance. Brands may help sellers to sell, but the process of branding also helps buyers to buy.

Even the most basic attribute of branding – its role as a *naming* device – helps buyers and sellers to create win–wins by streamlining communication. Everyday conversations would become extremely cumbersome if, each time we wanted to mention people or things, we had to stop to describe all their attributes in detail in order to identify them. You need names – concentrated packages of complex sets of information – to be able to have an efficient conversation. Likewise, with brands. You need them to have efficient commercial conversation.

Naming, matching and connecting: separately and together they are the source of many of the win–wins that make modern economies and companies prosper. And branding lies at the heart of them. So to suggest that somehow brands are 'bad', to be 'against brands' or to predict the 'death' of brands is simply absurd. If we did not have brands, we would have to invent them.

To the same degree, however, when we say brand narcissism destroys the fundamental win–wins at the heart of branding, we are not making a trivial point. What, then, are the causes of brand narcissism and how can these causes be tackled?

LOOK AT ME! MARKETING

There are four main causes of brand narcissism: structural, operational, motivational and methodological. The first cause is so familiar and obvious that we can state it very simply and quickly. But it would be a great mistake to confuse this simplicity with unimportance. A vital *structural* cause of brand narcissism is the way competition currently works, with many different sellers competing for the same buyers' attention, preference and custom. The 'Look at me!' nature of brand management and brand building is a by-product of the fact that many different sellers are crowding around each buyer, all focusing on how to get their particular message through. Cracking this clutter and crowding problem lies at the heart of finding a cure for brand narcissism.

'VALUE FROM OUR OPERATIONS'

The *operational* causes of brand narcissism have their roots in how modern companies create value. They do this by investing vast amounts of money, resources, skills, know-how and labour in corporate infrastructure, which they use to make products or services, which they then sell on the open market. The forms this infrastructure takes vary widely. It may be factories, pipelines, warehouses and shops, aircraft, bank branches and IT systems – whatever. Either way, creating such infrastructure is difficult and expensive, so it's a simple survival imperative that the firm generates a viable return on this investment.

Four things follow. First, the vast majority of most corporate managers' time and attention is necessarily focused inwards: on the operational challenge of how to make the most of these assets. Second (and equally naturally), when managers seek to 'make the most' of these assets they judge success or failure by their own internal criteria: the efficiency of their own internal operations, the returns generated on their own assets. As John Caswell of Group Partners puts it, what drives companies is the quest for 'vendor efficient supply' not 'customer efficient demand'. For these reasons the focus of management and the metrics of corporate efficiency are inherently inward-looking and narcissistic.

Third, companies naturally see value in terms of 'what comes out of our operations', not the value that is created in my life. There can be a big difference between the two. Take the simple examples of 'price' and 'cost'. When marketers talk about price, they naturally mean the price they charge: 'our price: the money we get from the transaction'. But this is never the same as the price actually paid by the customer. This price invariably includes other costs, such as those invested in sourcing and accessing the product or service in question: time costs, money costs, hassle costs. For example, if you value the time consumers spend travelling to and from grocery stores, searching for items in the shop, queuing and paying and so on, at the European minimum wage, this extra cost accounts for 20 per cent of the total grocery value chain. When marketers charge $1, the consumer actually pays $1.20 (calculations from Yrölä *et al*, 2002). But such calculations hardly ever enter brand narcissists' equations – because they see value as 'what comes out of our operations', not 'what happens in my life'.

Likewise, brand narcissists routinely define value in terms of the attributes of 'my product' rather than the attributes of my life. This creates all sorts of value blind spots. Henkel, Procter & Gamble and Unilever focus intensively on the attributes of their soap powders, but rarely look beyond these product attributes to the real need 'in my life', which is for fresh, clean clothes, ironed and ready to wear. (For a list of the main value gaps, see the box.)

The main value gaps

Industrial-age companies excel in producing certain forms of value – 'value from our operations': the sorts of value that can be made in factories and sold in shops. The inherent nature of 'value from our operations' means, however, that there are certain forms of value that the firm either cannot or does not want to address. These elements of value have, for the most part, been left to individuals to 'make' 'in my life'. They include:

▌ *transaction costs:* what it costs me in terms of time, money and hassle to search for, identify and purchase the value I want;

▌ *solution assembly:* what it costs me in terms of time, money and hassle to purchase, assemble and integrate different ingredients to realize the outcomes I want;

▌ *customization:* the dimensions of value I miss out on, or the extra time, money and hassle costs I incur, because mass-produced standardized value offerings do not align perfectly with my particular needs or circumstances;

▌ *buyer-centric information:* the sorts of impartial, comprehensive, easy-to-use information that helps me identify and source the value that's best for me – as opposed to the partial, biased advertising information that's presented to me by self-interested sellers;

▌ *where economies of scale fail:* areas such as clothes washing, plumbing or childcare where traditional economies of scale fail to operate;

▌ *authentic emotions:* my desire for emotional benefits such as genuine community, personal sense of purpose or authentic self-expression that the manufactured identities of traditional branding either do not address or do not allow;

▌ *personal asset productivity and maximization:* my desire to make the most of personal (as opposed to corporate) assets such as my time, my information, my energy, my attention, my money and property and my passions.

Finally, consumer rhetoric aside, the job of marketing in virtually all firms is to assist managers in the task of maximizing the value generated by our operations, by 'feeding' these operations with the orders that keep the firm alive and generate the returns it so desperately needs. Again, this is perfectly natural and understandable. But along the way it also subtly influences the role of marketing and therefore of brands.

Twenty years ago Harvard Business School professor Theodore Levitt saw the need to draw a distinction between marketing and selling. 'Selling focuses on the need of the seller, marketing on the needs of the buyer,' he wrote. 'Selling is preoccupied with the seller's need to convert his product into cash, marketing with the idea of satisfying the needs of the customer...' (Levitt, 1983).

But the narcissistic mindset has a knack of taking every such idea and insight and using it as a tool for its own purposes. Take the now-universal marketing clichés of 'focus on your customer' and 'understand and meet the needs of your customer'. At first glance, phrases like this seem the ultimate rejection of narcissism. What more can you do than focus on and understand the needs of your customer?

Yet, by definition a consumer or customer is someone who buys (or could buy) what we make. When companies 'focus on the consumer', what they are really focusing on is units of demand for what they are trying to sell. In this way 'consumer focus' is often nothing more or less than just another way of focusing on what we make: a company looking in the mirror of its own needs and operations. Likewise, when companies research 'the market' – another apparently outward-looking process – 9 times out of 10 they have already defined this market in narcissistic terms: in terms of what they are trying to sell. Again, what they are really doing is looking into the mirror of their own needs and priorities. Most market research fits the DSM IV narcissistic personality perfectly: the preoccupation with how well I am doing and how favourably I am regarded by others.

We can see the same narcissism running all the way through the traditional marketing pantheon. Take branding. By definition, a brand represents the product or service the firm is trying to sell. The brand is a manifestation of 'what we make' in the world outside. So when companies say they are now marketing- rather than production-driven, because they are now focusing all their efforts on building their brands, what they are really saying is that they are focusing all their efforts on... a manifestation of ourselves. They are polishing the mirror of their own activities and priorities.

As Doug Daft pointed out, for example, obsessing about the brand's personality, values, soul, DNA (the list grows longer by the day) can become an extremely convenient way of *not* focusing on the people the company is dealing with. Brand loyalty becomes the narcissistic quest to get consumers to worship a manifestation of the corporation, and customer relationship management the attempt to build a relationship… around the products we are trying to sell.

That is why, a decade and a half after Levitt, management guru Peter Drucker echoed his comments, declaring that marketing and branding were nowadays just a subset of selling. 'Marketing teaches that organised efforts are needed to bring an understanding of the outside, of society, economy and customer, to the inside of the organisation and to make it the foundation for strategy and policy,' he wrote in a *Forbes* magazine article (Drucker, 1998). '[But] marketing has rarely performed that grand task. Instead it has become a tool to support selling. It does not start out with "who is the customer?" but "what do we want to sell?" It is aimed at getting people to buy the things that you want to make.'

Brand narcissism, then, is not just a product of the need for brands to shout louder to gain consumers' attention. Its roots are operational, too, fundamentally affecting how companies approach the whole process of marketing and branding.

WHO ARE BRANDS FOR?

The third root cause of brand narcissism is *motivation*. It relates to the question 'Who are brands for?' The answer (consumer rhetoric aside) is that brands are built and owned by corporations to serve corporations' purposes. The brand is the property of the corporation (as trade marks, brands are intangible assets that are legally owned by companies to be bought, sold, invested in or milked to death as the formal owner sees fit). And its purpose is to help the corporation achieve its goals, eg to maximize profits or shareholder value.

Again, this is quite natural and understandable. Building a brand is an expensive exercise. The necessary market research, packaging, design, advertising, sponsorship, public relations and so on that are necessary for the brand to make the grade don't come cheap. So companies making such investments expect to earn a return on this investment. But one result is that the value of these activities is instinctively measured first and foremost in terms of value 'to me': the company. Take the following high-profile issues in marketing, for example:

▌ *Marketing effectiveness.* When companies talk about marketing effectiveness they naturally assume that effectiveness is defined from the company's point of view: how effective a marketing programme was in terms of achieving the *company's* goals, not the customer's. In marketing circles, 'marketing effectiveness awards' abound. But none of them bother to consider whether the marketing programme in question addressed or met consumers' go-to-market goals.

▌ *Marketing accountability.* Accountability is now a hot issue in marketing circles. How can marketing departments justify their budgets? How can they prove that the funds they have spent on, say, advertising have generated a decent return? The natural assumption here is that accountability means accountability to the company and its goals – not to consumers and their goals. After all, it is the company that spends its money on marketing, isn't it? Well, no. It isn't. This sort of accountability confuses 'those who actually pay' with 'those who write the cheques'. Marketing departments (or finance directors) may hold the purse strings, but consumers pay for all marketing and brand building in the prices they pay for products and services. Yet how many companies attempt to make marketing budgets and expenditures accountable to the customer? How well did that ad campaign generate a return for the person who funded it, the consumer?

▌ *Brand valuation.* Brand valuation is now a massive mini-industry in its own right. Its focus is entirely narcissistic. Companies are forever asking 'What is the value of my brand to me? Can I claim this value as my own, something I can put on my balance sheet?'

▌ *Lifetime value.* Lifetime value is now a key metric by which companies approach their customer relationship strategies. Typically, the aim is to focus effort on those customers with the highest lifetime value and to de-emphasize (even 'sack' or 'dismarket') those with low lifetime values. Of course, lifetime value means value to the company over time, never value of the company to the customer over time.

These examples show how narcissistic assumptions instinctively inform and seep through every aspect of modern marketing debate and practice.

But there's another angle to this question 'Who are brands for?' The win–win answer is to 'make a profit by delivering superior value to the consumer'. But the increasingly common answer is subtly different: 'to command a price premium'. With this answer the narcissistic mindset confuses the purpose of branding with its win–win effect.

Historically, superior margins were a happy by-product of successful brand building – successfully delivering superior value to consumers. But, as narcissism has taken root, increasingly the corporate purpose in building a brand is to justify a price premium: to charge more. The purpose of most image advertising, for example, is not to draw attention to a superior value offer, but to persuade consumers to pay more. In this way, brands have become a part of the industrial-age corporation's value extraction mentality. 'We extract value from the earth via our mines. And we extract value from markets (eg consumers) via our brands.' The narcissist sees all value in terms of potential value to me.

This value extraction mentality doesn't stop at price. It spills over into brands' approach to meaning and culture too. When marketers talk about emotional added value, they are already talking narcissistically. They are referring to the attributes of their brand, not real benefits for people. When a cleaning product presents us with 'good mother' imagery in its advertising, it is attempting to use the housewife's emotional commitment to being a good mother to drive sales of its brand – not to add emotional value in her life by helping her to become a good mother.

Naomi Klein's best-seller *No Logo* is a tirade against some of these excesses of brand narcissism. Brands' attempts to move into the spheres of culture and meaning – via tools such as sponsorship – are all about soaking up cultural ideas to turn these ideas into 'extensions of their brands', she complained (Klein, 2000: 28). It's about value extraction, a form of cultural looting: 'to nudge the hosting culture into the background and make the brand the star' (Klein, 2000: 30). Likewise, with fashion- and youth-oriented marketers' obsession with 'cool hunting'. Hunters hunt and kill to satiate their own needs at the expense of their victims. These marketers do the same with youth trends and cults – hunt them, and then kill them with their over-commercialization.

Once value extraction becomes the purpose of brand building, branding loses its original *raison d'être* – the win–wins that made it valuable in the first place.

SERVICE OR CONTROL?

The final piece of the jigsaw is the methods companies use to build brands, and how brands are meant to do their job: their *methodologies*.

In the era when marketing was born, there were no viable mechanisms for buyers – consumers – to send 'Here I am, this is what I want' messages to producers and sellers: messages that potentially contain all the information needed for efficient, effective matching and connecting. In the absence of this critical source of information, sellers had to fill the vacuum with their own 'top-down' marketing communications and activities. Marketing became a process of sellers saying 'Here we are! This is what we have to offer!'

The results of this historical 'accident' permeate every aspect of modern marketing. Marketing has evolved as a top-down process, where messages and information flow one way from seller to buyer. Marketing has also evolved as a seller's monopoly. Sellers take responsibility for organizing the core tasks of matching and connecting, so marketing becomes something that is done by sellers *to* and *at* buyers. That's why today the core marketing methodology is stimulus/response: seller stimulus designed to elicit consumer response. As the grand old man of marketing education Philip Kotler remarks in his latest book, the fundamental paradigm of industrial-age marketing is one of 'unidirectional control' (Kotler, Jain and Maesincee, 2002: 125).

This control over the marketing process – 'we do it all; we pay for it all' – naturally has its effects on the goals marketers set for their marketing programmes. Marketing became a *seller-centric* activity, done *by* sellers *for* sellers to achieve sellers' goals. For example, brands are supposed to be the end-product of a matching process by which the company aligns what it does to the needs of its customers. But if we look at the reality of marketing as practised day to day, we find that when it comes to going to market – once the company has made its product or service – now the overwhelming survival necessity is to sell it. At this point, the real goal of the company's marketing is turned on its head: from getting the company to do what the customer wants, to getting the customer to do what the company wants: 'Buy our product!' Marketing and branding become an exercise in attempted consumer influence and control.

That is one of the reasons why corporations are so keen to build their brands: because they see their brand as a means of extending the control that they influence internally and operationally beyond the boundaries of the firm to the marketplace. That is why marketing is so chock-full of the language of power and control: of campaigns and offensives, of 'targeting', 'precision marketing', response rates, pulling the right levers, pressing the right buttons, finding the right emotional triggers and so on.

It's also why so much emphasis is placed on certain mechanisms. Price and promotion, for example, are used by companies to influence consumer purchasing behaviours in their favour. Likewise with marketing communications, which in countless cases boil down to an attempted 'mind-cuckoo' marketing strategy.

The cuckoo inserts her egg in another bird's nest, and expunges that bird's own eggs from the nest, with the intention of getting the other bird to feed her chick. Advertisers seek to do the same with consumers' minds. They seek to insert their brand messages into the consumer's mind, to dislodge other rival and competing messages, with the intention of getting that consumer to feed their brand – to be 'top of mind': hence marketers' obsessions with measures like spontaneous and prompted awareness.

Mind-cuckoo marketing may not work half as well as most marketers may wish, but the intention is there. A large element of marketing communications is an attempt to control: to get consumers' perceptions, preferences, priorities and behaviours orbiting the brand – just as narcissists try to organize other people's emotions and behaviours to orbit their own egos. As Peter Drucker continued in his *Forbes* magazine article, as a tool marketing was originally fashioned to bring the outside to the inside. But since its earliest days it has been 'penetrated by the inside focus of management' who have used these tools in the belief that 'they can manipulate the outside and turn it to the organisation's purpose'.

ALL IS FORGIVEN... OR IS IT?

Boastful and vain, self-absorbed, selfish and controlling: these are how the structural, operational, motivational and methodological drivers of brand management manifest themselves in brands' behaviours. Yet at the same time, the origins and value of brands lie deep in the matching and connecting win–wins we discussed earlier. Both are true. Both are reflections of the same underlying reality. That is why the public has such a love/hate relationship with brands – why brands are both so universally popular and reviled, so universally sought after yet kept at arm's length and dismissed as 'mere marketing ploys', so universally trusted yet treated with suspicion.

Looking at the popularity, desire and trust that brands manage to generate, marketers routinely hope and believe that if only they could do a little more, better marketing – by building even stronger brands – the positives will eventually crowd out the negatives. But as we've seen the reality is quite different. More, better marketing is the source of both the positive *and* the negative effects. More, better marketing is part of the problem, not part of the solution. But the ideology of branding helps obscure this fact.

Like all truly successful ideologies, branding unites two divergent trends behind the same banner: of brands as vehicles of value (as former Unilever chairman Sir Michael Perry described them) and brands as vehicles of corporate narcissism. Both sides are convinced 'we must do everything we can to build our brands'. But they mean completely opposite things. Both sides coexist in the same companies and in the same individuals.

But neither aspect of this Jekyll and Hyde character is particularly new. It's been around since marketing was first invented. So why draw attention to it now?

The answer is, all is forgiven as long as branding remains a win–win process. If brands still stand for trustable sources of unique and superior value, and the process of branding helps both sides achieve better matching and connecting at lower cost, then the irritations and limitations of brand narcissism are a small price to pay. Trouble is, the opposite dynamic is prevailing. Brand narcissism is increasing precisely because the win–wins that underpin branding are declining. As the wins for consumers diminish, consumer enthusiasm and loyalty for brands decline. Marketing becomes 'less effective'. As a result companies find themselves under increasing pressure to regain the market share, margin and other benefits their brands once brought – and the narcissistic 'What's in it for me?' mentality moves centre-stage.

Increasing brand narcissism, then, is a *product* of declining win–wins, not just a cause. Why should this be? The causes of diminishing win–wins are familiar, so we'll allude to them only very quickly:

▮ *Market maturity.* Brands originally helped energize a virtuous spiral where increased demand fed through to improving economies of scale, to lower unit costs, to better value. As markets mature and overcapacity kicks in, however, increased investment in productive capacity generates more cost than benefit. Companies' ability to offer improving value diminishes. The virtuous value spiral begins to turn vicious.

▌ *Product parity.* Competition is all about not letting your competitor get ahead, so whenever a successful innovation is introduced it is quickly copied. This makes sustainable differentiation on the basis of 'demonstrable product superiority' ever more difficult and undermines the original role of brands as beacons of unique, superior value. As a result many companies have now begun to argue that branding itself is the source of differentiation. Yet, as soon as the brand's job is to hide sameness rather than express and communicate difference the win for the consumer evaporates. This destroys trust, rather than building it.

▌ *Information overload.* When marketing first started out, media markets were immature. In today's world of proliferating, fragmenting media, consumers are bombarded with selling messages. As a result, the beacon benefits of advertising – to help consumers identify and seek the sources of value they want – are turning into a cost and a chore instead: of sifting through information clutter.

▌ *Innoflation.* In their increasingly desperate attempts to find a source of differentiation, companies are increasingly throwing ersatz innovations at the market: not real value breakthroughs, but excuses for being able to claim 'new, improved'. Endless line extensions, gimmicky features, product variants and so on make the job of searching for the sources of genuine value that are right for me ever more tiresome. They complexify rather than simplify.

Brands generate win–wins by acting as trusted beacons of superior value. Separately and together, these developments are working to undermine each element: trust, the brand's beacon role and its ability to guarantee superior value. Crucially, however, each of these developments is beyond the control or influence of individual marketers and companies. They are *systemic* effects: the net result of many individual decisions by people who feel 'just compelled' to act in certain ways.

It's this that makes brand narcissism so toxic. The win–wins that underpin traditional brands are under threat anyway. Narcissism threatens to destroy them. So what can we do about it?

RESISTANCE OR IMMUNITY?

Like all diseases, brand narcissism has its own epidemiology. How badly companies are affected depends on their history, cultures, categories and markets. And there are things they can do to bolster their resistance.

One simple answer is constantly to resist the temptations of narcissism – constantly to strive to regenerate the win–wins of branding. A first step is to repudiate the 'product/service parity is inevitable' counsel of despair that justifies the now-common marketing argument that 'branding is now a substitute for product/service differentiation'. If an organization can no longer offer something special, it has lost its right to brand.

To resist narcissism we also need to recognize that a crucial job of win–win branding is helping buyers to buy as well as helping sellers to sell. It's the job of the brand (and the marketing communications and activities that support it) to help buyers navigate their way to and access the value they seek. Successful branding delivers *buyer-centric* information – addressing buyers' go-to-market needs and priorities as well as delivering seller-centric 'buy me!' messages. It also requires that we address customer transaction costs: the time, money and hassle I invest in sourcing the value I want.

In other words, as well as asking how well does our product/service add value to the customer, we also need to ask how well does our *marketing* add value to the customer. Not only must the *product* be 'worth buying', so must our marketing.

This isn't a trivial point. If you divide value creation into two broad buckets of 'making' and 'marketing' (or matching and connecting), a hundred years ago making accounted for 75 per cent of all economic activity, and matching and connecting accounted for around 25 per cent. Today the split is much closer to 50/50 with matching and connecting costs rising proportionately as making costs fall (see, for example, North, 1990: 28; Butler *et al*, 1997). Consumers pay for both these cost buckets in the prices they pay for products and services. But in the case of brand narcissism especially, they are paying ever more for ever less – indeed sometimes negative – value. Think clutter, confusion, hassle.

The rising cost of marketing, then, is not only a problem for companies. It is a problem for their customers too. Companies need to assess marketing effectiveness and accountability from the point of view of the people who pay for it: buyers.

A third crucial step is constantly to guard against the tendency to reduce 'consumer focus' to a process of staring into the mirror of the firm's own products and processes. Defining needs in terms of 'what we make' is very different to defining what we make in terms of identified needs. As we've seen, companies routinely talk the language of one while investing most of their efforts in the other. As we saw in the box of the main value gaps, many of the greatest unmet needs in advanced economies lie in areas that traditional business models either cannot or do not want to address.

But is 'constantly guarding' against the risk of disease enough? Probably not. The very definition of a systemic phenomenon is that it is created by the collective interaction of many separate parts. It is therefore beyond the power of any single part to transcend it. No individual advertiser can tackle information overload and clutter, for example. Systemic pressures drive companies to act narcissistically. So asking them to take a self-denying ordinance – to stop doing so – isn't going to solve the problem. If the answer was simply a better exercise of organizational will-power, branding wouldn't be in the state it is today. The problem has to be solved at a different level: by changing the way the system itself works.

TRANSCENDING BRAND NARCISSISM

Luckily, our current marketing system is pregnant with change. Its own evolution means that, perhaps for the first time, we now have a chance to tackle the underlying structural, operational, motivational and methodological causes of corporate narcissism. The following presents a bare outline:

▐ *Structural drivers.* Narcissism is a part of the brand manager's job description because each and every seller needs to grab the attention of potential buyers. As we've seen, this has its roots deep in marketing's history (in an era when the telephone was a revolutionary new device) when there was no efficient, effective way for individuals to say to companies 'Here I am; this is what I want' and when sellers filled this information void with 'Here we are; this is what we have to offer' messages instead. But today, thanks to a burgeoning information revolution, those original conditions are disappearing. As 'bottom-up' messaging becomes a reality, so the framework of marketing needs to adjust accordingly. New types of business, for which a core activity is eliciting, organizing and passing on 'Here I am! This is what I want!' messages, could soon transform the context and methods of marketing. The 'battle for eyeballs' is a hangover from the past. The battle for access to rich, up-to-the minute *volunteered* information *from* potential buyers is only just beginning.

▮ *Operational drivers.* The traditional firm falls into the trap of narcissism for two core operational reasons. First, value comes from what it does inside – 'from our operations' – so naturally its day-to-day focus is also inward-looking. Second, once it has created this value, it is driven by the imperative to realize this value by closing sales. Which is why marketers end up trying to get consumers to do what the company wants them to do – buy my brand!

But if we look again at value with fresh eyes, we see that all consumer value is realized 'in my life'. As individuals, each one of us is in the business of 'making our lives'. We are the factories, or producers, of personal value. What's more, we also own a range of personal assets with high market value. Media owners grow rich by organizing, aggregating and selling our attention, for example. Retailers wield supply chain power by organizing, aggregating and deploying buying power: our money. Financial institutions grow fat by organizing and aggregating our savings and cash flow. Direct marketing, market research, database and information companies earn their keep by organizing and aggregating information from and about us.

In other words, we can see that many of today's biggest, richest and most influential businesses trade in personal assets that have enormously high market values. Yet rarely do they do so on our behalf. Instead they treat us a mere 'resource' – like the ore in a mine – there to be extracted and used as *corporate* assets.

But now we are seeing the emergence of new types of business whose core task is to help individuals maximize the value they 'make' in their own lives – and who earn their keep by organizing and aggregating personal assets such as attention, information, money and time on behalf of the asset owner: the individual. Some people call these new business models 'consumer advocates' (see, for example, Mitchell, 2000; Zuboff and Maxmin, 2003; Mitchell, Bauer and Hausruckinger, 2003). Others call them 'consumer agents'.

Consumer agents can undertake many value-adding tasks, but their three core roles parallel those of any and every corporation: sourcing inputs, processing them to add value and realizing this value. Specifically, consumer agents:

- Elicit and organize 'Here I am; this is what I want' information to help individuals find and source the best possible value in the marketplace, to act as the individuals' professional purchasing department. Their job is to help the buyer buy, rather than help the seller sell.
- Help individuals maximize the efficiency and productivity of their life operations – such as personal financial management or home maintenance – by accessing, assembling and integrating many different products, services and sources of information. They act as personal 'solution assemblers'.
- Help individuals reach their personal goals – the outcomes they really desire. They act as 'passion partners', to help individuals maximize their own personal, emotional bottom line.

Each of these advocacy or agent roles points to a completely new and different business model. But for our purposes they have three crucial characteristics. First, their operational focus is 'value in my life', not 'value from our operations'. Second, they do not have a vested interest in pushing any particular product or service – their job is to make sure that individuals' interests are best served in dealings with brands and companies. Third, they survive because individuals invest valuable, monetizable personal assets with them – attention, information, money, time etc. In other words, they do not relate to the individual as a mere consumer of what we make. They relate to the individual as an investor: if they fail to deliver a return on investment, they go out of business.

▮ *Motivational drivers.* Ultimately, the modern brand business makes its money *out of* customers. Agents or advocates make their money *with* their customers. The focus of trust in traditional branding is the product: 'will it deliver what it says on the tin/advertising?' The focus of trust with agents/advocates is the relationship. Are they on my side or not? The agent business model – we only get paid if we represent the interests of our investor/customer – means the two parties' interests are fundamentally aligned, not in conflict.

▌ *Methodologies.* A combination of structural, operational and motivational drivers forces traditional brands down the road of attempting to control/manipulate the attitudes and behaviours of 'target' markets. They are 'push' businesses. Agents and advocates on the other hand are 'pull' businesses. Their job is to organize and facilitate the best possible response to the signals coming from their clients. While the one is inevitably controlling and top down, the other is equally inevitably facilitating and bottom up.

Put these elements together and we can see how emerging business models address the disease of brand narcissism, not at some superficial level but at a systemic level: by changing the way the marketing system itself works. Yesterday, brand narcissism may have been a 'necessary evil': the price we had to pay for extraordinary value creation. Tomorrow it will be an unnecessary evil, and therefore unacceptable. Brand owners will need to adjust mindsets, distribution channels and perhaps even revenue streams and business models to prosper in this emerging environment.

But prosper they will, because this emerging marketing system also unleashes all manner of new win–wins. By unleashing the flow of rich, up-to-the-minute information from buyers to sellers, consumer agents create the opportunity for companies to re-engineer how they go to market and massively to reduce the waste they currently incur in both making and marketing. By 're-engineering' the way matching and connecting work, agents and advocates allow traditional makers to concentrate on what they are good at – innovation and efficient production – without having to invest so much time, money and effort in the often vain attempt to find the right 'targets', grab their attention, influence them against their will and so on.

Brands will always prosper as signals of specific forms of value. But the process and content of branding is about to change. Radically. We are ready to move beyond brand narcissism.

REFERENCES

Butler, Patrick *et al* (1997) A revolution in interaction, *McKinsey Quarterly*, 1
Drucker, Peter (1998) Management's new paradigms, *Forbes* magazine, 5 October
Klein, Naomi (2000) *No Logo*, Flamingo/HarperCollins, London
Kotler, Philip, Jain, Dipak C and Maesincee, Suvit (2002) *Marketing Moves: A new approach to profits, growth and renewal*, Harvard Business School Press, Boston, MA

Levitt, Theodore (1983) *The Marketing Imagination*, Free Press, New York

Mitchell, Alan (2000) *Right Side Up: Building brands in the age of the organized consumer*, HarperCollins Business, New York

Mitchell, Alan, Bauer, Andreas and Hausruckinger, Gerhard (2003) *The New Bottom Line: Bridging the value gaps that are undermining your business*, Capstone-Wiley, Oxford

North, Douglass C (1990) *Institutions, Institutional Change and Economic Performance*, Cambridge University Press, Cambridge

Senge, Peter M (1990) *The Fifth Discipline: The art and practice of the learning organization*, Century Business Books, London

Yrölä, Hannu *et al* (2002) Taming the 'last mile', *International Commerce Review: ECR Journal*, **2** (2), Winter

Zuboff, Shoshana and Maxmin, James (2003) *The Support Economy: Why corporations are failing individuals and the next episode in capitalism*, Viking, London

4

Branding for good?

Simon Anholt and Sicco van Gelder

In this chapter, we consider the role of brands and branding as creators of wealth, and ask why, despite the evident desire of many people and organizations in developed countries:

■ to help poorer countries become richer;
■ to achieve this by the transfer of wealth-creation skills rather than handouts;
■ and despite a growing sense that corporations in rich countries need to 'give something back' to the world and behave less selfishly than they have in the past.

These techniques are never – or almost never – recognized as useful skills to transfer to poorer countries.

We argue that brand building is a vital technique for companies and governments in the developing world to learn if they wish to use the forces of globalization to their advantage rather than remain perennially its victims.

But we also raise a note of caution that here, as in so many areas of development, it is essential that the countries now learning and wielding these skills do so more responsibly, more sustainably and more efficiently than has usually been the case in richer countries.

The beneficial effects of transparent and responsible branding – creating inclusive and effective communities out of companies, and a host of related benefits that spread out into society at large – are simply too powerful to be wasted. It would be a tragedy if, in transferring these skills to the companies and countries that really need them, the error of treating brands merely as creators of economic rather than cultural and social well-being, for the very few, at any cost, was perpetuated instead of eliminated.

INTRODUCTION

Globalization, the process of increasing economic, social, technological, regulatory and political interaction between societies across large parts of the globe, has over the years been praised and blamed for much that is good and much that is bad in the world.

One of the most vocal of globalization's recent detractors has been Naomi Klein (2001), who accuses global corporations, and by extension global brands, of bullying poor developing countries into providing them with near slave labour. Johan Norberg (2001), a Swedish anarchist turned liberal, defends global capitalism as a system that has lifted large parts of the global populace out of abject poverty and presents plenty of evidence for that claim. Although he admits that there is still a lot to be done to eliminate poverty, degradation and hunger, he concludes that this is possible precisely because we can learn from experience how to fight these ills. Indeed, one of the co-authors of this chapter claims in a recent book (Anholt, 2003) that brands can play an important role in redressing the imbalance of wealth between developed and developing countries.

Our position is that neither globalization nor branding is inherently good or bad, and that attaching 'moral' or 'ethical' labels to either shows a very limited understanding of what they are and how they work. Globalization is a societal process that has been occurring for several hundred years and, where the increase of interaction has been free and voluntary, has allowed people from all over the world to benefit from various forms of exchange: ideas, goods, services, culture. Branding is a way of thinking about how an organization aligns its goals and abilities with the demands of its stakeholders. When an organization manages its brand or brands in such a way that they balance stakeholder demands and meet or exceed expectations in doing so, people benefit. The world becomes an ever so slightly better place to live in thanks to what is called value creation. Value is created when people reckon that a brand offers them something worth their while and they are persuaded to provide something in return, eg their time, money, attention, allegiance, brainpower and so on. Value is thus an intangible substance made up of qualities like trust, reassurance, excitement, snobbery, efficiency and so forth. Value creation is not the same thing as making money, but making money is often the result of creating value and a prerequisite for sustaining an organization's value-creation activities.

There is no reason why the practice of branding, and its value-creation benefits, should be confined to developed nations – apart from the fact that people in the lesser-developed ones do not yet have enough of the required knowledge and skills. To correct this imbalance, such expertise must be passed on to entrepreneurial people in developing countries.

THE CASE FOR KNOWLEDGE AND SKILLS TRANSFER

We believe that what we have learnt in 'advanced' societies about creating value through branding can and should be transferred to less-developed nations in order to improve the lives of their populations. If organizations in these countries apply brand thinking to their activities, they will be better able to provide their stakeholders with what they want. This may entail:

▍ better value propositions for their customers, which can lead to greater customer loyalty, attracting more and better customers, the ability to charge higher prices and so on;

▍ improved working conditions for their employees, as the organizations realize that their people are instrumental in taking the brand to their customers;

▍ increase in share prices as branding demonstrates the continuity and vitality of the organization to investors;

▍ increased appeal of the organization to suppliers, as well as potential employees, who feel secure and proud to be working for a trusted and respected organization;

▍ development of the local community as more means become available to invest in health, education, infrastructure and the like;

▍ local, regional and national governments benefiting not only from an expanded tax base, but from the reflected glory of flourishing brands in their constituencies.

Each individual brand will, of course, have different impacts on different stakeholders. But there is absolutely no reason why the beneficial effects of branding should be restricted to the developed world, or why the role of less-developed nations should be as mere suppliers of commodity goods and labour to rich companies from rich countries.

One very visible benefit of better branding in developing countries would be the rise of export brands, directly tapping the wealth of consumers in rich countries – truly a pipeline of economic 'aid' directly linking the donor and recipient, providing clear and immediate benefits to both parties. But such cases are still the exception rather than the rule. Many poor countries remain, and are likely to remain, enmeshed in a pattern of economic behaviour that keeps them poor: selling unprocessed goods to richer nations at extremely low margins and allowing their buyers to add massive 'value' by finishing, packaging, branding and retailing to the end user. In many cases, this process helps deplete the source country's resources while keeping its foreign revenues at a break-even level at best.

But building an export brand requires more funding, marketing expertise, ambition and chutzpah than many emerging-market companies can lay claim to. Still, organizations that only operate locally have much to gain from branding, and the same value-creation process applies to local brands as much as to export brands. Indeed, building a powerful domestic brand may often be a more urgent priority: local brands constantly need to fend off foreign brands encroaching on their territory and the best way to achieve this is often by developing a brand that better meets local demands and is more sensitive to local cultural conditions.

As the glossy image of multinational and especially Western-owned brands begins to wear a little thin, local brands may well find that they have an unprecedented window of opportunity to state their different and attractive credentials. One of the authors of this chapter argues in the book *Global Brand Management* (van Gelder, 2003) that brands are influenced by various local structural, cultural and motivational conventions, and that the choice of abiding by or challenging these factors may provide specific value to consumers. A further effect of this situation is that strong local brands become more and more likely to be selected by foreign brands as co-brands or as component or ingredient brands.

There are many obstacles that can impede the development of healthy local brands. One significant problem is the issue of proper legal protection of the brand. Hernando de Soto (2001) argues that it is the complex and peculiarly Western system of legally protected property title that has enabled trade in the West to burgeon into capitalism on a major scale, and the lack of such a system that keeps the great wealth of parts of the 'developing' world in unmeasurable, non-negotiable and unrealizable form (you can't take out a mortgage, for example, against a property for which you hold no formal legal title). De Soto's argument clearly has its application to the issue of brands: without the protection afforded by intellectual property legislation, and the right of a manufacturer to protect its namestyle, it would be impossible for the value of a brand name to be considered a quantifiable asset of the business. Without this asset the market capitalization of a company like Xerox, for example, would be a mere $481 million rather than $6.5 billion.[1]

However, even in places with rather weak legal protection of intellectual property, local brands can thrive. A good example is China, where brands like Tsingtao, Haier and Legend have (largely) depended on their local markets and despite stiff competition from powerful foreign brands have nonetheless managed to create substantial brand equity, which now stands them in good stead as they move out on to the international market.

Multinational brands often create this entirely beneficial (and entirely unintended) side effect: their presence in countries around the world has the power to 'inoculate' local brands against powerful competition, teaches them world-class design, quality, packaging and marketing standards, and helps to train them for success on the global marketplace.

Along with the transfer of branding knowledge and skills, foreign and local companies who wish to practise branding must also realize that this brings added responsibility: responsibility for delivering on one's promise, meeting expectations, behaving in an ethical manner, contributing to the community and generally being held accountable for one's actions.

CHARITY VERSUS RESPONSIBILITY

If branding provides all these benefits for organizations, whether they are from a developed or a less-developed nation, there is always the flipside of the organization's responsibility for all activities undertaken for and by the brand.

Many companies support worthy causes financially or otherwise but, however laudable charity may be, it does not constitute organizational policy. As the great donations of 19th-century robber barons to education and culture show, the way a company is run can be totally disconnected from the causes it supports (*Economist*, 2002). Even today, as Bill Gates shells out his personal wealth to charity, Microsoft's monopolistic tendencies are generally not considered the epitome of good governance.

We identify three types of responsibilities that can apply to organizations: a general form of responsibility, a sector- or category-specific form and a brand-specific form:

▌ The *general* form of responsibility encompasses such issues as business ethics, employee treatment and the environmental impact of an organization's activities. All organizations should be aware of these issues and act to ensure a minimum standard of conduct. These minimum standards may, of course, vary across time and place: what is considered acceptable in China may not be in the United States; and what is considered acceptable now may not be acceptable in 10 or 20 years' time. For this reason, organizations need to keep a finger on the pulse of the societies where they are active in order to remain abreast of these ever changing standards.

▌ *Category-specific* responsibility is relevant to sectors or categories that have a specific impact on societies. Often, manufacturers in certain categories will join hands to limit the detrimental effects of their products or services to society. For example, manufacturers and importers of alcoholic beverages in the Netherlands have established a foundation to help combat the abuse of their products,[2] although the actual effects of such sector-wide initiatives will often be contentious.

▌ *Brand-specific* responsibility encompasses specific societal issues that are directly related to the organization's brands. The benefits that an organization derives from branding have a flipside: a responsibility that is the inverse of the benefit. Many of the world's biggest corporations have been, and apparently continue to be, blind to this particular form of responsibility. How could Nike, the epitome of consumer self-actualization, overlook the fact that its footballs were sewn together by indentured child-labour in Pakistan? In this case, this probably had much to do with the then much touted ability of Nike to concentrate on the juicy bits of business (eg branding, design, marketing) and leave the gritty business of manufacturing to others. The public at large did not see things this way and decided that Nike was responsible.

We have so far in this chapter discussed three seemingly separate threads: global branding, the transfer of branding knowledge and skills to developing countries, and brand-specific responsibility. We argue that there is a clear relationship between these three: global branding offers an opportunity for accelerated socio-economic development for people in developing nations; this process needs to be advanced through turning over relevant available know-how to those people who are likely to make use of it; and this should not lead to a repetition of the mistake so often made in 'developed' countries – treating branding as a superficial endeavour that is aimed at glossing over cracks in the way organizations deal with their stakeholders.

WHERE DOES THIS LEAD?

We feel that the time has passed for grumbling vaguely and unproductively about 'brand bullies' – and, indeed, for grumbling about the people who do the grumbling. It is time for a positive initiative to help organizations – whether they are companies, governments, NGOs or community initiatives – learn how to take advantage of the benefits of branding while staying fully aware of the ensuing responsibilities. This transfer of skills and knowledge should be aimed at improving the lives of the stakeholders of these organizations through value creation that is aimed at providing them with the means of emancipation. Emancipation, as we see it, is a process of liberating people from their daily burdens and providing them with the opportunity to shape their own lives and those of their families. The means of emancipation can consist of better wages, education, healthcare, infrastructure, security, cultural engagement, and the list goes on.

There are several ways in which branding skills and knowledge can be transferred to less-developed nations, and each has its own specific advantages and drawbacks. First of all, there is the possibility of sending branding and marketing experts to Third World and former Communist countries as volunteers to aid local organizations in their brand-building and marketing activities. This is the basic intention behind an initiative called 'Aidvertising', which one of the authors of this chapter is launching in the United Kingdom.³ The advantage of this approach is that direct hands-on expertise can be delivered to those in need of such know-how. The main stumbling blocks for such an approach are the potential for miscommunications and misunderstanding due to cultural differences, the possible mismatch of what the branding professional has to offer and the local organization's needs, and the unfamiliarity of the volunteer with local circumstances. Most of these issues can be remedied by the proper selection of candidates (eg only those with sufficient multi-country work experience) and the thorough examination of the organization's requests and carefully matching that with one or more professional volunteers. However, this is only an option when a short intervention is likely to have the desired effect – for example where a local company is having difficulties moving its branding efforts ahead.

The second approach is to encourage multinational companies (MNCs) to transfer their local branding knowledge to local organizations, and these might include the suppliers or distributors of the MNCs. One interesting scenario might be where a big brand-owning corporation, anxious to reassure the public that it genuinely supports ethical labour practices in its overseas manufacturing, could help its manufacturers to develop their own brands alongside the corporation's. The deal could be that the brand owner gives design, branding and marketing expertise to the manufacturer in return for a stake in the new brand; the corporation could even act as the new brand's sole distributor for the developed world, and position the brand as a companion to its own. Whatever the ultimate success of the new brand, the corporation has proved its integrity and commitment to social justice in a highly visible and imaginative way; if the brand succeeds, it owns a valuable stake in a growing brand and positive new brand equities deriving from its close association.

A project like this would also provide the corporation with many more free column-inches in the international media than it can possibly achieve with yet another grudging 10-cent pay rise for its sweatshop workers in the Third World. A lot of the 'ethical' gestures that big corporations make are just that – gestures – and fail to convince an increasingly sceptical public: this is mainly because they are reactive (a scandal is uncovered, and the corporation does something to put it right), and tend to give the impression of an evil global corporation that would prefer people not to think of it as evil, rather than a global corporation that actually isn't evil. Of course there's a risk attached, and potentially a high cost, but that's in the nature of benevolent gestures: they don't mean a thing unless they cost you something.

By helping their local business partners to apply branding in these and other ways, the MNCs may help them to become more professional and better able to act as local or regional representatives of the global brand. In addition, the branding of such business partners provides the MNCs with an opportunity to employ some of these brands as so-called benefit brands, branded ingredients or components that enhance the main brand. And by helping their business partners to benefit from branding, the MNCs can also shift some of the brand responsibility towards them. In other words, the use of branding provides local companies with a higher profile and should subsequently involve increased accountability of behaviour.

The third and perhaps least direct approach to branding skills and knowledge transfer is to aid national, regional or local governments to brand themselves. This implies helping them understand the strengths and weaknesses of their territories in terms of natural and human resources, and determining how best these can be applied to tourism, export branding, inward investment, foreign relations and representing culture (Anholt, 2003). The question of a country's image crops up over and over again in marketing literature these days, and it's clear that countries (and, for that matter, cities and regions too) behave, in many ways, just like brands. They are perceived – rightly or wrongly – in certain ways by large groups of people at home and abroad; they are associated with certain qualities and characteristics. Those perceptions can have a significant impact on the way that overseas consumers view their products, and the way they behave towards those countries in sport, politics, trade and cultural matters; it will affect their propensity to visit or relocate or invest there; their willingness to partner with such countries in international affairs; and whether they are more likely to interpret the actions and behaviours of those countries in a positive or a negative light. In short, the perception of a country determines the way the world sees it and treats it, and the more enlightened and expert a government is about branding and 'reputation management', the better it will be able to use these effects to its advantage.

A good example of successful 'nation branding' is Singapore, where the government set a clear agenda for knowledge intensification, starting with import substitution in the early 1960s, followed by an export orientation from the middle of that decade, accompanied by a shift to high-tech industries, followed by a shift from skills-based to knowledge-based industries in the 1970s. From the 1980s onward, Singapore assumed a greater role in regional growth and development using the skills and knowledge it had acquired. In the 1990s, Singapore strove to become 'The Learning Nation', thereby clearly articulating a purpose for the nation brand (Hampden-Turner and Trompenaars, 1997). In the present decade, Singapore is trying to encourage its citizens to rise to the next level of know-how: how to apply creatively all their learning.

But among the most dramatic illustrations of the combined power of brands from a country and the branding of a country are Japan and South Korea. Japan went from a nation shattered by war to the per capita richest OECD member in less than 50 years; the Republic of Korea had the same GNP as Cameroon – indeed, was substantially worse off than North Korea – in the 1960s, yet is now the United States' eighth-largest trading partner and the eleventh-largest economy in the world. Between these two countries, many millions of people have been lifted out of poverty, and it is hard to reconcile these facts with the view that international trade does not help growth and growth does not help the poor.

Not coincidentally, both countries produce world-beating brand names in valuable and profitable product sectors, notably consumer electronics, information technology and motor vehicles.

None of this has happened by accident. Economists often assume that such miracles are primarily the results of free trade, whereas developmental capitalists put it down to industrial policy and systematic state intervention to support growing industries. In these cases, it would appear to be the latter rather than the former: both Japan and South Korea have followed a policy of first excluding foreign imports in the market sectors that they have earmarked for development, then copying and improving on the foreign products, and then doing everything possible to encourage the export of branded domestic products.

Of course, in these and in many other cases, one can endlessly debate whether the commercial brands have done more to build the country brand or vice versa, and which came first, but the reality appears to be that the rise of both brands is intimately and intricately linked: the brands help to build the country's image and the country's image helps to build the brands. The more consistent and planned the effort that a country's government and private sector put into developing both, the more likely these two effects are to build upon each other and create a powerful and seamless whole.

Obviously, the approaches we have discussed are neither mutually exclusive, nor are they likely to succeed independently. Unless national, regional and local governments in developing countries provide an environment conducive to entrepreneurial initiatives by people within public, private and non-governmental organizations, no amount of nation or commercial branding will change the lot of the population. Likewise, unless (foreign) corporations at least tolerate – and preferably encourage – local companies to gather the fruits of branding, there is little incentive for them even to try their hands at it. Finally, even if companies in developing nations successfully employ branding to create wealth for themselves, when they fail to pass on the benefit to their stakeholders they face a public backlash that will defeat their ability to sustain their newfound prosperity.

THE WAY FORWARD FOR BRANDING

The value that branding adds to products and services may not be tangible value – unlike sales, products, factories, land, raw materials or workforces, you can't measure it very easily, which may be one reason why governments, NGOs and even companies have been quite slow to recognize its enormous potential value to the developing world – but it is good currency for the simple reason that it enables producers and sellers to charge more money for their products and services over a longer period. Brand equity is a multiplier of value and, as such, represents a substantial advantage for its owner: it's as good as money in the bank. You can borrow against it, buy it, sell it, invest in it and increase or decrease it by good or bad management.

The concept of intangible value is a well-established one in our capitalist system, and doesn't make brands any more suspect or less valid than any other form of commercial worth.

This additional value is not a trivial phenomenon; it forms a substantial part of the assets of the developed world. According to some estimates, brand value could be as much as one-third of the entire value of global wealth: according to Interbrand's latest survey of the *Most Valuable Global Brands*, the intangible assets of the top 100 global brands are together worth $988,287,000,000: just a shade under a trillion dollars. To put this almost unimaginably large number in context, it is roughly equal to the combined gross national income of *all* the 63 countries defined by the

World Bank as 'low income' (and where almost half of the world's population lives). To be fair, not everybody is happy with systems that create tangible measurements out of intangible quantities, but few would doubt that brand value represents a massive part of the wealth of the 'first world' today.

How is it conceivable that such a major source of wealth and wealth creation has consistently been overlooked when the fairer distribution of wealth is under discussion? There are two likely reasons for this.

The first is that the marketing industry has never really understood its own power to make a difference. Corporate social responsibility, for the marketing profession, has seldom got beyond reactive or panicky 'cause-related' initiatives – never, it seems, has the marketing industry sat down and taken a good, hard, strategic look at its future role in a changing world and its huge responsibility for helping to create much of the injustice that still surrounds us. For marketing services, the occasional 'pro bono' charity campaign has been the extent of most companies' contribution. This must now change.

The second reason is a widespread ignorance about what brands do and how they work. One doesn't need to stray far from the marketing department in a brand-owning company – in many cases, a short walk to the finance department is sufficient – before one encounters a profound misunderstanding about the role and purpose of marketing generally. The default belief about marketing and brands amongst non-marketers, as evidenced by Naomi Klein and her vast readership, is that marketing is essentially a refined and insititutionalized form of lying: it's the art and science of adding a coat of worthless gloss to worthless products, tricking people into paying more money than strictly necessary for products they don't need in the first place. Klein's passionate condemnation of the 'brand bullies' confirms what marketers have known for some time: branding is something that people outside the profession don't and won't understand; the vocabulary is too inflammatory for the times we live in; the risks of being misunderstood (let alone making grave mistakes through applying the marketing model too narrowly) are too great.

It's not surprising that marketers are so misunderstood. Marketers are in the habit of talking in a pretty cavalier fashion about the techniques of persuasion, coldly classifying people into consumer types, controlling the 'drivers of behaviour' and so forth: a vocabulary that, to outsiders, can sound outrageously cynical, arrogant, even sinister. Not for nothing did

Vance Packard's book *The Hidden Persuaders* – and dozens like it – have so much success: we, the 'public', have always preferred to believe that we are being clinically manipulated by forces unknown than simply to admit that we enjoy spending our money, and not always wisely.

If the power of brands and marketing to do good is not to become another casualty of the great 'anti-corporate' and 'anti-global' muddle, it is now essential that the branding and marketing community concentrates on teaching the world that brand value is far more than this, and that it has the potential to contribute substantially more to the planet than it has done in the past.

REFERENCES

Anholt, Simon (2003) *Brand New Justice*, Butterworth-Heinemann, Oxford

Economist, In praise of the unspeakable, 18 July 2002

Gelder, Sicco van (2003) *Global Brand Strategy: Unlocking brand potential across countries, cultures and markets*, Kogan Page, London

Hampden-Turner, Charles and Trompenaars, Fons (1997) *Mastering the Infinite Game*, Capstone, Oxford

Klein, Naomi (2001) *No Logo*, Flamingo, London

Norberg, Johan (2001) *In Defense of Global Capitalism*, Trimbo

Soto, Hernando de (2001) *The Mystery of Capital*, Black Swan, London

NOTES

1   According to Interbrand's 2001 survey, 93 per cent of Xerox's market value is attributable to goodwill.
2   Stichting Verantwoord Alcoholgebruik (STIVA).
3   For further information about Marketing VSO, Aidvertising and related projects, please contact Simon Anholt at simon@earthspeak.com.

5

Brand sustainability: it's about life… or death

Tim Kitchin

Allow me to set the scene…

The earth is an ecosystem, which had been evolving for around four and a half billion years until the arrival of humans. Marine algae had had things pretty much their own way for a very long time.

Then, around 6 million years ago, the hominid species arrived with a grunt and a belch, probably evolving first in Africa and migrating north. Homo sapiens, the modern human being, appeared around 100,000 years or more ago presumably saying something like 'Have a nice day' or 'Would you like fries with that?' and began to make hay (not literally of course – that came later).

By 3,000 years ago there were already 100 million of us, and by the end of the dark ages – around AD 1300 – the total number of humans had crept up to 360 million. Around that time, as a direct result of technology, things really started to take off. In just 700 years, our species multiplied to 6 billion individuals, and we are currently increasing at the rate of around 80 million a year – roughly equivalent to the population of Germany.

If we imagine the life of the earth as a single day – New Year's Eve for example – we have just added 5.6 billion people at one-hundredth of a second before midnight – just in time to finish singing 'Auld lang syne'. 'Shall old acquaintance be forgot…?' Shall they? I wonder. In the next 50 years, the UN expects the party to swell by another 3 billion.

So why does any of this matter? It matters because the 6 billion have already trashed the joint, because nobody knows one another, because no one can talk above the sound of the blaring promotional music, because a gang of axe-wielding bikers in the corner ate all the pies, the fire exits are all blocked by Gucci fur coats and nobody thought to bring any aspirin for the morning.

It matters because, during the last 150 years (one-400th of a second of our metaphorical party-day – lips just parting for that long-awaited kiss), we have directly altered 47 per cent of the earth's land area. The United Nations now estimates that biodiversity will be under threat in over 70 per cent of the land area by 2032. It matters because 24 per cent of the earth's mammals are officially threatened with extinction, and because we already consume more than the total fresh production of the sea every single year. It matters because 900 million people are malnourished, 1.2 billion lack clean water and 2 billion have no access to sanitation (UNEP–WCMC, *World Atlas of Biodiversity*).

And it gets worse. Even the most optimistic of global scenario-builders only aspire to halt the acceleration of degradation. No scenario that I have seen implies that these maltreated ecosystems can be rehabilitated. Nor can we take it for granted that we will suddenly acquire the detailed insight and clarity of belief needed to see such a renovation to its end.

This matters because the holy trinity of global harmony that should get us out of this mess – pervasive free market capitalism, a common judicial framework and effective global collaboration forums – are at best 'unproven' and at worst inadequate for the purpose. What Thomas Homer-Dixon (2000) refers to as the 'ingenuity gap' may just be widening irrevocably.

Most importantly of all, this ecocontext matters because of the 'wake-up and smell the napalm' feeling it should give us all in our daily lives. Unless we accept our joint and several liability for this future and begin to address the sustainability of all human systems, we stand little chance of tackling the most complex system of all – our symbiosis with spaceship earth... destination unknown... arrival time yet to be announced.

Against this apocalyptic backdrop, how are responsible CEOs to manage their affairs? How do they help sustain the systems in which they are personally enmeshed – family, community, organization, market and nation? How does a 60-year-old global CEO promise a bright future and possibly a pension to a 16-year-old apprentice, or any future at all to the 10-year-old enslaved employees of the company's suppliers?

How do CEOs create a sustainable future for their organization and those to whom it has made explicit or implicit promises? Where do they start? With branding, of course.

THE ROLE OF THE ETHOSYSTEM

Start with branding? I beg my pardon! Of course, I realize this may seem an unlikely departure point but, as my co-authors have pointed out, brands are simply ideas with names on. In psychological terms, they are supremely effective vessels of complex meaning. If achieving human harmony and common purpose is a precondition for survival, then brands are going to have a very big part to play. Brands drive relationships, relationships liberate knowledge, knowledge generates insight, insight drives innovation, innovation drives transactions, transactions create value, which reframes the brand and so on, and so on, *ad finitum humanensis*.

Brands frame our understanding of the world. They carry information and context and purpose from one person to the next. Within organizations as in nations, brand-affinities condition the way humans relate to one another. They help set the terms of their collaborations and their mutual expectations. Not for nothing was there an 'HP way' at Hewlett-Packard.

If knowledge is to be turned into insight and thence into smarter decisions, then responsible brands must be there to guide and inspire us. To save the ecosystem we must first salvage our ethosystem – with purposeful brands at its centre.

> The steps are laid down by the prophet who says, 'unless you believe, you shall not understand'.
>
> (St Augustine, *De Libero Arbitrio*)

THE GREAT BRAND PURGE

Before discussing brand sustainability any further though, we need to submit to a brief, but painful, brand enema. The business world in general, and the marketing world in particular, is filled with brand-think toxins, accumulated over several decades. These toxins have nothing to do with brands themselves, but everything to do with how they have been used by the organizations that apparently 'own' them. They need to be purged (see Figure 5.1).

Brands originated as a means of claiming ownership of possessions (cattle and so forth), and have subsequently come to be used as a stamp of authenticity to help sell products. Since a brand's value comes from its ability to apply a consistent premium to a customer transaction, brands have gradually come to be seen as having a financial value in their own right, and so, ultimately, have come to be owned by investors, who buy and sell them. This so-called brand equity is primarily created through mass advertising, which inscribes messages in the mind of customers. The discipline of branding is thus about maintaining a constant flow or 'current' of inspiring images flowing to consumers' heads to create differentiation. By protecting this space in the mind, brands sustain loyalty. Now purge. Ouch.

STAKEHOLDER-MANAGED BRANDS

Brands are not created by management, certainly not by investors, nor even by customers, but by stakeholders – all stakeholders. This is not a trivial observation or a semantic nuance, but a full-on Kuhnian paradigm-shift, with far-reaching consequences. Stakeholders manage brands, not companies.

But if stakeholders truly own the brand, and are altering it day by day around you, then the 'big brand question' for our 21st-century CEO becomes: 'What exactly are they using your brand for?' Is it fit for these new purposes, whatever they are? And if not, then what rights and duties of intervention do managers have in these values-shaping conversations?

Figure 5.1   Existing brand management

As with any organism, an organization's highest purpose is survival. And the only way to survive is to facilitate sustainable (ie win–win) value exchanges between itself and its stakeholders. The goal of a corporate brand, and even product brands, is 'simply' to offer a positive context for these value exchanges.

It follows that all serious attempts at brand management should be directed towards value facilitation: leading stakeholders to shape the brand they need to minimize transactional and relationship risk – and improve their alignment of purpose. However, as my co-authors have also stressed, the new responsibility of brands in this multi-stakeholder environment is only just beginning to emerge. We have a lot still to learn and much more to do.

A MULTI-STAKEHOLDER PERSPECTIVE ON HOW BRANDS WORK

In everyday life, brands are simply bundles of ideas, permitting the rapid exchange of meaning within conversations. 'England' is a brand just as much as 'Nike' or 'Microsoft' or 'Islam' or 'biodiversity' or 'science'. This brand meaning will be more or less commonly held, depending upon the consistency of each individual's actual experiences and their wider personal context. The meaning will also depend upon the specific decision individuals are trying to make. Hence the question 'What do you think of Microsoft?' has a very different meaning in a courtroom from the one it has in an office, or on a trading floor, and a different meaning again in a computer store.

Brands therefore exist not as a 'current' of promotional imagery but as a 'voltage' of individual understanding. They are sparks across the gap between what stakeholders hear and what they actually experience, in the here and now. But they also guide future expectations. While the value offered by a brand can be clearly evaluated here and now, the quality of an organization's future is inferred from the consistency of its brand values. Across the trust gap between what the stakeholders expect and the behaviour they observe, these brand values come to life.

If both these present and future gaps get too wide, then power ceases to flow around the stakeholder system. Too narrow and there is no spark –

and no (e)motive force in the relationship system. Managing relationship systems is a delicate art.

Brands also create decision context. They allow stakeholders to make transactional decisions (to interact or not to interact) based upon the belief gap they observe between promise and delivery (this is their *brand image*). But they also facilitate relationship decisions (to trust or not to trust) based upon the trust gap between what stakeholders believe a brand implies about itself and how they observe it behaving (this is their individual version of *brand reputation*) (see Figure 5.2).

Let's ground this discussion in reality. A brand like Andersen did not topple purely because of legal action, nor even because of false value promises in its advertising. It crashed down because it had not understood the expectations of it in the wider world, and had made no efforts to manage the gap between those expectations and its own institutionalized behaviour. Its trust gap was too wide.

The Andersen example also illustrates the third and final 'gap' that post-purge branding has to manage. Stakeholders make their ultimate affinity-decisions about a brand (to support or not to support) based upon the clarity and consistency of purpose that a brand declares and exhibits to others. They mentally resolve the gap between how a brand is talked about and how it appears to treat others. This is their commitment gap, based almost entirely on second-hand evidence. To commit truly to a brand, stakeholders try to assess the authenticity with which that brand acts across its entire relationship network. Because that network is largely invisible to them, they use proxies (analysts, media, friends and family) and symbolic gestures (philanthropy, leadership declarations, physical

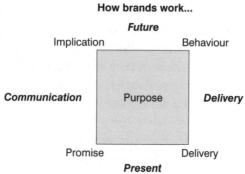

Figure 5.2 How brands work

ambience) to assess the honesty of a brand they are committing to (see Figure 5.3).

As a consequence of this delicate interdependence, comprehensively failing one stakeholder may ultimately bring down relationships with all the others. Even when no direct transactional promise has apparently been breached this fragile impression of honesty can be destroyed overnight.

In hindsight, Andersen appears to have misprioritized partner profits over the interests of all other stakeholders: Enron's investors as the most obvious example, but even over its own employees. Andersen failed to comprehend and manage the sustainability of its brand system. In so doing, it found itself irrevocably compromised within its stakeholder network – what Richard Edelman has called 'the sphere of cross-influence' (www.Edelman.com, The relationship imperative). Within this sphere, Andersen was not only brought down by conflicts of transactional interest, but also conflicts of relationship intent. Its stakeholders simply did not share a common purpose – transparently shared, debated and resolved.

A QUESTION OF SENTIMENT

The Andersen situation is further complicated, of course, by the question of sentiment – the prevailing climate of public opinion. Could Andersen have survived this crisis at another point in time? Did the dotcom

Future Brand Management...

Brand

Perceived promise (↔) Performance

Image

Expectation (↔) Behaviour

Reputation

Authenticity (↔) Observation

Relationship

Brand should be managed here...

Figure 5.3 Future brand management

meltdown raise levels of cynicism beyond breaking point? Did 11 September reduce acceptance of moral turpitude? Did Afghanistan raise people's consciousness of interdependency? Do people just love to hate accountants? All of the above may be true. What is certain is that this brave new world (of decentralized brand ownership, mutually interdependent value-webs, interventionist stake-takers and intangibles-dependent enterprises), with its almost imperceptible changes to the emotional 'climate', will have an enormous impact in brand opportunity and risk.

We can think of these eddies of sentiment as turbulence in the ethosystem – the web of aspirations, responsibilities and social norms that binds us together as humans. We are moving from centralized promise-management to decentralized reality-based branding. Brand context now needs managing as much as, if not more than, brand content.

The most pressing strategic challenge for 21st-century organizations is to learn to adapt their culture and processes to the short-term fluctuations in the ethosystem while maintaining a steady evolutionary purpose. Shaping and interpreting the interface between these internal and external worlds is the role of 21st-century brand management. This is the essence of brand sustainability. This sustainability dialectic manifests itself in many incarnations in many ways: 'tight vs loose', 'stable vs agile', 'DNA vs senses', 'substance vs form', 'responsive vs focused'. Sustainability depends upon resolving these conflicts – on finding the Third Way of Branding. The built-to-last (Collins and Porras, 1990) companies of the future will learn to respond to present relationship threats and opportunities, while remaining focused on a clear and harmonizing purpose.

WHAT IS BRAND SUSTAINABILITY?

'Sustainability' is an overused word of course. It should mean the ability to survive in perpetuity. More often than not, in business terms, it seems to mean reducing the acceleration of carbon gas emissions, or opening a few wind farms, or decorating a new village hall, or perhaps donating money to let someone else redecorate the village hall.

The remainder of this chapter will argue for the strongest and broadest possible meaning of the word, on the assumption that it will inevitably be diluted in any practical application. I will draw an analogy between the identifiable principles of environmental sustainability, and their branding equivalents – the capabilities that brand leaders will have to develop in order to protect their intangibles assets in perpetuity. These capabilities and competencies, for sustainable branding, are collectively known as 'brand-learning'.

Deep sustainability seems to rely upon five core principles: adaptability, sensitivity, fit, relevance and systemic collaboration:

1. *Adaptability.* Adaptability defines an organism's ability to change its underlying form to meet new circumstances.
2. *Sensitivity.* Sensitivity describes its capacity to sense and interpret change and adjust future decision making accordingly.
3. *Fit.* Fit defines an organism's ability to adjust its role in the food chain – changing its source of nourishment, for example, if a long-established prey becomes too difficult to catch.
4. *Relevance.* Relevance describes an organism's significance within the entire ecosystem.
5. *Systemic collaboration.* Finally, to ensure true sustainability, collaboration is necessary. Collaboration encapsulates the ability to alter the nature of interrelationships within the ecosystem. Setting aside conspiracy theories about mice running the planet, it is fair to say that only humankind possesses the necessary ingenuity to address this final challenge.

If brands are to continue to carry valuable meaning for stakeholders, they must address each of these sustainability principles. Each sustainability criterion has a clear branding equivalent:

Sustainability principles	Brand-learning capabilities
Adaptability	Organizational agility
Sensitivity	Market sensitivity
Fit	Value fit
Relevance	Brand relevance
Collaboration	Stakeholder collaboration

Brands are the oil in the organizational machine. Only by harnessing and managing these five capabilities together will brand owners retain a say in their own future, as well as managing their present. If relationship capital is the engine-room of an intangibles economy, only learning brands will be confident of avoiding a breakdown.

Organizational agility

Organizational agility defines a brand's ability constantly to adapt the ways in which it delivers to the changing needs of its stakeholders. This learning imperative applies at an emotional and ethical level just as much as it does at a functional level. Unless organizations can evolve stakeholder-responsive processes, a brand's belief-gap will gradually reach breaking point as brand promise and brand delivery diverge.

The fact that organizations have to evolve by developing improved processes and procedures seems like a truism. And the importance of organizational learning has long been recognized. However, it was probably most persuasively argued by Peter Senge in his seminal work *The Fifth Discipline* (1990). In making such a compelling case for the importance of the 'fifth discipline' of systems thinking, Senge identifies four other adaptive disciplines that organizations must learn:

▌ shared mental models;
▌ personal mastery;
▌ shared vision;
▌ team learning.

Senge argues that by embracing these disciplines a learning organization can develop a capability for improved decision making and renovation. This capability emerges as both an individual and collective ability: 'Shared visions emerge from personal vision', he declares.

In the world of the learning organization, individuals know themselves, their role within the team and the higher purpose of the collective. But more than just knowing their role in the system, like well-informed termites, they actually have to learn and internalize these desired norms, assimilating them through a process that Senge refers to as 'metanoia' – a mutual empathy picked up from the 'ether'.

However, successful organizational learning also presupposes a common experience of brand. Brands are the invisible carriers of Senge's metanoia. Brands crystallize personal duties and communal vision. It is the brand that creates 'the way we do things round here' and determines whether an environment feels 'authentic'. Brands, which live purely in the minds of stakeholders, are enablers of organizational learning but are also shaped by that learning. Senge would appreciate the symbiosis of that relationship.

Creating a sustainable brand relies upon the ability of an organization to change its present structures and forms, by building shared mental models – not only with its employees, as Senge envisages, but increasingly with its suppliers, partners, investors, regulators and even the media.

Market sensitivity

If organizational agility is all about the adaptability of the underlying substance of an organization, then market sensitivity concerns itself with the surface form. Market sensitivity determines how well an organization senses its environment and how fast it can adjust its behaviour. Like a chameleon, a sustainable brand must be able to sense its changing surroundings and respond, ideally with chameleon-like speed, to its changed context. The shape and function of the chameleon doesn't necessarily change one iota, but its surface form adjusts to fit in with its environment.

In organizational terms different degrees of sensitivity are desirable. Sensitivity must be managed in balance with the other attributes of sustainability. However, at the most extreme, organizations must be prepared to cannibalize or even abandon their entire business to survive.

At this extreme end lies IBM's decision to become an integrated services business, or at its most trivial the ability of Hush Puppies to reinvent its 'comfort' positioning as a means of leisuretime self-expression. Just like the chameleon, in these cases, the underlying nature of Hush Puppies has not changed, but its decisions and stakeholder interactions have adjusted to a new and compelling threat – or indeed an equally compelling opportunity.

If sensitivity is about continuing to mesh with the ecosystem, adapting diet, finding new shelter or developing new techniques of hunting, then market sensitivity is about meshing with the ethosystem. Organizations, communities and nations that perfect this will consistently adapt their behaviours to meet the shifting demands of all their stakeholders.

Value fit

If stakeholders are not promised something meaningful and do not feel they are being listened to, they will take their belief, their loyalty and ultimately their money elsewhere. This is the stark reality that drives value – alignment. 'Make me a proposal!' 'Show me you understand me!' 'Convince me you care!' 'Show me some compassion!' At the most basic level, these are stakeholders' human demands.

Luckily a multi-billion-dollar advertising and communications industry has evolved to help organizations make inspiring and empathic promises to customers. To date, this industry has not seen it as its role to engage stakeholders beyond the customer group. Nor has it always seen the importance of grounding these promises in a deliverable reality. Nor, finally, has this industry recognized that alignment is not a one-time process. 'Convince me you care' is not about producing a bunch of flowers on my birthday, but about a consistent and transparent demonstration of listening, understanding and assimilating my needs. In short, value fit or value alignment is about maintaining a meaningful dialogue with all stakeholders. The purpose of that dialogue is to lay the ground rules for a sustainable relationship where all participants get enough of what they want, but also accept transparent trade-offs, in return for a future undertaking to build and sustain a beneficial relationship.

However, in order for any stakeholder to go deeper into a relationship, there will need to be more than just belief in the truth of brand promises. At one point or another in any relationship comes a call for trust. 'Will you lend me the money to start a new business?' 'Will you look after my friend if I recommend him to try your company?' 'Can I trust you to make clothes as well as dumptrucks?' These open questions are not simply resolved on the basis that a brand has always kept its promises. They depend upon trust, which is created when values are reinforced through sensitive behaviour.

> Men live upon trust.
>
> (John Locke)

Brand relevance

Brand relevance does what it says on the tin. By ensuring that the values that drive a brand are those that best unite its stakeholders, organizations lay the foundations of their own future. They ensure they stay relevant to the lives of their stakeholders.

An iconic example of sustained relevance is BP's bold decision to adopt the 'Beyond Petroleum' heliotrope identity in its re-branding in 2000. This visual display is simply the pinnacle of a wider strategic decision to stay attuned to its stakeholders' gathering concerns. The same old BP core processes remain – it extracts and sells oil – but different stakeholder interfaces, more open dialogue and much improved decision criteria are evidence of BP's genuine intent to understand the values and expectations of its community of influence. Gone, or going at least, is the arrogance of tell-and-sell marketing. Instead BP is moving, as fast as a complex multinational can, towards pervasive ethical engagement.

However, only by maintaining this alignment of values will BP sustain its brand. By working continuously and sensitively at values alignment, organizations can shape expectations that are fair, that can be achieved and, most of all, that stand a chance of inspiring collaboration – the fifth and final principle of sustainability.

Stakeholder collaboration

> The very shaping of history now outpaces the ability of men to orient themselves in accordance with cherished values... Men sense that old ways of feeling and thinking have collapsed and newer ways are ambiguous to the point of moral stasis... In search of selfhood they become morally insensible, trying to remain altogether private men. Is it any wonder that they come to be possessed by a sense of 'the trap'.

These powerful words were written in 1959 by C Wright Mills. Mills's own solution to this moral and emotional stasis was to argue the need for a 'sociological imagination' – a systemic understanding of the world that seeks to balance our interpretation of biographical and historical contexts. By viewing the world through a sociological filter, he argued, personal and social duties would crystallize and concerted collective action would become possible.

Forty-four years later his concerns ring even more true. The personal search for meaning seems ever more elusive, our sense of social duty ever more utilitarian. Mills's contemporary Talcott Parsons (1951) speaks of the importance of social equilibrium – a balance of behavioural norms and values that are sustained through socialization and social control. But neither author can remotely have envisaged the fusion of state and commerce that the last half-decade has wrought. The world they looked out upon was of increased power for the nation-state, increasing rationality, increasing human control and increasingly tight definition of roles. All these trends are now being reversed.

We now inhabit a complex socio-economic world where marketing-led commercialism permeates every corner of our lives and begins even to colour our interpersonal values. Attempts to ignore this new reality are doomed to failure. Even deep sociological words like 'community' or 'kinship' now have rather less to do with human connection and rather more to do with marketing or web-service strategy.

In 2003 our challenge is now to acquire a 'brand imagination' – a systemic understanding of our world that fuses organizational sociology and commercial ideology. We need to understand how the processes and disciplines of 'value' impact our collective 'values' and vice versa. As I type, McDonald's has just declared its first quarterly loss in 20 years. A few million dollars falling the wrong side of a line is no great problem, but the symbolism of a brand tipping too far away from the value demands and values of its stakeholders is very powerful. McDonald's is taking root-and-branch action to stem its losses, but its problems are not unique. To holders of this 'brand imagination', typical challenges of the coming age will be all-pervasive in scope and psycho-social in nature:

∎ How do brands earn the right to survive?
∎ How well can brands crystallize the values of the organizations that promote them?
∎ How should brands best acquire the values of their users?
∎ Are brands products of their societies or creators of those societies?
∎ How do brands earn the right to co-opt the energy of their stakeholders?
∎ How do brands inspire human beings to create better social structures?

And most importantly of all: how can brands foster stakeholder collaboration? Stakeholder collaboration is defined as the capability of a brand to shape the coherence of an entire market through inspiring and triggering multi-stakeholder collaboration. This systemic learning process means creating and sustaining a clear and common brand mission. Stakeholder collaboration means building and sharing a common vision for all stakeholders. Most of all, it is about nurturing and sustaining the delicate interdependencies among stakeholders that constitute brand context.

Any successful attempt to create a sustainable brand relies upon understanding the brand's role within an entire set of overlapping value systems: markets, communities, societies, supply chains and demand chains. True sustainability means understanding and developing the purpose of a brand for the benefit of all stakeholders. To attain sustainability, a brand must offer a vibrant, evolutionary purpose for all stakeholders – a continued learning process that will only be sustained in an environment of relationship transparency (see Figure 5.4).

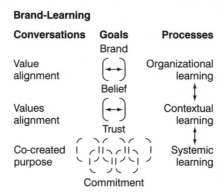

Figure 5.4   Brand-learning

THE FUTURE OF SUSTAINABLE BRANDING

In conclusion, striving for brand sustainability means managing delivery as well as promise. It means shaping behaviour as well as expectations. And most importantly of all, it means carefully and substantively evolving a common purpose among your stakeholders (see Figure 5.5).

Perfecting the art of brand sustainability amounts to nothing less than the development of a total intangibles management strategy – managing the flow from value to values and back again. Specifically, it requires organizations to set aside existing structural models of intellectual capital and revisit them through a 'brand imagination' – as a set of overlapping systems containing 'assets' of at least five different capability clusters (value fit, market sensitivity, organizational learning, brand relevance and stakeholder collaboration).

Breaking down these intangibles management competencies and then reclustering them into core competencies reveals three generic asset

Sustainable Branding

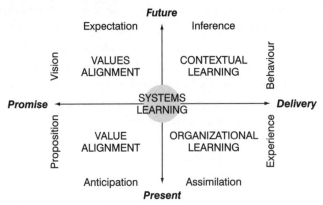

Figure 5.5 Sustainable branding

classes within each capability: *drivers, enablers* and *protectors*. These categories have minimal overlap, but extensive interaction. Analysis of all 15 (3 × 5) clusters (see Figure 5.6) therefore represents a total picture of brand sustainability, as perceived by any given stakeholder.

Only by managing all these capabilities together will an organization develop and protect its intangible assets. And only by actively managing all its brand-learning capabilities together will organizations stand a chance of developing sustainable relationships.

The capabilities and their classes are:

▮ *Brand relevance.* The ability of an organization to attune itself to the values of its stakeholders.
　– *Clear value.* The clarity, relevance and consistency of a brand's values.
　– *Visible leadership.* The influence and credibility of key brand advocates.
　– *Social commitment.* The authenticity and resilience of a brand's social engagement.
▮ *Value fit.* The ability of an organization continually to evolve a compelling and relevant offer to its stakeholders.
　– *Value innovation.* The inventiveness and self-confidence of a brand's market proposition.
　– *Customer intimacy.* The insight and empathy that a brand demonstrates to customers.
　– *Operational excellence.* The competence of a brand to deliver reliably and consistently.

EP = Energizing Purpose, **SC** = Social Commitment, **RT** = Relationship Transparency, **EE** = Employee Empowerment, **MI** = Market Influence, **CV** = Clear Values, **BV** = Brand Vibrancy, **VI** = (+ve) Value Innovation, **VL** = 'Visible' Leadership, **PC** = Productive Culture, **OD** = Open Dialogue, **CI** = Customer Intimacy, **OE** = Operational Excellence, **KO** = Knowledge Optimization, **TL** = Thought Leadership

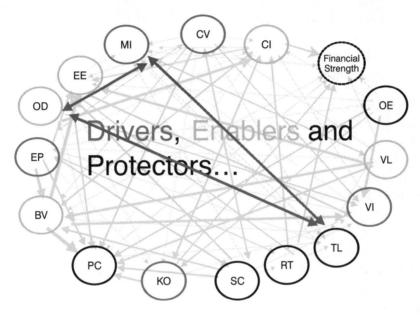

Figure 5.6   Interaction of drivers, enablers and protectors

▮ *Market sensitivity.* The ability of an organization to anticipate and manage shifts in 'sentiment'.
  – *Market influence.* The power and influence of an organization within a marketspace, and outside it.
  – *Open dialogue.* The availability and receptiveness of an organization to stakeholder feedback.
  – *Thought leadership.* The capacity of an organization to shape expectations of both performance and behaviour.
▮ *Organizational agility.* The ability of an organization to adapt its structures and processes to fulfil its vision.
  – *Knowledge optimization.* The effective creation, interpretation and deployment of knowledge at point of need.
  – *Employee empowerment.* The rights and abilities of employees to respond to stakeholder need.
  – *Productive culture.* A supportive and challenging environment.

▮ *Stakeholder collaboration.* The ability of an organization to facilitate collaboration among key stakeholders.
  - *Energizing purpose.* The clarity and human relevance of a brand 'cause'.
  - *Brand vibrancy.* The anticipation and excitement generated around a brand – by a brand.
  - *Relationship transparency.* A visible commitment to maintaining win–win stakeholder relationships.

By understanding all stakeholders' perceptions of the attributes in the list above, an organization would achieve a firm understanding of the strategic risks and opportunities it faces in sustaining its brand over time. These intangibles clusters represent the health of an organization's assets, as experienced or inferred by its stakeholders.

By tracking the connectedness of these competencies, and the interconnectedness of stakeholders themselves, an organization will begin to build a picture of its interface to the world and its own relationship to the ethosystem – its umbilical cord to the world.

To truly address our interconnectedness is a never-ending journey. But even never-ending journeys need to begin. Unless we wake up as individuals to the challenge of managing our ethosystem, our chances of managing the ecosystem seem very slim indeed.

> Unless someone like you cares a whole awful lot, things are never going to get better; they're not.

> (Dr Seuss, *The Lorax*)

REFERENCES

Collins, Jim and Porras, Jerry (1990) *Built to Last*, Random House Business Books, London
Homer-Dixon, Thomas (2000) *The Ingenuity Gap*, Jonathan Cape, London
Mills, C Wright (1959) *The Sociological Imagination*, Oxford University Press, Oxford
Parsons, Talcott (1951) *The Social System*, Free Press, New York
Senge, Peter M (1990) *The Fifth Discipline*, Random House, London

6

Brand, dynamic valuation and transparent governance of living systems

Chris Macrae

The dynamic valuation task of the living system analyst is to map whether organizations are spinning virtuous life spirals or vicious death spirals. Sounds spooky, but it is actually one of our human rights to know, identify and openly share and care about true relationships. Transparency mapping brings to the surface the kinds of assumptions that lesser number crunchers have sought to conceal over the years that globalization has evolved. When we think of firms like Andersen, the metaphor that comes to mind is one of a new world of human value exchanges put in the monopoly hands of cartographers who almost deliberately sketch lands in wrong areas. What immense control you can have of the business globe when you cause most people to sail off in the wrong direction – away from either a new economy or an improved society.

Brands were one of the most common intangible vehicles navigated into murky waters so that a few vested interests could perpetuate their process models. It is now depressingly evident that many of the powerful ways of performing 20th-century branding have turned vicious: against customers, employees and pensioner investors. The global forms of these costly brands are also a major cause of conflicts between local cultures around the world.

However, the newly discovered mathematics of transparency mapping (Macrae, Mitchell and Gordon, 2003[1]) makes win–win governance practical. Managers, economists, policy makers and opinion leaders of organizational systems can now design and steward brands that respect living system dynamics. Win–win is a natural human construct that means that, when you make different promises to two or more groups of people, you are doing so knowing how to keep all of those promises because they are mutually reinforcing. Today we can – and must – conceive promotions and deploy media that go well beyond mere image-making lifestyles. Total Brand Corporate Responsibility models purposefully focus on reality making to promote win–win relationship exchanges between people in ways that connect human inspiration and network greater value (Macrae, Yan and Kitchin, 2003). We invite readers of this book to benchmark and innovate human-focused brands, but first let's flashback to where we have just been – a most unpromising beginning to any new millennium: one that brings new urgency to my father's chilling 1984 prediction written from his editorial desk at *The Economist*: by 2005 the gap in incomes and expectations between rich and poor nations would be recognized as humankind's most dangerous problem.

Imagine a quarter-century-long career during which you see worse and worse organizational practices in the areas in which you have most experience. Something like this has happened to me as a mathematician and expert in how to charter investments made in corporate brand architectures (Macrae, 1996). Knowledge-age leaders could be developing organizational identities and living value systems in ways capable of sustaining the trust of all global and local stakeholders, as well as those that owned the shares.

Instead, surveys around the world collected for the top managers' own summit, World Economic Forum 2003, show people's trust in large organizations at record lows. And Naomi Klein (2000) is much closer to the truth of the global logo story than *The Economist* (2001) in reporting that the motives driving many world-famous brands involve putting extreme monetization before people's rights and needs. This is odd because in the golden days of the industrial age we can find leaders like Henry Ford declaring that the company that is only motivated by profits is unsustainable.

No apologies in this chapter for reverting to the first person. We need to picture a change to The System involving the participation of all our 'I's', eyes and other human senses we were given to make a difference within this world and in every local community we play brand roles in as customers, service-people, knowledge-people, owners and open policy makers of the kinds of places and spaces we want our children to live in.

> Focusing exclusively on financial objectives distorts the structure of [organizations]… and in ways that ultimately jeopardise them. This is the most important business lesson of the past decade.

> (John Kay)

In a stroke of verbal chicanery, accountants have been using the name 'intangibles' to refer to the hi-touch human connections of organizations wherever their numbers governance rules. In the mass media age, where increasingly small groups of powerful people have sought control over everyone else, verbal chicanery is one of the depressing communications diseases that has increased among media and structural suppliers to organizations. For example, whenever someone presents me with a technological system for customer relationship management, the first thing I have to check is whether it is really customer transaction management. This is the vicious technology-assisted process of how fast you can screw the customer. It works like this: make an excuse to get information from the customer so that you can later use it to transact the most money at times of greatest need or least knowledge or high time pressures.

Similarly, stakeholders are subjected to verbal confusion that numbers people go on to compound audit quarter upon quarter. See how employees are promised they can achieve great teamwork by knowledge sharing but are charged as costs by accountants whose very business models make great teamworking people the first to be cost-cut and fired. In the United States, state lawyers out of Delaware have decreed that the sole responsibility of corporate boards of global organizations is to shareholders.[2] Yet when you look at the mathematics of their fancily named shareholder value analysis, the modelling is often driven for and by speculators – with long-term investors, such as you and I as future pensioners, being taken to the cleaners. There was an idea in many dotcoms that could have merited slow and careful communal evolution but not in the hands of the dotbombers and flippers[3] and superbowl ad executives whose union became one of the greediest tribes of speculators the world has ever been forced to witness. It was so much so that e-branding has become a dirty word, as has the new economy, even though there are many human freedoms and newly productive value exchanges to be built through openly interactive media. All of this has been put on hold until we progress totally different governance from that which the new millennium inherited from the old.

In testimonies in 2002, Alan Greenspan was right on the money when he stated there is a missing governance system, without which there will be many more highly valued reputations like Andersen that will disappear, seemingly worth fortunes one day and nothing the next. It is critical that we see that transparency is not about a corrupt few boardrooms, but increasingly an organizational myopia spreadsheeted across whole organizations. The box summarizes the challenge of non-transparent governance systems. This is not particularly complex stuff but its systemic impact deeply conditions our human natures and the fabric of societies.

Why would any organizational brand expect trust – let alone have goodwill worth millions or billions of dollars – if:

1. the brand's system is governed by measurements that compound distrust/risk instead of detecting it?
2. the most knowledgeable people in that organization do not know what makes or breaks the trust of those people it serves or who have a stake in its sustainability?
3. the organizational brand repeatedly fails to protect itself from common cultural diseases where employees are too shy to pass bad news up the organization and too shy to ask co-workers who lie or otherwise abuse people's trust to behave better?
4. it does not know which of its worldwide partners may be putting people at risk by cutting corners?
5. it has no gravity because its leaders have no context-specific metrics for valuing unique purpose and the difference we make?

We need transparent brand leadership models if we wish to see the emergence of true 21st-century economies. We need organizations designed to sustain valued win–wins across their community of stakeholders by integrating the branding of trust flow with other human flows such as: how well is my time used as the recipient of a service product? Or how can I learn to create value as the participant in a knowledge-standard product?

Instead current governance monopolized by global accounting is still tracing the pattern set out above. It has become the precisely defined mathematics for disconnecting trust and seeding destruction across living systems. We require that it makes way for shared governance in which accounting numbers are moderated with a transparency mapping system. Both systems' information can be audited at every period and then contrasted. Where conflicts appear, quality decisions can be openly made by leaders. The focus of the dynamic valuation can be seen through the community of stakeholders who invest their trust by valuing relationships with the brand. In fact, before the aberration amplified by television's broadcasting age with its cost stagflation of mass media, Peter Drucker in his classic, *The Practice of Management* (1956), had defined marketing's duty of care as that of sustaining the value exchange of the company.

It is a pity that business schools have recently deserted Drucker's work as the primary text that emphasizes an organization's core responsibility –and social licence – to endeavour consistently to make human progress. Did we really need to suffer the likes of Enron to expose the claim that the world's largest organizations merited respect simply because they must have been efficient to become what they are? Wrong. Power has always been the primary mathematical variable begetting big organizations, and power can be used to good and bad ends. From Saddam Hussein's viewpoint, the organization of Iraq was very efficient until it ended. It was extremely efficient for the few, and shocking, inhuman and deadly for the many.

I make this point for several overlapping reasons. First, the transparency of organizational systems has become an issue of deep democracy for every person on this earth. Second, nations are as much brand systems as global corporations. Both, in their biggest forms, now exercise superpower commands over our whole world – able to exchange value in ways that could be of communal win–win benefit to billions who directly or indirectly invest their trust, or taken over by the greedy of spirit whose closed objective is to make losers out of the many so a few can profit from 'transactioneering'. Third, our generation is today confronting the challenge: to understand how networking technology connects all human freedoms in real and virtual ways. We are at the cusp of compounding systems that could blossom, or ones that destroy everything that you and I might mean by a better future.

New media have always provided revolutionary opportunities and threats. Think what Hitler did as the most extreme practitioner of the power of the radio wave. Think again how global networks and webs are influencing every second of people's online lives and have become insepa-rable for many knowledge workers. What Buckminster Fuller has called humankind's final examination[4] rests in this first decade of millennium 3 with reuniting all the world's major religious brands in the shared golden rule – relationship reciprocity revolving around the lifetime process of human give and take. If we let the Old System compound its take–take brand powers any further, it may not just be more costly to turn the open-knowledge world round later. Civilization's social fabric may have rotted beyond repair into everyday terror or big brotherdom in every locality.

Before mapping transparency's governance systems, here are five stories reported from my working journeys through this last quarter-century – each seems to me to provide further evidence that organiza-tional forms are being branded and administered in patterns that are the opposite of serving what most people want:

∎ the researcher of global consumers and local societies tale;
∎ the brand-learning systems tale;
∎ the knowledge capitals and policies tale;
∎ the preferred futures tale;
∎ the mathematician and risk governance tale.

The researcher of global consumers and local societies tale

In the 1980s, I worked in 30 countries in a company that assembled the first million-hour interviewing databank of how consumers and cultures responded to brands and expressed subtly different needs. In those days, senior management listened to our research, even adjusting sub-optimal brand mixes as and where we could feed back clear customer demand for something different. Then numbers came to corporate town both at the level of managers' PCs and at the level of big number-crunching market research formats. The nuances of local cultural understanding evaporated from globalizing consumer companies and their marketing. I left the market research business the day the company I had worked for got taken over by Robert Maxwell – a man whose number-crunching opaqueness and management dictatorship later became notorious.

The brand-learning systems tale

My experience in the 1980s took me to Japan for two years. There I found a different model from Western product propositioning. Essentially, Japanese corporate brands united the learning architectures of their workers in a unique organizing purpose. It is this and only this connection that when systemized totally can make the brand a proxy for all the intangibles/human wealth of a company and its unique competences. In a conversation I had with Gary Hamel in 1994, we coined the name 'brand architecture' to clarify his research that banner brands act as the roof, while core competences act as the floor: these two integrating systems enable leading, large organizations to find unique ways of communing growth for all stakeholders. However, the brand valuation algorithms sponsored by accountants have nothing to do with this future system dynamic nor the holistic integration required for every employee and leader to live and learn the brand. In fact, brand valuation algorithms use mathematics that negatively correlates with understanding whether a brand is growing or declining. I worked in the consultancy arm of a Big 5 firm for several years and was effectively fired for not being prepared to endorse such attempts to reduce a brand organization to a number instead of auditing the company's SWOTs as a means of evaluating its promises, values and vision.

The knowledge capitals and policies tale

In the history of intangibles valuation, 2000 was a landmark year. On both sides of the Atlantic, senior policy institutes (Brookings in Washington, DC and the High Level Intangibles and Intellectual Capital Group of the European Union) revealed the crisis in intangibles measurement. These reports blew the whistle on global accountants' competence to measure the human valuation dynamics of companies, pointing out that precisely opposite sorts of governance mathematics would be required. In personal interviews with the coordinators of both reports, I was interested to hear that they had not sought any testimonies from the communications industry whose valuation algorithms for brand they found as offensive as I did. Instead they listened to an emerging new breed of intangibles expert, identified by the term 'knowledge management', who have built up a capitals language for policy makers on all the hi-touch drivers of growth such as an organization's intellectual capital, people's lifelong learning needs in developing human capital, communities and other cultural needs for spaces where social capital can be nurtured and so forth. I have spent the last three years translating back and forth what I used to know about brand-learning systems and which terms knowledge management experts use instead. For example, at the time of writing I am content editor on knowledge management and emotional intelligence for the European Union's knowledgeboard.com and open assembler of the research curriculum on intellectual capital for the proposed Europe-Wide Network of Excellence known as Knowledge Angels. Our values as a movement charged with integrating intangibles research and practice across Europe are:

▌ to build on smart relationships;
▌ to act as a living system;
▌ to be open, transparent, excellent;
▌ to think big.

The preferred futures tale

Back in 1984, I collaborated with my father, Norman Macrae of *The Economist*, on a futures history[5] of the first four decades of a networking world. Our main future scenarios hold up quite well as of this date:

▌ Networks would turn out to be a greater productive freedom for humankind and system changer than even the invention of the steam engine.
▌ By 2024, if we people got there, the world would be a far better place, where people were transparently rewarded for what they contributed; where everyone had access to learning and making a difference with their special human qualities; where geography would have become virtually no barrier to any entrepreneurial or social collaboration people could imagine bringing to reality.
▌ Old powers might use every manoeuvre to block these new opportunities for people.
▌ A crunch point for the world would turn around 2005: 'By 2005, the gap in income and expectations between rich and poor nations had become

man's most dangerous problem, and one whose resolution became the prevalent internet conversation and action agenda amongst all caring customers and peoples of the world.'

What we can add now, which we did not fully understand then, is that this becomes the mother of all global branding responsibilities. It is now obscene to think of any global brand company spending a billion dollars a year on image making and none on promoting real responsibilities within the collaborative knowledge of its people. Companies in the same industry should compete on benefits but never on responsibilities. To take just one example from the top 10 most desperate needs in the poor world: fresh water. Coca-Cola – if it is the leading brand of liquid – would be best advised to set up the mother of all knowledge collaboration centres on how to get fresh water to every person in the world. It should involve Pepsi in this collaboration. It should involve governments, grassroots reporters, water utilities and everyone in networking information and insights into the politics of water until solutions are found. If Coca-Cola is saying that the younger generation wouldn't reward such a brand with loyalty for coordinating such a promotion, then the company clearly has lost all understanding of the desires of young people.

The mathematician and risk governance tale

I earned a first class honours degree in mathematics and a postgraduate diploma in statistics. I was taught that mathematicians have the following responsibilities:

▌ not to overclaim a standard's precision beyond its original context of use;
▌ to care about keeping assumptions in view especially where interpretations made would impact many people's futures;
▌ not to use the mystiques of mathematics to further their own vested interests.

Global business accounting has lacked transparency on all of these criteria. Those who believe that precision comes from navigating organizations by this means are perpetrating huge risks. These are the root causes of many depressing human relationships and widespread organizational implosions. With the exception of when a measuring company loses its own bond of respect with society as Andersen did, I find non-transparent governance to be a tragic indicator of how sick The System is and how widely it now handicaps human productivities and joys. These days wherever you encounter a global brand you should assume it is part of this value destruction unless it can provide you with open evidence that it is not guilty.

RESTORING BRAND AND ORGANIZATIONAL TRANSPARENCY – THE MISSING GOVERNANCE SYSTEM

Over the last three years, together with co-authors of *The Map*, I have conducted over 100 interviews with experts on all aspects of organizational relationships and dynamic system valuation. Our concern has been to specify a governance system that is the opposite of every feature of this profile of global accounting by numbers:

▋ Global accounting by numbers is transactional, ie harms relationships.

▋ It separates silos, ie causes disintegration and destroys the true values needed for knowledge-sharing cultures.

▋ Precision is achieved by ring-fencing the past as a static observable. This breaches the reality that intangibles valuation is about a system dynamic that is already compounding predictable future consequences.

▋ It reinforces inertias and vested interests, eg the past's powers get most share of business cases and budgets even as they decline in value and increase in cost.

▋ It rewards non-transparency between people and across stakeholders.

▋ It causes mistrust by burying the most vital human assumptions, eg accounting people only as costs.

▋ It loses context of leadership vision because it blindly applies a one-fits-all standard.

▋ The more precise it is believed to be, the less innovative and fit the organization's learning dynamics become.

Just as the 1980s became a time for benchmarking quality systems, today companies urgently ought to benchmark how to regain trust through committing to shared governance. Traditional accounting and transparency audits should both be done independently at every cycle, and then the reports of each openly contrasted so that quality decisions are made. Given the current state of immaturity of much global brand governance, the leadership team should expect to have to judge conflicting feedback. For example, the highest jumps in numbers in the last reporting period are precisely the ones that transparency mapping suggests a leadership team should double-check for organizational well-being before encouraging other units to learn from such high performances. That way Andersen could have spotted the misconducts of its Texas unit many cycles before it became a terminal behavioural cancer to the whole firm.

MAPPING TERRITORIES FOR TRANSPARENCY GOVERNANCE

In testing the system shown in Figure 6.1 we have refined five territories of relationship understanding that have in many cases gone completely missing from global accounting by numbers. Two territories represent systems of stakeholder demands and two, knowledgeable productivities.

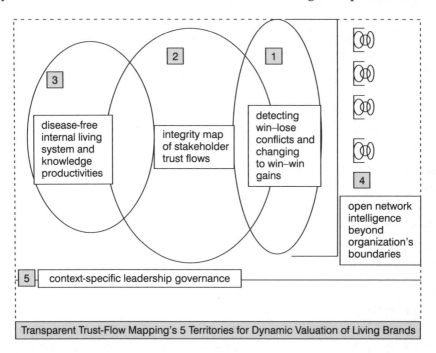

Figure 6.1   Transparent trust flow mapping

The fifth is an overall composite providing a see-through map of the whole organization's world of dynamic value. The missing governance needed to restore faith in a company's brand demands and core productivity competences looks like this:

■ *Demands* (aka relationship capital of brand):
   – Detect and resolve stakeholder conflicts in every audit cycle.
   – See the whole picture of what makes or breaks the trust of how each stakeholder segment values its relationship with the organization.
■ *Productivities* (aka knowledge of living the brand):
   – Steward the health of the internal organizational system versus commonly occurring disease spots of living systems, eg bad news does not flow up the hierarchy without relentless encouragement by leaders.
   – Openly share relationship maps beyond the organization's current borders with the best partners in current services to stakeholders or in permitting the company to progress its vision.
■ *Unique context* (aka unique organizing purpose and brand essence of the total living system):
   – Deeply understand the uniqueness of the organization's value exchange context with its community of stakeholders and why no other organization can achieve this. Reinforce this right to lead by governing through context-specific metrics and controlling the integration of all media (market serving and knowledge producing) in a way that lets no supplier vested interest reign, however big an impact it once had on the way the brand evolved.

Lessons from transparency governance and open brand-knowledge architectures

As people become familiar with the mathematics of brand and knowledge transparency models, they find its human laws can be applied to globally networked markets that govern:

■ 85 per cent of wealth production;
■ up to 100 per cent of all monetary risk;
■ all social wealth such as learning, peace, creating one world where we can be proud of our environmental responsibilities to – as well as freedoms for – our fellow human beings.

To restore the focus of organizational systems on people there needs to be a meta-disciplinary approach based on different perspectives. As well as brand and knowledge, there are risk, reputation, emotional intelligence, all sorts of organizational learning and design frames, future scenarios and environmental intelligence, as well as such areas as drama, psychotherapy and anthropology. Experts from each perspective merit a place in any territory of transparency that connects with behavioural, learning or communication dynamics they can help systemize. There is also a need for a simple but holistic transformation, so that a company learns to value its global/local perspectives and its real/virtual modes of production. Both the human and the network-age competences we need for the future have been cut out of organizations by global accountants – something that will be very difficult to reverse in the future. One way to picture the simultaneous restoration of human flows we now require is to ask organizational change facilitators and co-creativity people to connect all the feedback loops they believe a healthy organization will need to thrive on.

Pictures like that described can provide valuable insights as to how to heal today's global system. Using the idea of interrelationships, any organization's dialogue about its strengths, weaknesses, opportunities and threats should be:

▌ as continuously energetic and emotionally intelligent as any person who lives a full life with great purpose;
▌ as inclusive and as interactive as the Internet must be in facilitating the worldwide creativity of people in a way that multiplies local diversities;

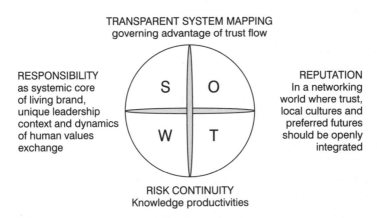

TRANSPARENT SYSTEM MAPPING
governing advantage of trust flow

RESPONSIBILITY
as systemic core
of living brand,
unique leadership
context and dynamics
of human values
exchange

S | O

W | T

REPUTATION
In a networking
world where trust,
local cultures and
preferred futures
should be openly
integrated

RISK CONTINUITY
Knowledge productivities

Figure 6.2 Company of interrelationships

▌　as locally respectful of relationships with all people as any human codes you hope your children will grow up to practise.

The greatest leaders will systematically ensure that every organizational cycle begins by detecting emerging relationship conflicts and resolving them. Responsibility defines an organization and reputation is earned by leadership that win–wins the trust of everyone it impacts. In a networked world, it is far more efficient to have everyone doing the company's marketing because they love the company than seeking to control their thoughts, perceptions or access to networks.

The mathematical rules of dynamic brand valuation can make number crunchers uncomfortable but most other people are more self-confident in good human behaviour. The first law of brand risk – hereby dedicated to the Andersen brand – is that stakeholder relationships are so interconnected that one really rotten relationship can destroy the value of the whole, even if you counted it up yesterday as being worth many billions of dollars. In fact, rather than add, subtract and separate, dynamic relationship capital obeys patterns of multiply, connect and compound over time. The bad news of this is the possibility of zeroization if any stakeholder values you as zero; the good news is that growth can be sustained as greatly as the depth of your unique human purpose is needed. There are opportunities for companies not only to achieve brand market leadership but also to open network leadership, where all audiences are active participants in the development of the organization. This is particularly noticeable when we look at the principles of integrating internal and external media (the opposite perspective of mass broadcasting). Here we should not take the perspective of the company but, as with much innovation, the perspective of the customer. The company must learn and co-create, not impose.

SUMMARY

Technology's worldwide computer-based powers of intelligence and communications already exist. We have no more chances of reversing this engine of value multiplier – that connects all the greatest demands and productive freedoms of our human race – than the Luddites had of drying up steam. If we deploy the brand as a transparent catalyst for change in a

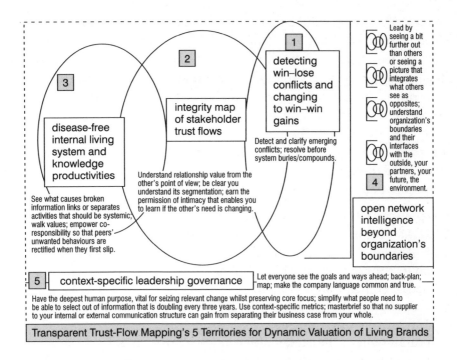

1 detecting win–lose conflicts and changing to win–win gains

Detect and clarify emerging conflicts; resolve before system buries/compounds.

2 integrity map of stakeholder trust flows

Understand relationship value from the other's point of view; be clear you understand its segmentation; earn the permission of intimacy that enables you to learn if the other's need is changing.

3 disease-free internal living system and knowledge productivities

See what causes broken information links or separates activities that should be systemic; walk values; empower co-responsibility so that peers' unwanted behaviours are rectified when they first slip.

Lead by seeing a bit further out than others or seeing a picture that integrates what others see as opposites; understand organization's boundaries and their interfaces with the outside, your partners, your future, the environment.

4 open network intelligence beyond organization's boundaries

5 context-specific leadership governance

Let everyone see the goals and ways ahead; back-plan; map; make the company language common and true.

Have the deepest human purpose, vital for seizing relevant change whilst preserving core focus; simplify what people need to be able to select out of information that is doubling every three years. Use context-specific metrics; masterbrief so that no supplier to your internal or external communication structure can gain from separating their business case from your whole.

Transparent Trust-Flow Mapping's 5 Territories for Dynamic Valuation of Living Brands

Figure 6.3 Transparent trust flow mapping in 360-degree detail

living system of trusted interrelationships, we can design win–wins that unite the global intelligence of computing and the local intelligence of human sensing. Society and business can both win. The richer world can gain from promoting the poor world's interests until desperate global divides are history.

We are embarked on a journey whose impacts on human meaning and learning would have sounded like extreme science fiction less than a generation ago. We must change our communications agents – 'the brands' – and our time machines – 'the organizational systems' – inside out. If we fail, those one-way communications controllers that count the production of things as more important than multiplying the trust flows between people will lead us to be branded as the most destructive generation in the history of this place and space we call earth.

You can find out about free general tours of transparency mapping governance at www.valuetrue.com. Co-authors of this book and our membership at CBO Association will also be hosting special events for readers – for news updates please feel free to e-mail me, Chris Macrae, at wcbn007@easynet.co.uk. Just as in the 1980s most large companies decided in union that their physical quality systems were immature and collaborated in fast-track benchmarking of improvements, today there is a huge need to benchmark intangible governance value systems. We aim to help people get started secure in the knowledge that early comers will both gain economic advantage and discover that social models of doing good can be some of the best concepts for any worthwhile global company – or start-up with aspirations to make a difference – to brand and promote its purpose through.

Specific area contacts are:

- company HQ in USA/UK: Chris Macrae;
- HQ in Nordica: Nicholas Ind, Thomas Gad;
- HQ rest of Continental Europe: Sicco van Gelder;
- HQ southern hemisphere: Jack Yan;
- nation brands: Simon Anholt;
- brands promoting collaboration around a top 20 world cause: Jack Yan, Tim Kitchin, Chris Macrae;
- brands where the stakeholder network does much of the brand's marketing because they know everyone can trust it's the best: Alan Mitchell;
- brands that wish to rediscover trust in their founder's culture or something deeply humanly inspiring: Chris Macrae, John Moore.

REFERENCES

Drucker, Peter (1956) *The Practice of Management*, Harper Business, New York
Economist (2001), Pro logo, 6 September
Klein, Naomi (2000), *No Logo*, Picador, London
Macrae, Chris (1996) *Brand Chartering Handbook: How brand organisations learn living scripts*, Economist Intelligence Unit/Addison Wesley, Harlow
Macrae, Chris, Mitchell, Alan and Gordon, William (2003) *The Map*, John Wiley
Macrae, Chris, Yan, Jack and Kitchin, Tim (guest eds) (2003) *Journal of Brand Management*, Special double issue, Total Branding of Corporate Responsibility (TBCR)

NOTES

1   Transparency communities at www.valuetrue.com.
2   See Margaret Kelly, http://www.business-ethics.com, Campaign for Economic Democracy.
3   See Jim Collins, Built to flip, http://www.fastcompany.com/magazine/32/builttoflip.html.
4   See Buckminster Fuller, Final examination, http://www.bfi.org.
5   See http://www.normanmacrae.com/netfuture.html.

7

Authenticity

John Moore

Four hundred years ago, Shakespeare gave us the ethical principle 'This above all: to thine own self be true' (*Hamlet*, I iii 78) but, with a delicious sense of irony, had it articulated by Polonius, as slippery and untrustworthy a character as you could wish for. Perhaps this is the challenge of authenticity: it's quite easy to talk about and not so easy to do. If authenticity is hard for people to achieve, it is even harder for businesses.

Yet developing greater authenticity will help future organizations to be more effective at satisfying human needs. It will help us to respond to a world where people's faith in marketing has fallen to new lows, as we simply fail to engage with the claims advertisers make. The humanity has been driven out of most branding programmes, replaced by an ever-growing list of clever-sounding jargon and 'tools' designed to manipulate rather than engage with consumers. It seems to me that the cleverer these tools seem to be, the more trust is compromised and real human value destroyed.

In common with my co-authors, I do not believe branding is inherently either good or bad. However, in order for it to play a positive role in society, branding must adapt to respond more responsibly to real human needs.

Without authentic communication among the human beings inside and around brands, little of worth can be achieved. With authenticity, the unique creative abilities of human beings can be released to create real value.

This chapter is divided into three parts:

∎ Part One: What authenticity is, and what gets in its way;
∎ Part Two: Why authenticity is becoming more important;
∎ Part Three: What businesses can do to benefit from authenticity.

As a frail human being, I'm aware that there may be some repetition of ideas between these sections, but I hope this structure provides at least some coherence to my thinking as it stands.

PART ONE: WHAT AUTHENTICITY IS, AND WHAT GETS IN ITS WAY

So what is authenticity?

I would define human authenticity as the willingness to speak the truth, as you see it. You may be right, you may be wrong, or it may be just a matter of opinion – but you call it as you see it. And your behaviour is consistent with your statements.

For human beings to organize effectively to meet their needs they must be tolerably honest with each other about what they need and what they can contribute. They need to show their vulnerabilities and needs as well as their strengths.

Authenticity should not be confused with piety. Human beings are volatile, temperamental, social creatures. Our social identities and behaviours are not fixed; it's in our nature to be quirky and unreasonable and 'inconsistent' at times. Indeed, one of the benefits of authenticity is that it allows us to be honest about our defects instead of trying to live up to impossible ideals. (In fact, it is in their failure to match up to idealized images that so many brands fail.)

What gets in the way of authenticity?

Woody Allen once described his ambition to 'forge in the smithy of my soul the uncreated conscience of my race. And then see if I can get them mass-produced in plastic' (Allen, 1975). This brilliantly summarizes the approach of business to the concept of authenticity – and the thinking that puts so much branding and marketing at odds with the creation of real value for human beings.

As I reflect on what causes inauthenticity, I think of three overlapping factors:

▌ social conditioning;
▌ the misuse of language;
▌ the confusion of fantasy and experience.

Social conditioning

Tom Heuerman, in his online article on authenticity,[1] explains how social psychologist Solomon Asch conducted experiments to investigate what human beings will do when confronted with a group that insists that 'wrong' is 'right':

> When alone, 99 percent of the people chose the obviously correct response to a question. But in a group, 76 percent betrayed their own judgment and sided with the majority (who were confederates with the scientist) at least once during 12 trials. And 37 percent of the subjects' responses were incorrect across all trials. Asch warned of a 'tendency to conformity in our society so strong that... people are willing to call white black.'

This urge to say not what we believe is true, but instead what will make others happy, is probably at the root of a great deal of marketing failures where too much is promised and not enough delivered.

The definitive study of conflict avoidance, and its consequences, was Irving Janis's famous analysis of the Bay of Pigs disaster. John F Kennedy presided over a cabinet made up of people with formidable and robust intelligence. Yet these great minds managed to persuade themselves of the efficacy of invading Cuba – a decision that with hindsight was absurdly dangerous. Janis studied how the group managed, subtly, to suppress doubts and concerns – creating the illusion of unanimous enthusiasm for a project where really there was no consensus. They had the illusion of trust, but not the reality.

There are many versions of Groupthink in marketing. You can experience it in bandwagoning by consumers in focus groups, or in agencies convincing themselves desperately of the brilliance of their latest ideas. This Groupthink is encouraged by marketing's inbuilt tendency to wishful thinking and its love of image making: participants in the marketing process lose their ability to express their real views in favour of their desires to fit in.

I recall attending a meeting with top marketing people in a soft drinks firm who debated whether they could position their product as 'a connecting beverage'. They eventually concluded that consumers might not buy this. I then suggested that this wasn't really the point. Did they themselves believe it? They instantly said not. It is typical of marketing people to have discussions about what *other* people might be persuaded to think, without stopping to notice what they themselves actually think of the proposition.

Most brand failures start not with a failure to communicate with customers, but with failures of communication inside organizations and between organizations and consultants.

A culture of sycophancy colours the relationships between brand managers and their agencies. I have sat fascinated at meetings where a client sits with an agency, has an amiable conversation and agrees an outcome. The agency then leaves the room, and then – only then – the client people roll their eyes to the ceiling and express their frustrations and their low expectations of what will result. I have also sat in agencies where their people return from similar meetings, bewailing the failings of the client. Amazingly, none of this supposedly 'negative' stuff gets dealt with; it just festers quietly.

Relationships become dull and false as participants suppress their real ideas and feelings, perhaps out of a fear of giving offence or alarm. Needless to say the output of such relationships is the off-target, over-promising, insincere ads that clutter our daily lives.

What they need is much more honest conversations with each other, and with all stakeholders. There should be fewer promises made and a greater willingness to challenge and be challenged.

The misuse of language

In the world of branding and marketing, the degree of adaptation has reached extraordinary levels, to the point where words start to lose their meaning altogether. The role of language is to represent our experience; the better it does this, the better we can understand and, crucially, empathize with each other. Marketing slogans contribute to a degrading of language.

For instance, early in 2003 Coke's Chief Operating Officer, Steve Heyer, gave a keynote speech on the future of marketing. In this he stated, 'Coca-Cola is refreshment and connection' (*Advertising Age*, 6 February 2003). In similar vein, Interbrand blandly confirm that 'Kelloggs is now synonymous with health and vitality' (Clifton and Maughan, 2000). Such sloganizing is widely regarded as harmless hype. However, I believe that such utterances contribute to an atmosphere of unreality in which lively debate does not take place.

It seems to me to be a bit like Chinese children, at the height of the Cultural Revolution, singing 'Chairman Mao will live forever!' To engage with organizations that adopt absurdities as mantras would require anyone to have to suspend their normal ways of thinking. The consequence is not the fervent support that is hoped for, but a culture of falseness and disengagement.

Mark Barden, of agency Barden and Jelly, recalls why his partner Jelly stopped working for Coke: 'Sitting in one of those airless beige conference rooms, drinking his mandatory caffeinated, carbonated beverage with 20 grams of sugar, he nearly choked when the Coke executive leaned in close and said, "Jelly, this year we're going to own Ramadan." Shortly after that he did quit advertising.'[2]

I think that, for every Jelly who quits with his feet, there are dozens who stay physically in organizations but quit with their spirit and enthusiasm confronted with such bizarre unreality of conversation.

Stalwarts of image-led branding sometimes claim that their work contributes to the general fun of life. And yes, we can all point to the occasionally amusing ad we have seen. They go on to suggest that greater authenticity will lead to greater boredom: I believe the opposite is true; much conventional branding tends to support phoney organizational cultures that are deeply boring and unengaging.

The confusion of fantasy and experience

In his great poem 'If', Kipling wrote of the need to 'dream, yet not make dreams your master'. These wise words should be taken to heart by anyone responsible for marketing.

Many of the problems people deal with in psychotherapy are attributable to the mismatches between their *actual experience* of the world, and the way they represent that experience. For instance, a woman struggles in social situations and feels uncomfortable. She tells herself that she lacks social skills, thinks of herself as 'not normal'. From this idea about herself, she reinforces her sense of awkwardness and a vicious cycle sets in. Some would say the answer is social skills training – confirming her idea that there is something wrong with her. In fact, she may do better to be more accepting of her response rather than fighting it.

Likewise, most brands live in a world of fantasy and concepts divorced from actual experience – and seem to encourage the rest of us to do so too.

This was reinforced for me just the other day in my gym. There I sat, pedalling away on my stationary bike, when I noticed that one of the TV channels had been replaced by a corporate video for the brand my gym belongs to. It presented a series of rather beautiful people having deeply satisfying and healthy gym experiences, in pristine rooms with caring and attentive coaches.

What on earth could be the purpose of screening this fantasy to someone who is actually participating in the real, somewhat less ideal, experience? I was, in fact, quite content with my surroundings until presented with this soft-focus fantasy of beautiful people. The real gym was perfectly functional and the actual experience was fine – at least until I compared it with the Shangri-la gymnasium of the screen: this video fantasy of the marketing department that oozed inauthenticity through every pixel. And the incident captured the futility and stupidity of so much brand building – the presentation of ideals that aren't real, which either (a) encourage derision or (b) make us unhappy with something that was perfectly OK before.

Marketing experts seem ambitious to build a sort of fantasy value that outruns their reality. Recent work by Kit Kat in the UK attempts to tell us that the brand is not a mere chocolate bar, but a symbol of our willingness to take time off work and look after ourselves. Yet given the multiplicity of brands, however are we supposed to store and process all these complex ideas? In a world where buying chocolate becomes a lifestyle choice, where can we find time to think about things that actually matter to us?

Marketing gurus delight in the fantasy of brands. They tell us that without these brands our world would be dull and empty. Rolf Jensen's *The Dream Society* (1999) opines: 'In the years lying ahead, the market for fairy tales will see a booming expansion... We will have to abandon our way of categorising products according to their immediate function.'

Jensen seems to think this is a great thing. To me, it's depressing. I would like to reserve the limited capacity of my brain to buy things based mostly on what they actually do for me. Finer human emotions and dreams I would like to reserve for human relationships. It's crazy for us to live in a world where each bar of chocolate or cup of coffee has to carry its own leaden symbolism.

Crucially, if I want to attach additional sentimental value to a bar of Kit Kat or a can of Coke, then please let me do it for myself. It's offensive for some advertising person with a bit of pop psychology to try to manipulate this fantasy on my behalf.

Inauthentic brands reduce our ability to create value

The consequence of branding gone mad is to reduce the lives of the human beings involved to ones of empty symbolism, disconnected from reality. The consequence is that our ability to find satisfaction in things and relationships is diminished.

In a sign of the impoverishment of our working lives, professional services guru David Maister reckons that only about 20 per cent of consultants actually like their clients or like their work.[3] US research by Gallup in October 2000 showed that 26 per cent of respondents said they were engaged in their work, 55 per cent said they were not engaged in their work and 19 per cent said they were actively disengaged at work.[4] The rise of image-led branding has clearly played its part in this depressing failure of our working lives to create a sense of satisfaction.

PART TWO: WHY AUTHENTICITY IS BECOMING MORE IMPORTANT

Branding has been pursuing its shallow image-building for a number of years. (Chapter 3 explores the follies of this kind of narcissism in more depth.) Whatever the ill effects for society, it appears on the surface to have made satisfactory business sense for some companies. But – thank goodness – society is changing.

Our trust in authority is shifting, as the survey from the United States shown in Table 7.1 confirms. Whilst our trust in ourselves remains high, our faith in media is in steep decline. And whatever trust we once had in advertising has all but vanished – so that it's just about on a par with used car salesmen!

In such an environment, people are getting hungry for services and products they can rely on, things that do (to quote a famous UK ad) exactly what it says on the tin. Similarly, the loyalty of employees can no longer be taken for granted. The most common reason why employees are negative and cynical about the way they are managed is because the company articulates one set of values (usually hopelessly idealistic) and manages by a completely different set. So what is said and what is done are different.

I can see you!

One of the more interesting effects of the Internet has been the huge increase in the scrutiny and 'outing' of businesses. Among the first to point this out were the authors of the Cluetrain manifesto (www.cluetrain.com) – who bluntly point out that organizations are going to find it harder and harder to maintain false images in a talkative, networked economy.

I recently checked out a couple of fascinating US Web sites. The first, www.vault.com, maintains frank bulletin boards, one per company, where anyone can post just about anything they like about what they think of the

Table 7.1   Levels of trust in the United States

	1987 %	2001 %
My own abilities	80	85
TV news	54	26
Salespeople in clothing stores	23	7
Corporate advertising	20	3
Advertising	8	3
Used car salesmen	15	2

Source: Yesawich, Pepperdine and Brown/Yankelovich Partners National Travel Monitor

business. Perhaps more extraordinary is www.internalmemos.com, where employees are posting internal memos – good and bad – that circulate in their business. In such an age, I am not sure we can ever speak of an 'internal' communication again.

If you're really unfortunate, you may find your business gets its own 'hate' site, such as www.btopenwoe.org.uk or – even blunter – www.chasebanksucks.com. I recently tried putting 'Sunny Delight' into a search engine, and found as many hostile sites as official ones. The rumour about the girl who turned orange after drinking the stuff puts in an appearance. As I write, I have enjoyed www.badpension.com, one man's brilliant tirade against his pension provider's charges.

Perhaps the most passionate and optimistic voice of the new transparency is Yahoo's Tim Sanders, author of *Love is the Killer App*. He believes:

> The most profound transformation in business… is the downfall of barra-
> cudas, sharks and piranhas and the ascendancy of nice, smart people with
> a passion for what they do… At a time when more of us have more
> options than ever, there's no need to put up with a product or service that
> doesn't deliver, a company that we don't like, or a boss we don't respect…
> It's almost impossible for a shoddy product, a noxious company, or a
> crummy person to keep its, his or her sad reality a secret anymore.
>
> (Sanders, 2002)

Quite suddenly, business finds itself transparent in ways inconceivable even a decade ago. I don't think most marketing people have really caught up with the implications of this – but there are a lot of naked emperors out there who are going to be looking for answers. And they won't be listening to any old-style tailors either!

More of the same won't work

Oddly, the prelude to this new transparency saw the rise of 'brand strate-gists' who abandoned straightforward expressions of what businesses do and what they believe, in favour of complex image building. Now this is not the place to discuss the pros and cons of individual brands, but overall I see a failure to offer consumers real value, covered up by image building and wishful thinking.

As a result, we live in a world where we are constantly having to decode communications from businesses. As someone who has run a lot of focus groups, I can bear witness to the high level of scepticism of the average consumer. It's not that they are offended by the inauthenticity of advertising

Table 7.2 Dysfunctional branding

Many fundamental principles of marketing and branding would be regarded as deeply dysfunctional in person-to-person relationships. Here are a few examples:	
Marketing Shibboleth	**Therapeutic Interpretation**
'Put the customer first.'	A wife who always puts her husband first (or vice versa) is likely to have a deeply unhappy marriage. Oddly, both partners will be unhappy because none of us really enjoy the company of sycophants (even though a lot of brand managers spend their time in the company of such people).
	At extremes, in relationships this leads to battered spouse syndrome.
	Or both partners may try constantly to please the other and neither finds out how to satisfy him or herself. This leads to dull marriages that end in affairs.
	The general label for this kind of behaviour in real relationships is *co-dependency*.
'Differentiate or die.'	Branding puts far too much effort into differentiation. But this is simply another way of being co-dependent, because we allow our identity to be dictated by others.
	An individual whose main purpose is to be different often wastes energy on pointless cosmetic changes instead of realizing that the easiest way to be different is to be true to yourself. Many brands lack any sense of purpose, which can be the key to standing out. This is manifestly the case with banks like Barclays with its absurd giantesque advertising with Anthony Hopkins.
'Consistency of presentation is vital.'	It's absurd that companies produce multi-volume manuals to control the exact colour scheme for their logo. This is like the dysfunctional adolescent who is obsessed with appearance to the point of bulimia or anorexia. Instead of building self-esteem, they undermine it.
	And no sensible employees want to be guided by a rule book. They want to be inspired by example. Presentation is completely secondary to behaviour, as the British Airways tailfin and Consignia examples demonstrate.

– they have simply learnt to filter out and ignore most of what companies try to tell them, or translate it into what they assume is real.

It's an interesting human characteristic that, when engaged in unproductive behaviour, our reflex response is to do *more of what is already not working*. Similarly, in a climate of suspicion, some marketers seem to think the solution is:

▌ to shout more loudly to try to drown out the competition;
▌ to find more exciting and impactful ways of telling the same old half-truths about their products;
▌ to develop ever more cunning research techniques with preposterous claims to penetrate the consumers' unconscious mind – and tweak it to make them buy more product.

The result is a 'tragedy of the commons' in which more elaborate fantasies are unloaded on the public, with ever diminishing resonance.

David Lewis (2001) argues that we are moving from a time of hype to one of buzz, which he summarizes as shown in Table 7.3. This underlines the weakness of conventional brand thinking.

PART THREE: WHAT BUSINESSES CAN DO TO BENEFIT FROM AUTHENTICITY

It's a human failing that we are often reluctant to express our deeper feelings and desires for fear of being vulnerable or looking foolish. In work, we try to keep up a façade of 'professionalism' rather than admit to doubts or fears. It calls to mind the old proverb of Jacob the Cobbler:

Table 7.3 Buzz and hype

	Buzz	**Hype**
Style	Democratic	Autocratic
Content	More likely seen as truthful	More likely seen as devious
Typical media	Conversations, Web sites	Advertising
Examples	Rumours, gossip	Press releases
Reaction	Trust	Distrust

Jacob is just a cobbler.

If Jacob cannot be a great lover, that is not a tragedy.
If he cannot be a fine warrior and leader of men, that is not a tragedy.
If he cannot be a wealthy merchant, living in luxury, that is not a tragedy.

But if he cannot be Jacob the Cobbler, that is a tragedy.

In a network economy of great transparency, all marketing rests on a series of real human conversations and relationships. These more authentic relationships must start inside organizations – and arguably inside each of our own minds.

As with Jacob the Cobbler, it is a challenge for you, dear reader, and me, sometimes to drop our social masks and reveal ourselves more fully. As Terry Cooper, the founder of Spectrum, a psychotherapy practice in London, once explained to me: in order to manipulate others, we first have to manipulate ourselves. (Just think for a moment about how it feels deliberately to lie to someone.) (Some people would talk about this as about choosing to have an authentic relationship with yourself – an idea that sometimes makes me feel squeamish but is, I think, quite powerful.)

At the next level, any organization where people are frequently inauthentic and manipulative in their dealings with each other and suppliers is not going to succeed in being authentic to customers.

So what can we do?

Now developing authentic relationships with other humans, under the pressures of business life, is not easy. And it's not my purpose here to present a simple formula that guarantees success in developing authenticity. Any single formula will inevitably be an oversimplification of what must remain a highly fallible human process. Nor am I saying that we have to be 100 per cent authentic the whole time – that would be an absurd demand of any human being.

What I want to do is suggest some approaches I have used to get behind the masks people wear inside organizations, as well as the masks organizations themselves put on. It's my experience that such approaches contribute to far more satisfying and productive work and can help organizations build brands of substance and value, not illusions and deceits.

Vulnerability and status games

The biggest reason humans find authenticity difficult may be that we so dislike being vulnerable. To avoid admitting our needs, we try to satisfy them by indirect methods, which can be very energy consuming.

One of the interesting concepts from improv (improvisational theatre) is that of status.[5] Much great comedy rests on confrontations between characters of different status, frequently when someone playing high status is inadvertently humiliated by someone of much lower status. Basil Fawlty and Manuel from *Fawlty Towers* would be a classic example.

The world of business gets stuck in monotonous high status. Small businesses are not small; they are 'specialists'. The third-ranked company in its sector will be 'a leading' provider. The result is usually dull and uninspired communication. And the real trouble with all this high status is that it blocks real contact. I don't show you what I really feel and you don't show me what you really feel. We can try to guess what we want but there isn't much chance of either of us being happy. Playing high status gives us the illusion of power and control but prevents the kinds of relationships from which we can learn and grow.

Much modern business is always striving to perfection: beautifully presented products, promises of superb service and great prices. But as humans, we all know perfection is not possible. And those of us with perfectionist streaks will know how unhappy such aims make us. The great thing about authenticity is that, practised well, it actually releases businesses from the requirement to be perfect.

The low-cost airlines have been big beneficiaries of cutting through this nonsense with under-promise. They are (relatively) cheap and offer a matching level of service. Easyjet seems to revel in the ITV series that frequently demonstrates its human shortcomings. With no investment in CRM and frequent-flyer pseudo-loyalty, they seem to have created a more realistic relationship with customers. Of course, Southwest Airlines takes the biscuit for no-holds-barred self-mockery. After a bumpy landing on one flight, the flight attendant announced: 'We ask you to please remain seated as Captain Kangaroo bounces us to the terminal.'

Part of this ability to manage imperfection is that authentic businesses do not depend on the outside world for approval – even though, paradoxically, they often earn it.

Play to human strengths… and 'weaknesses'

Human beings in an organization must be able to express themselves more freely. With that ability, they can work to challenge and adjust whatever bureaucratic or ideological framework happens to be in vogue, so that the organization remains responsive to the needs of its participants.

Given the strong tendency of businesses to favour command and control, what's needed is a balancing intervention in favour of practices and ideas that play up to our human strengths.

Techniques from the worlds of improv and psychotherapy focus attention on what creates real satisfaction in human relationships. They are simple in design and allow us as humans to create subtle and rich connections. (In contrast, most management consultants peddle ludicrously complex techniques that only serve to crush the subtlety and versatility of human relationships.)

For example, I recently worked with a niche furnishing business. I was asked to help the sales team become more effective but quickly discovered a series of misunderstandings and anxieties between them and management. I started using a simple concept created by family therapist Virginia Satir. Called a temperature reading, it is designed to help couples or teams to examine the nature of their relationship by going through a simple and consistent agenda.

This starts with appreciations, and works its way through new information, puzzles, complaints with recommendations to wishes and hopes. Without going into detail, this relationship tool allowed all concerned to give voice to deeply felt but as yet unexpressed needs and concerns – many of which could be easily resolved once exposed to daylight. None of these were emerging in conventional daily meetings.

Actors in improvisational theatre have learnt how to create compelling scenes totally spontaneously, with no script. In doing so, they have inadvertently stumbled on principles that are a powerful antidote to the prevailing mentality that stifles the power of the human spirit in organizations.

Get business people playing a few of the warm-up games that improv actors play and strange things happen: the energy level of the group rises and often laughter bursts out. Gradually, people get better at creating greater spontaneity in their communications and their emotional state changes. They start to experience the power of (forgive the jargon) co-creativity.

For example, take a game called 'one word story'. A group of players sit in a circle. They make up a story, to which each contributes only one word at a time before passing to the next player. After a few stumbles, most story circles start producing funny and satisfying stories, yet no one is really in control and everyone must acknowledge that they have contributed to the outcome: arguably the holy grail of team building, within minutes of first trying. And people can be encouraged to ask: what if my working relationships and meetings could be more like this?

Improv also often gets participants to play status games. It invites them to explore how to play high status (for instance by quoting illustrious authors or famous acquaintances, adopting a more fixed gaze, holding one's body relatively still) and then low status (perhaps by fidgeting, looking away from the other person, stuttering) – and then to find all the positions between the two. For many people, simply to become aware of how they play status can be a revelation, one that encourages them sometimes to drop patterns that impress but isolate, in favour of ones that open and connect.

It is possible to take these ideas and use them to help groups of people interact more openly and also to generate new ideas about how they as a group interact with other stakeholders in an organization.

In praise of 'negative' emotions and conflict

Bad news: if you want passion in your organization, you can't pick and choose what form it takes. You might get laughter but you might also get tears; you may get enthusiasm but you'll also have to deal with anger.

I remember taking part in meetings to steer a £30 million two-year branding project in which everyone was very polite. One day, a skirmish broke out as someone (me) started openly to criticize some of the work. Arguments broke out, until the brand director intervened and expressed his disappointment that the normal spirit of teamwork seemed to have failed us.

Of course the 'normal spirit of teamwork' was code for a spirit of denial, where doubt and challenge were suppressed in favour of the illusion of unanimity. As the cause of the skirmish, I soon found myself marginalized from the process. One participant subsequently revealed his strategy at these meetings: to sit there and not allow the wrenching of his stomach to become manifest in any discussions.

The inauthentic meetings resulted in inauthentic marketing to consumers. This campaign, which shall remain nameless, is one of the most spectacular rebranding failures of modern times, and was canned by its financiers after two years of negligible results.

Yet the teamwork exemplified is exactly the type that many businesses inculcate. A friend recently told me that at Hewlett-Packard there was something called the 'Hewlett-Packard nod', which meant the passionless assent of people unwilling to state their real views. In contrast, I hear that at Intel employees are encouraged to practise 'constructive confrontation'.

An authentic organization will not be anger-phobic and stuck in conflict avoidance. It will see conflict as a potentially creative opportunity. Most of us have had unpleasant and painful experiences of conflicts. We may, for instance, associate conflict with violence or psychological cruelty. As a result, we may feel the wisest strategy is to avoid conflict.

Unfortunately, by avoiding conflict we often make things worse, allowing small resentments to build up over time to the point where we may feel furious, helpless, desperate or resentful – or perhaps a powerful cocktail of all four.

I take a more optimistic view that conflict can be positive. It can be an opportunity for a relationship to change and move to a more rewarding level; it can also provide us with rare opportunities to gain insights into our own and other people's behaviour – insights that can be of lifelong value. Sometimes, what feel like intractable feelings of hurt can change into much more satisfying ones.

Methods of alternative dispute resolution such as mediation are making great headway in business, in preference to the nasty and expensive alternative of litigation under the adversarial court system. The same principles can be deployed widely in an organization to encourage richer relationships between individuals.

The adoption of such principles can lead to a rehabilitation of the idea of conflict from something that is always dangerous to something that can be positive. A culture that encourages and supports challenge is likely to be one that identifies and resolves conflicts of interest far more quickly and effectively.

A challenge to convention

In my view, what supports authenticity is thinking that values human relationships. At its most extreme, such thinking may challenge the conventional economics of brand consultancies and ad agencies, which depend on claims to control and manage relationships on behalf of their clients. What's needed is an approach based on facilitation rather than agency, a style that relies on improving the quality of human contact to allow participants to access more of their innate resources for connecting – instead of claiming to do it for them.

Sadly, many consultants make their money not by challenging their clients but by placating them. In the tale of the emperor's new clothes, the tailors get well paid for their empty flattery. For the small boy, virtue may have been its own reward – but that won't be enough to motivate most people. Businesses need to be willing properly to value challenge and insight over frenzied activity that only confirms the status quo.

I also believe that the transition will not be easy and may at times be chaotic. In my own life, the challenge of authenticity is presented on a daily basis; it is not one I will ever clearly pass or fail. This chapter is – and I think must be – only a partial analysis of the issue but I hope that it can stimulate the sort of questioning and uncertainty that is often the prelude to change and growth.

REFERENCES

Allen, Woody (1975) *Without Feathers*, Random House, London

Clifton, Rita and Maughan, Esther (2000) *The Future of Brands*, Macmillan Business/Interbrand, London

Jensen, Rolf (1999) *The Dream Society*, McGraw-Hill, New York

Lewis, David (2001) *The Soul of the New Consumer*, Nicholas Brealey, London

Sanders, Tim (2002) *Fast Company*, February

NOTES

1   See http://www.amorenaturalway.com/pamphlet_15.htm.
2   See http://www.authenticbusiness.co.uk/docs/articles/apg.htm.

3   See http://www.fastcompany.com/online/58/shortcourse.html.
4   See http://www.gallup.com.
5   Robert Poynton of On Your Feet explores this in depth at www.oyf.com.

8

What's brand got to do with it?

John Caswell

BROKEN PROMISES: SHATTERED DREAMS?

No one wants to help me go where good things might be found.

(Brian Wilson, I just wasn't made for these times, Pet Sounds,
14 February 1966)

The sense of frustration, disappointment and fear I feel that exists in the business world today is palpable. Fragmented, constrained, defined, siloed, splintered and segmented into oblivion, today's organizations (and the employees and customers who rely upon them) are ever more dysfunctional and disconnected from one another.

We face what chemists would call a 'sublimation' of meaning. The solid truths and measures of a mass-broadcast, command and control age seem to have not even paused to become fluid – they have simply transmuted straight into gas – as ethereal as forgotten dreams.

I'm not alone, I know, but that doesn't make me any happier about what's going on in the name of business, or even worse what is perpetrated under the auspices of branding and the often total disconnection between them. Nor do I accept the commonplace patchwork of systems and all too convenient 'applications' to resolve this randomness of strategy.

Is it the business of branding or the branding of business that is at fault? Or neither? Of course the answer is both.

I no longer believe it is constructive to deal with the effects of these disconnections in isolation from their causes and in isolation from one another. Relentless innovation and organizational re-engineering are all very well, and crucial to human progress. But what is required – simultaneously – is a little renovation, ingenuity, creativity and some constructive support.

So what's the problem anyway? A typical conversation going on in the head of your average CEO

The first thing to get to grips with is that there are many questions for any CEO to grapple with, almost certainly too many. Many potential answers as well. If brand people with their own specialism aim to provide answers for clients, well that can be a very subjective and precipitous path to tread too.

Of course we should start with what the customer wants, what does he or she need or aspire to from us and our products or service? Now that's a great question but what does the consumer actually feel? What perception exists? What sentiments are out there? When during the day does he or she really consider your product – if at all?

Hmm, that's a bit more tricky.

There are 6 billion people on the planet so we had better try to imagine what they need and want from us. And who are these people? What are they like? Where do they live? What marks out their community? How might we refer to them – categorize them if you like? What are their vital statistics? What are their CVs like? Are they similar to one another or markedly different? How should we group them? How should we classify or manage them? Is that feasible anyway?

Now, does the database strategy we have in place 'map' to these criteria? Or does the company hold insights that relate to the most profitable customers in ways in which they can perhaps talk to them more valuably? Are they growing as sectors or segments? Can the business decide whether these communities are in decline or are they static? Can they address each segment differently? Can they rank all of these needs and wants to each category or type of potential customer? What would they be able to do if they did? Would they create different services and products?

Now that's getting interesting.

Well, OK, if we could arrange and organize the value metrics of all of this then that's great but then it just gets more complex. Each of these individuals has countless ways in which to get to the product through a retailer, a wholesaler, online, direct through an intermediary, a club, an association, in fact third parties galore. And then what about the influencers like the media, trade associations, local government, the press. So much chatter, so many influences however well intentioned, often out of the control of the business.

Ah, it's just getting too difficult.

And what are these stakeholders' needs? What are their business interests? What are their imperatives? How do they describe their problems, their 'points of pain' as we might call them? The point is that we have to speak very differently to the business community and show that we understand them, even build specific services and solutions for them. This is becoming of increasing importance in ensuring that we build business as cost-efficiently as possible and finesse the demand chain through which our ultimate customers can gain access to our products and services.

Furthermore the enterprise has constantly to consider the pure product, its current positioning, the competition, the 'commodity of everything', the systems of manufacture, the resources, the services, many of which are often still unformed or nascent. How much time is devoted to thinking about the current business model, the price, the value, the way in which the business describes itself? It's interesting to listen to the 'What do you do for a living?' answer they give as that is often proved to be way out. How can the business better create an improved and differentiable experience for their partners and alliances, their customers across all of these channels, the call centres and data centres? What about improving the training and consulting they may do to support their sales?

OK, so now they have considered all of the complex conversations they may have and that are inextricably associated with their products, services, channels, channel needs, communities of need and customer needs, what should they be saying they really do now it's all added up? What's the big idea behind their business? Should they actually refer to what they *actually* do in the light of all this somewhat differently? Could they have a whole new language to describe what they do? I would say so.

The reality is that most consumers are pretty tired of the same old stuff being addressed to them. They get communication fatigue. Customers get bombarded by thousands of new messages every day. I heard that the average consumer receives over 20,000 messages every day. Let's have a go at saying something fresh and different. Please.

So clearly CEOs really do have a lot to think about. Yet how can they prioritize it all, how can they make certain decisions and how can they make those decisions to the benefit of everyone: the enterprise stakeholders, the customers, the environment, the society and sustainable for the good of long-term success of the business?

This is clearly not easy and really does provide any organization with a set of very difficult decisions. Many of these decisions could be almost paradoxical. We most certainly live with paradox all around us. If you think about it, almost everything that you consider in business or in everyday life has its opposite energy with a win for one invariably meaning a loss for the other. Subjectivity rearing its head again perhaps. This win–lose struggle is a massive drain of energy, and causes frustration and inevitably the failure to appreciate reality. The counter-intuitive behaviour of social systems further compounds paradox. Things can get worse before getting better, or vice versa. You can win or lose for the wrong reason, and actions intended to produce a desired outcome may, in fact, generate opposite results. What we could really do with is far better 'decision quality'.

Given all of the above 'striving for alignment', it's now very important to integrate the external messages within this bigger picture, the awareness, the generation of leads, their conversion, the retention and long-term relationships and support of newfound customers. The continuous 'mantra' of integrated communication and tactical customer acquisition is important, yes, but at least we could make it a pleasant and coherent conversation for our customers, couldn't we? And surely advertising isn't the only way to do things any more, is it?

Oh, and then perhaps we should remind ourselves of what we were aiming to achieve: those business imperatives. Will they be changing now that we actually begin to understand all of the issues we are setting out to address? They just might.

Moving on…

So have we described the totality of what an integrated business, brand equation and brand framework might look like? A new mould? Well, maybe, with a clear language, we'd be getting closer, but as we all know to our cost, business plans were probably fixed at a particular time and perhaps also at a time when external observers were brought in. It's usually all gone a little bit off the tracks by now.

What can we infer from all of this?

Disconnectedness and misunderstanding.

At the core of organizational disconnectedness is the similarly core problem of both verbal and visual language. Instead of verbal content uniting organizations, in reality we see business and brand *bad language* creating a flow of 'dis-content' through organizations that fundamentally confuses and divides people. The lack of a commonly acceptable language or 'framework' for businesses is becoming a real yet unseen threat to business and global systems.

For almost 20 years I have been dealing with the effects and the fallout from the toxic waste of failing to address this issue of deliberate disconnectedness and shared misunderstanding. I've learnt this lesson through bitter first-hand and often costly experience and then developed and applied the solutions I describe later on in response to it. I believe we need a fundamental shift from just the creation of content – to a vital liberation of context.

In describing a piece of the total solution to this in the following pages, the aim is to catch a glimpse of a very real and achievable world in which branding can reconnect to a serious business agenda, and in which businesses can successfully exploit the strengths and relationship opportunities that brands can create. This is about liberating value.

By building on insights into the nature of human understanding, I merely offer a very simple and clear strategic approach that can help resolve so much of the problem of fragmentation and corporate indecision. It can help take us, finally, beyond 'branding' as the forcible imposition of a fake reality and into something honest and truthful: positive context.

This simplicity is in direct contrast to the unnecessary complexity of conventional IT, management consulting and branding solutions traditionally thrown in the face of such a crucial issue: our growing remoteness from one another and the institutions that surround us. Resolving this is of course critical to the future of our planet – its necessary economics and most importantly its humanity.

The individual and the collective?

I think I now need to paint a personal picture of the background as to why I got to where I am. This frustration of fragmentation is based on the realization that actually we are all becoming immune to content and increasingly so. We are in some way separated even from our own reality. We are in many ways and especially so in business and on so many more occasions isolated, completely alone and entirely without a context within which to piece it all together and make sense of it all. I think we must each assume personal responsibility for re-establishing this context.

At the root, we are all somewhat subject to the illusions perpetrated on us by circumstances beyond our control, by the industry of 'branding', and are in actual fact the unwitting subjects of this traditional phenomenon of the commercial world. To my mind all this business processing, the strategy setting and the definition of goals should be a critical and fundamental part of any brand strategy, fully understood and embraced by those inside the business where possible and *not* solely left to self-serving service providers with their own agendas to fulfil.

In addition, and adding more complexity, each divisional team within each enterprise will use its own 'context', with an often wildly differing language, and base its individual 'strategy' on data that are interpreted according to the department's point of view. Naturally enough, many people will have their individual perspective on how to achieve their own objectives. This is madness.

This situation, common in almost every business on the planet, actually displays utter inefficiency, is a criminal waste of shareholders' cash and is a 'best-in-class' recipe for an explosive and very public failure. To understand properly the isues as a whole the resolution surely must be to get a fuller and more objective picture of what's going on.

If this were done the organization could also then develop 'real' solutions: ones it not only understands and subscribes to but not necessarily those that primarily suit the service provider or sets of 'advisers'. This newly refreshed organization might then deliver those valuable experiences to customers it keeps talking about. Interestingly, and sadly all too seldom admitted, is that many boards just lack the sense of this. They just don't admit that they don't understand how to make things better.

The double frustration is that they will turn to *any* available seemingly rational explanation as to just why they may be in difficulty or decline, or why they are being trampled by the competition or losing share: whatever suits them to explain the phenomena, in the absence of first-hand experience, reality or facts.

Fiefdoms and follies

In the hundreds of board-level conversations we undertake, I sense an implicit misunderstanding caused by an individual's perspective and point of view when compared to the condition of the systems of the business or the community. To put it another way, I feel an entrenched protectionism displayed by senior managers to blur the effects of any misunderstandings or dysfunction and as a result I see them try to place barriers or smoke screens around their actual hold over what is going on around them.

We are, I believe, each of us linguistically constrained inside our own heads, never knowing if we fully understand or if we are being properly understood. We lack any check or measure other than a result or a nod of the head, perhaps a shake of the hand. This certainly seems to give some people a rather false sense of security or even insecurity. In addition the longevity (or rather shortevity) of senior managers or politicians in their role and their ability to perform at full power with all the market change and rate of uncertainty thrust upon them is a further contributor to the integrity of the enterprise, the wider market system and its subsequent success or failure.

The implication of this is an increasing transience and fragility of organizational meaning, captured momentarily in words, but having no lasting meaning for the people of the organization. What organizations face instead is continuous uncertainty and a fragile state of the known values that are culturally important and so they just get lost, subsumed or shifted within this continuous change.

This amounts to a 'systemic failure' of language and indeed a failure of 'numbers' to capture and connect an organization's people, processes and purpose. As all organizations and communities are the sum of their entire moving parts, people, products, structures, strategies and so on, very few companies or nations have flexible or rapidly adaptable enough strategy. Also, they are confused by the distinctions between tactics and strategy and remain solely focused on dealing with effects rather than causes. This is in every sense a very complex environment within which to make change happen or stick.

In light of all this disconnection, organizations talk glibly about knowledge being powerful. I worry constantly about the hijacking of knowledge management by software companies and others. Controlling knowledge and information may well be of value to some, but what I believe we should be aiming for is comprehension and literacy in the whole business-brand strategy and its values across the entire organization.

In order for organizations or societies properly to comprehend and manage their opportunities and create winning strategies, they will need the 'fullest' picture. In most organizational systems we are constantly told that this is simply not possible. In too many it is deemed impractical, indeed it is even actively made impossible as divisions are incentivized and compelled by the organizational structure to deal only with divisional issues. They have no way of connecting across the system to achieve their common targets.

Worse still, the potential collaborative value and human motivation to achieve that collaboration, the 'internal brand', is boiled out by lack of meaning, purpose or reward. The result is depression, waste and frustration in many cases. Were there a way of compressing all of the waves and stages of innovation, vision, motivation and delivery by organizations then I propose it would require cross-organizational groups who are powerfully cascading ideas and actions and collaborating in meaningful ways both up and down the organization in a language that discards the traditional structures and approaches of everyday business and branding.

We are a long way from such an ideal. But an active start point requires a full and aggregated view of the current state and then the co-creation of shared mental models of the 'journey' the organization must take towards a more valuable, deliverable and believable future.

WHO CAN CREATE A SOLUTION? AND HOW?

First let's determine what we think the successful enterprise of the future needs.

The 'owners' of systems – clients or social communities – want to see real return on the investment of their energy, which, in the case of most businesses, equals dollars – in everything they do. This is often the only 'criterion' for success within the current system of economics. We are endeavouring to find opportunities to construct and introduce measures for the intangible values beyond dollars and you will have found much spoken about this elsewhere in this book. Furthermore organizational custodians continually want to reduce cost and increase performance across all aspects and throughout all measures within the system.

We know that in fact custodians are looking for breakthrough in all areas. They need to win and then maintain competitive advantage and efficiency in all areas of the enterprise. They want above all to grow, and to find the best way to restructure their resources and systems, people and processes in order to capitalize on the opportunity they have defined. They need to reduce their risk both in identifying the proper solution and in its consistent delivery 'on time', 'on budget' and 'on all given criteria'.

To achieve their goals, organization leaders know they need to get closer to customers, influencers and decision makers, build better relationships and respond to expectations and needs. But in the multimedia and multi-channel world this has become immeasurably more complex and therefore needs more innovative, imaginative and wholly more human solutions.

In the present and future enterprise the new leadership teams will also be demanding increasing transparency of strategy and real-time understanding of objectives and opportunities and of whatever is deemed the 'scope of works'. And of course all of this understood by the whole enterprise. We see corporate governance issues are increasingly dominating the agendas, corporate and social responsibility objectives rising up the list; what will be done?

These new managers will always want to lower the cost of actions, planning time and inefficient and unnecessary project management. They will continue to need fast and expert intervention and the provision of the relevant expertise on a just-in-time basis. They demand excellent service, clarity over measures and proper controls.

Yes, leaders need to create a commonly shared purpose and objective in their enterprise and one that can dramatically increase the likelihood of success in this delivery of change. Yes, they will need to build and refresh their agenda in terms of this wave of reinvigorated interest in corporate governance; yes, they will need to demonstrate a new truth thereby building 'trust' and belief in themselves, their market and their financial community, but by creating more than rigour in the management of the enterprise. But they must now actually do it! What leaders do not want though is more technology, more presentations by consultants or more complexity in the process of transforming the business, or more risk in the form of inflated promises and hollow, husk-like customer relationships built on momentum and bribery.

What is the new reality for the 'suppliers' of brand or business solutions? What do they need?

A leader's supposed partners, the suppliers of brand solutions, want guaranteed new business growth and mostly they want an opportunity to do better, more rewarding work. They need to show clients how to generate and accelerate value fast, not introduce increased consulting confusion and unnecessary expenditure. They need to develop a full and extended relationship that has respect and trust. They need a fast and differentiated approach to developing their solutions.

They also must seek ways to educate and involve teams of senior managers and deliverers in order to ensure full understanding, essential to successful results. They need to find a way of overcoming perceptions of expensive consulting solutions, silo and agenda-driven solutions, low-value delivery and execution-based solutions. They need advice objectivity and solutions, but only those really adding value to the systems. In overview, their interests would seem to coincide with those of leaders, but silos, language and deception can often get in the way. Fragmentation again rears its head. Content overrides context.

Clearly there is a need to overcome misperception, misunderstandings and all of the language barriers, politics and semantics that often plague and undermine the typical long-term engagement and project. The irony is clear; the branding community has fallen foul of its own image: its brand.

Managing the moving parts

We all know that it's only possible to stay in control of *all* the moving parts for short periods of time. Whilst technology and innovation are helping here, major initiatives aimed at staying ahead of the curve are very expensive and difficult to manage.

This is particularly true when needing to manage the individual needs of people or operating units, local governments, the moving parts of the value chains and the many external players and partners involved in all complex systems. In addition benchmarks and industry standards (often quoted as measures of performance) can also be a false sign of achievement as they too are also changing constantly and cause much stop–start in their infrequency or are misaligned in their involvement with/by the enterprise.

The usual linguistic and numerical rigidity of management, social or government process and structure also leads to distress in the system in that the current systems are notoriously unsuited to wholesale community-driven change and therefore revert to rigidity and inappropriate pressure in varying degrees across the divisions of the business or the strands and seams in the social system.

Positive and negative context

What seems increasingly clear though in this fragmented world is that performance increase and competitive advantage in systems do not come from conventional business processes, most of which remain constant over long periods of time. There is simply too little understanding by the people involved in the down-draught of these systems.

My repeated assertion is that a new cross-organizational dynamic must emerge to interrupt these processes, and the energizing force behind that dynamic is *positive context*.

Fixed business system structures that demand a strict adherence to highly ordered and dogmatic process, business plans and fixed objectives mean that any enterprise is both difficult to transform as market needs dictate and also does not allow for the creativity, experimentation, innovation that stakeholders require. Nor are they adaptive enough to the customers' constant need for the next new thing. Ingenuity is a powerful dynamic and needed now like never before.

The status quo is 'energy sapping' and a negative context.

So how do we build a new relationship framework?

And an end to all this frustration.

I created a series of visual frameworks built on a set of 11 pieces of logic within which to think 'outside the box' and cause consensus and understanding within it.

The primary objective of Contextual Mapping© and Progressive Framework Methodology© is to get the organization leaders and partners, of whatever denomination, into the most important and meaningful conversation possible. By reframing conventional goals, imperatives and means within a common visual and verbal language, organizations can avoid and resolve any linguistic misunderstanding and friction that come with most highly agenda-ed discussions.

The aims of such an intervention are straightforward:

1. Complete understanding and a team-wide belief in the capability to deliver the objectives, co-created and refined throughout each iteration.
2. A framework upon which to build assets. From the insights collected, build a set of hypotheses from which to increase chances of success and mitigate risk.
3. A common and committed set of tasks throughout the teams all understood by the people who have to help to deliver them.
4. Increased richness in the quality of the solution through broader analysis of the 'whole'.
5. Consistent planning and programme management across and supported by the whole enterprise or social system based on proven techniques of value management.
6. Deep diving into the causes of the problems and removing the temptations of superficiality and effects of problems.
7. Remove the risk of solutions looking for problems and fitting the situation to convenient 'closed solutions'.
8. A common language that increases efficiency of operation and can be sustained and developed very fast and over long periods of time.
9. Disclose fully the differences between divisions or individuals in a respectful, innovative and valuable way.
10. Spot early weaknesses in the current infrastructure thereby avoiding and preventing problems rather than waiting for the dysfunction and disconnections to cause larger problems.

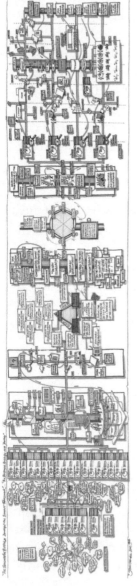

Figure 8.1 The 'live' drawn co-created discovery map

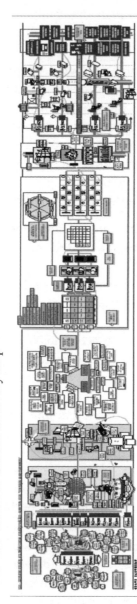

Figure 8.2 The outcomes are digitally stored for ongoing hypothesis and inferences to be worked through by the teams

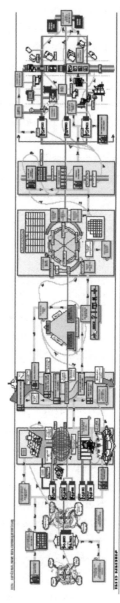

Figure 8.3 Clarity and focus emerge once the development map is created after the initial intervention and resulting synthesis are done

11.   Embrace creativity across the entire business system.
12.   Assess *all* of the opportunities and properly understand the stress points across the whole enterprise and system.
13.   Begin to identify the real values and strengths and drive for coherence amongst the team to create a shared focus around strategy, tactics, implementation and direction.
14.   Build powerful relationships at senior level to overcome political and systemic imbalance.
15.   Show how innovative, properly thought through and integrated thinking is achievable through engineering a common frame for agreement and purpose.

Through our own organization's approach using our techniques and frameworks the aim is to create a new world beyond branding. We deliver 'constructive interruption', which accelerates organizational self-transformation. By fusing a visual vocabulary with a universal business equation our aim is to crystallize and carry meaning and motivation right across an organization. To that extent, our interventions and their effects are 'of the brand', but they also 'are the brand'. Brand, after all, is the totality of organizational meaning.

By intervening in the status quo to reframe, reconfigure and remould the totality of an organization's purpose within the minds of its leaders (and partners), we aim to build a broader and deeper constituency of purpose around the brand. We 'co-create' pictures that frame the energy of organizations and make things happen.

'You are what you edit': the power of positive context

Almost all the issues we face in our work with clients across the world and all of the misunderstandings that we have discussed here seem to me ultimately related to context, whether personal or organizational. We therefore now desperately need new and more innovative approaches to tackle both of these *together*. Content and content management just doesn't seem to help. It just doesn't figure. Why, when there is so much data and information knowledge and reference material so liberally available, does decision making not improve? Why are consumers no better served? Or at least no more fulfilled? Why are decisions made in isolation of the whole argument or all the facts? Why are so many people in the businesses so demoralized and so desperate for things to change?

I don't really understand it. People from every walk of life and every discipline, people I respect so much and with so much experience, seem so prone to make decisions based on their own best practice. I believe it's probably worst practice when it lacks proper context.

My definition of context may well suit my argument and I make no apologies for that but I believe it mounts up to having the best view of all your surroundings. I believe it amounts to being in receipt of all the facts about the whole case or the whole. It's expected for advisers to have a vision. They are the 'experts'; they should know what they are talking about; they do it every day, have a specialist skill. They have their lingo, their terms, their jargon; they have an industry language and by and large they all speak it very well.

We've described here how the inhabitants of boards and owners of systems badly lack this common language and they have no shared framework. Would-be purveyors of 'beyond branding' techniques must now start by putting themselves in the mind of our mythical organization leader who is so confused or, if not, is so wilfully complacent.

The call for help

To validate and refine the equation (see Figure 8.4), most CEOs will call for help. Often they simply won't have access to qualified data nor sometimes even know where to look for the resources to change the status quo. This feeds nervousness, an inability to know what to do about the realities, which might be creating a downturn. Worse, they will get a 'professional's' opinion from just one point of view or another: a self-propagating and unstoppable spiralling of decline.

Each member of a board represents a different skill sector: finance, manufacturing, sales, marketing, technology and if you are lucky sometimes these days even human resources. Despite the 'borrow your watch to tell you the time' accusations, management consultancies are actually great at having a (fairly anodyne) point of view; so are analysts, the media and marketing advisers of all varieties. Overdosing on advice is a real skill of the average board. Actually, learning to tell the time, as an integrated team, on your own watch is probably the most useful skill a board can develop.

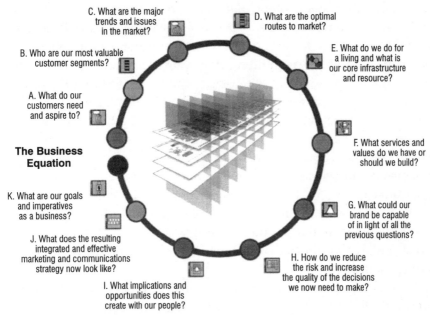

C. What are the major
trends and issues
in the market?

D. What are the optimal
routes to market?

B. Who are our most valuable
customer segments?

E. What do we do for
a living and what is
our core infrastructure
and resource?

A. What do our
customers need
and aspire to?

**The Business
Equation**

F. What services and
values do we have or
should we build?

K. What are our goals
and imperatives
as a business?

G. What could our
brand be capable
of in light of all the
previous questions?

J. What does the resulting
integrated and effective
marketing and communications
strategy now look like?

H. How do we reduce
the risk and increase
the quality of the decisions
we now need to make?

I. What implications and
opportunities does this
create with our people?

Figure 8.4   The brand-business equation: Progressive Contextual Mapping©

A favourite quote, and one that is so relevant and plays so wonderfully to the underlying premise of postmodernism, is amazing as much for what is being said as to the era when it was said. Albert Einstein said this at around the turn of the last century: 'Perfection of means and confusion of goals seems to me to characterize our age.'

And thus we foster trillion-dollar consulting industries to refine our ability to achieve meaningless objectives. What is the real goal? What are the objectives? Are they the right ones? What will drive the potential success of business? Who will care? And should they?

Answering these questions on intent and integrity requires a cross-organizational conversation that simply cannot be held within existing organizational language. And certainly the richness of these conversations cannot easily be conveyed through conventional 'preach and teach' internal marketing.

The 'visual' imperative: how Contextual Mapping© can take us beyond branding

All my life I think I have found it easier to think and construct thoughts visually rather than in any other way. In fact for me I am not sure there is any other way to think about complex issues (just to make my point again). I look back and in my head I cannot remember any occasion where the record of my life's activity is anything other than a visual one. Of course it's added to multidimensionally when taste, smell or a sound adds to the impact and clarity but for me the primary record is always a visual one.

Words, mission statements, volumes of strategies, performance targets, whilst of course still important, don't figure much in my memory. Instead, I have images and associated moments, triggered by sensual associations: fragments and snapshots, linked by a common purpose and acting as a rich narrative to my life – biography and history in a jumbled slide show.

With due deference to Proust, I think of Contextual Mapping© as 'the active premonition of things future'. By formalizing and moulding context we create an organizational biography. This, surely, is the essence of what branding should be.

Contextual Mapping© is a perpetual, dynamic process. It is all about business, it's all about brand, it's all about systems and it's all about people. And it's about time, in every sense: the transition from brand present to brand future, and the ability for the brand continually to learn and adapt to shifting context in order to get there, both internally and externally, both individually and collectively.

Well, actually, it's all about managing the systems that surround us to create harmony and access a truth that is smothered and fragmented. My assertion is that, without interrupting existing entrenched processes and adopting fresh multi-sensual frameworks to accelerate dramatically understanding of the connected enterprise, we will fail to build humanly sustainable businesses.

The world of 'beyond branding' is where context matters as much as, if not more than, content.

9

Anthropology and the brand

Ian Ryder

> To manage brands is to manage society – if we can capture a moment it is
> surprising the catalytic changes we can make.

Anthropology may seem like a strange word to be including in a book that
seeks to push the leading edge of brand thinking, yet the only strange
thing is the extent to which it has previously been ignored. As the social
science that studies the origins and social relationships of human beings, it
is a central discipline that explains much of how brands work through the
many societies and cultures across the world.

Let me just ask you a question or two. As a CEO, CxO or other senior
manager, do you really care about issues of sustainability? About why
your customers and other stakeholder groups behave the way they do?
About why you and your fellow managers and employees behave the
way that you and they do? After all, with the average tenure of a CEO
now down to around two years, where is the incentive to take the long-
term view?

Well, you should care, if only as a human being on our planet for the
briefest of moments. The world is evolving and you and your brand are
integral parts of this pattern. Let me share some reasons why working
with the natural systems of the world are both essential for corporate
success and also can make you feel good as well!

The word 'anthropology', perhaps, has poor brand image itself as it sends images of apes, hominids and the old TV zoologist Desmond Morris. Yet despite his TV image, Desmond Morris was one of the leading anthropologists of his day, writing such books as *The Naked Ape*, in which he points out:

> Homo sapiens has remained a naked ape nevertheless; in acquiring lofty new motives, he has lost none of the earthy old ones. This is frequently a cause of some embarrassment to him, but his old impulses have been with him for millions of years, his new ones only a few thousand at the most – and there is no hope of quickly shrugging off the accumulated genetic legacy of his whole evolutionary past.

(Morris, 1994)

In other words, when we are considering brands and people, to ignore our history is to ignore our humanity. Although the targets of our brand may pretend to be advanced beings, those earthy motives keep reappearing. To be brand experts, we must see people as evolving creatures who are doing the best they can, within their limiting evolutionary constraints. Most importantly, to understand the drivers, conscious and unconscious, of both ourselves and our customers/stakeholders is critical to optimizing business performance.

There are three contexts within which we can examine the anthropological impact on our brands, and these are reflected in the sections of this chapter:

▌ *Outer systems* are the forces of nature and society that act upon us, our actions and brands.
▌ *Inner systems* are the deep human drivers through which we are motivated, understand and decide.
▌ *Outer constructions* are the resultant actions that brands can take, bridging the outer and inner systems to create business, social and evolutionary success.

OUTER SYSTEMS

Evolution is the driver of change. We have prospered as has no other species, yet our accelerated development has its price in the anchors that drag behind us. We still have, for example, the famed 'fight or flight' reaction that primes us for ferocious physical action whenever we are surprised, annoyed or frightened. Our primitive emotions are still strong current realities for us, and we are at the beck and call of a subconscious that prods us into strange and unpredictable behaviour, from the mad dash in the days before Christmas or the backlash of betrayed consumers (names like Ratner and Hoover come to mind).

Further than this, we are social beings who have found that, for survival and growth, togetherness beats aloneness hands down. The price of this is conformance to social norms, and the threat of exclusion has become a potent weapon. Let us consider these two issues, of evolution and society, and how they relate to brands.

Evolution

Despite the fact that 72 per cent of people in the United States do not believe in evolution (including Presidents Reagan and George W Bush), it has been proven as a powerful force that is at the root of much change. According to neuroscientist William Calvin (1997), there are six elements in the evolutionary process – all of which have implications for brands:

1. *There is a pattern*

   In animals and people, the root patterns are in the DNA helices that we pass to our children. This principle was taken further by Richard Dawkins when he described the 'meme'. A meme is a single idea or thought that spreads in genetic ways. Memes are themselves memes. This notion has since blossomed into the entire discipline of memetics, including its own journal (at jom-emit.cfpm.org). The now-traditional search of Google offers a mere 40,500 pages on the subject.

   Brands are patterns, too. They are also memes, containing specific and differentiated ideas about companies as well as their people, products and services. 'Bentley', for example, says 'refined power'. When I go to a Bentley showroom I expect refined service. 'Wal-Mart' says 'cheerful low cost' and, whether visiting Asda in the UK or one of the many US stores, I do not expect their people to be wearing Armani suits, but I do expect them to give friendly advice.

2.   *The pattern gets copied*
With ideas, copying occurs when other people learn of the idea. Memes thus act as 'thought viruses' with the more powerful memes, such as those that appeal to common interests and fundamental needs, spreading further and faster. Thus news of wars and deadly diseases spreads like wildfire, whilst the invention of a new type of house-brick raises few eyebrows outside of the builder's yard.

Brands get copied in the memetic sense. As we communicate the brand and people tell one another about it, it spreads through the populations of both carriers and targets. Brand managers should thus think closely about the impact of their brands on common needs and interests, as well as the ease with which the message can be passed on to others.

3.   *Variations occur in the patterns*
As genes evolve they do experiments and mutate into different forms. Nature's experiments are random and incremental. Small genetic modifications occur at a balanced rate that protects the population at large from damaging distortion whilst giving different genetic make-ups a chance of making the big time of widespread copying.

This happens with ideas too. When you tell them to other people, or even recall past thoughts, the received thoughts may be subtly or somewhat different from the original ideas. Brands fall into this category. Like Chinese whispers, each transmission goes through an interpretation process (perception of actual experience) that leads to a stream of mutation. A well-designed brand message and strategy are so clear that this distortion is minimized.

An implication for brands is that close attention should be paid to the cognitive and social processes of people who perceive and retransmit the brand message. Accidental distortion can cause great damage (and, occasionally, great assistance) to the brand.

4.   *There is competition*
Ideas fight both one another and established concepts for the prize of development and use (only 1 in 56 new product ideas actually succeed). Good ideas spread more rapidly as they are told and retold. Ideas that are weak or difficult to understand are given less consideration. Brands compete for mind space more than billboard space, and a well-*positioned* brand will establish a differentiated and defensible hill in the minds of its targets.

5. *There is a complex environment*

The business environment in which brands operate is indeed complex, as is the internal territory of the minds of the target population. A well-designed and managed brand will naturally navigate these muddy waters. Further, a well-designed organization, although complex, will naturally support and align with the brand itself.

Biologist Ross Ashby defined the 'Law of Requisite Variety' in 1956, when he showed how, for a species to survive in a given ecology, it requires to have at least the complexity of its competitors in order to counter all of their attacks. The same is true of businesses and brands. A brand requires sufficient complexity to survive in its environment. A part of that complexity is to maintain the apparent simplicity of a clear message whilst maintaining the underlying capability both to fend off attacks and to provide for complex needs. New Labour in the UK did remarkably well in grabbing a wide central political territory with a fresh, open and youthful image that pushed the previously powerful Conservatives into a perceived dour corner of ageing corruption.

6. *Successful variants get varied more*

When an animal mutates successfully, evolution seems to pay particular attention to it, performing additional experiments. Perhaps unsurprisingly, humans are the most rapidly evolving species. Out of interest, the second most evolved group are birds: the dominion of the air has given them a huge advantage in reaching food and travelling distances with which other species cannot compete.

Brands also come and go, and smart companies pay close attention to the success of their brands. Brand variants do have a limit, and brand extension (dilution) can weaken the original memes. With care, however, in-brand variation can be used to create the commercial equivalent of ecological space-packing, filling the shelves with different variants of the base brand (how many variants of Colgate are there?).

The implications for brands are several. First, as people, societies and ideas evolve, then brands must change with them. A brand that once allied itself with the greatness of the British Empire would be seen as jingoistic and distasteful. Robertson's jams had a 'golliwog' as a brand icon that was hugely successful, but social and political-correctness pressures caused them to remove it from their corporate identity. Secondly, the brand itself may play the lead role as it evolves, perhaps with the evolution of its masters, such as where the personal growth of Richard Branson led to the increase in social responsibility associated with the Virgin brand.

Brands may also evolve as their parents change. Mergers, acquisitions and divestitures lead to the combination and splitting of people, ideas and brands. Brands can fade or die out this way. Beecham's was a 'family' pharmaceutical with its famed and quirky 'powders'. It then became the B of SKB and has since faded below even this as Glaxo stole its place in the more recent GSK. In the way that there is now a discipline of evolutionary genetics, so also is there interest in the notions of 'brand genetics'.

Brands have life cycles even though they are often much longer than product life cycles. Brands are born and they die. Even the whole discipline of brand management can be viewed in this way. In the post-Klein era, there are claims of the death of brand, but such bold statements are somewhat exaggerated. *The Economist* also tried this back in 1992 and 'Marlboro' Day' in April 1993 almost proved the case, but journalistic fervour is no replacement for reality. True, short-sighted companies do cut back on managing brands but, like the dotcom claim that strategy was dead, such prophetic statements are blind and suicidal. Brands have always been and always will be an integral part of our human context. Brands are created from the perception that your customers and other stakeholders have of you. To leave these perceptions to chance is to leave the future of your company to the fickle hand of unmanaged fate. Always remember that there is no such thing as an unmanaged brand: if you do not do it, the market or your competitors will do it for you!

Society

Evolution has made us complex social beings in which there are two competing forces. First, we are descended from primates who lived in tribes and lived on readily available fruits and berries. We can observe the apes today as they leisurely move in large groups from tree to tree. They have strict hierarchies and clear social rules. Any ape that tries to jump the pecking order is asking for a beating or worse. The second force comes from the period when we left the forests, shed our hair and started walking upright. As hunters, we still lived in tribes, but the males now had to go out and hunt for meals, taking great risks and using thoughtful wiles to trap their faster and fiercer prey. Females, meanwhile, stayed at home to tend the slow-growing family.

We are thus driven by both hierarchy and loose, but intense, collaboration. We eat both in the primate sweet snacking and the carnivorous hot gorge. We both pair-bond and opportunistically mate with the partners of absent colleagues.

This social complexity is both a minefield and a goldfield for brands. The complex social rules and behavioural patterns are all pathways that brands must tread. As with the Bible or the Koran, you can use social rules to argue for or against pretty much anything, although the degree of your success can be highly context-dependent. To weave the brand into the fabric of social networks means socializing the brand, creating it as an integral element of how things happen. This can be seen especially in lifestyle brands, and particularly those targeting the young. Marketing methods *themselves* have been branded to suit, such as 'permission marketing' and 'guerrilla marketing', and authors such as Seth Godin have built their personal brand on a basic understanding of anthropological forces. There are arguments, with some but not total validity, that refer to the 'brand resistance' of Generation Y (10- to 25-year-olds). These would argue that, because of the huge volume of 'messages' delivered to this group every day of their life, coupled with the range of products available, they have become inured to our brand communications and are less brand loyal. Importantly, the argument runs that they want to be 'individuals', which would preclude anything that resembles 'uniform'. I said there was some validity in this argument and there is. Certainly, and thankfully, there is a growing awareness of the damage that major corporations can wreak if they continue as in the past and ignore the wider global tapestry of which they are an integral user and creator. They do not want to put up with this and wish to see change, and this is good. But for those with a responsibility also to create wealth (as distinct from value, which is equally important and linked) we cannot ignore the subliminal drivers that come from way back in our genetic make-up that tell us some of this argument doesn't work. Tell me, what is a bare midriff, low-cut trousers and tank-top if not part of today's Generation Y 'uniform'?! Parents may ponder when they last managed to escape buying their son or daughter those vastly more expensive Nike/Gap trainers or cargo pants because he or she 'couldn't be seen dead in *those*'. Let us not forget or ignore the most basic and strong anthropological drivers of our brand management in our rush to fix the future, as much as it really does need to be 'fixed'.

Societies themselves are now demanding that corporate governance systems have the transparency that permits evaluation of a company's (brand) performance on more than the 'old economy' accountants' and analysts' favourite quarterly earnings! Total corporate responsibility (TBCR) has moved into the boardroom and will, of necessity, become a key strategic thread to be woven into the patchwork quilt that is the brand as presented to all its stakeholders. The Enron, Worldcom, Andersen and other collapses that gave birth to the Sarbanes–Oxley Act in the United States in 2002 caused a watershed in corporate governance that has changed both the manner in which companies must manage their brand, and the leeway that society will permit corporations in their selfish pursuit of profit and power. Corporate citizenship is now more powerful at shaping company perceptions and reputations than either brand quality or business fundamentals – we must deal with it.

To manage brands is thus to manage society, which of course we can never do. At least we can never do it completely, yet if we can capture a moment it is surprising the catalytic changes we can make. Linux and the open software movement thus challenged the might of Microsoft. Akio Morito defied research to launch the Sony Walkman, and Nokia/Motorola and others destroyed our public 'privacy' for ever with the ubiquitous mobile phone. And when Martin Luther King had his dream, he encapsulated the aspirations of black America and spread his brand around the world. Wouldn't it be wonderful if you and your organization made a similarly outstanding contribution to the world?

The social construction of the brand

Brands start off with the *intent* of the brand marketers and senior managers in a company, which is typically itself built through a socializing process of market research, product competencies and many conversations within and outside the company.

The *espoused brand* then continues its social journey, constantly evolving in subtle ways as it is translated into action by everyone who is involved in the delivery and reception of this espoused brand. Enactment is still not the brand in its final form, although it is a step closer than the intent. It is the difference between Argyris's (1993) 'espoused theory' and 'theory in use'. You are what you do, not what you say. Company values are the totality of what their people do, not a neat list of values on the Web site.

Brand messages can take many tortuous routes before they reach their final destination of the minds of target customers and stakeholders. Everett Rogers (1995) described (and Geoffrey Moore (1999) expanded upon) the process of *diffusion*, where segments such as innovators and early adopters adopt new concepts before more cautious groups accept them.

The theory of social contagion has been known since at least Le Bon's 1895 study of crowd behaviour. More recently, marketers have more overtly courted the magic of fads and fashions and the positive catastrophe of the 'tipping point', as Malcolm Gladwell (2000) calls it. Brand perceptions are spread through social networks, where Emanuel Rosen (2000) identified the specific roles of 'hubs' and 'connectors' of intermediaries who spread (and evolve) the word. This is particularly true in the early days of a product – for example, 65 per cent of early Palm users heard about it from friends. It is in this diffusion and socializing that the *social reputation* of the brand is made.

As an integral part of modern diffusion, the media, especially non-advertising journalism, can have huge effects in creating social meaning – both positive and negative. With the stroke of a pen or, particularly, a carefully edited image, new spins of meaning can reach millions of people, heroizing or vilifying a product or an entire company. This is just one reason why transparency is essential. The media love beating up brands on behalf of ordinary people (and we love them doing it too!). An exposé of a corporate cover-up or disaster makes great news and can quickly do serious damage to the reputation of a brand. The list is large and well known: Perrier, Union Carbide and Exxon Valdez, just to name a few. Even those companies that have long sought social responsibility can be tripped up by a moment's misunderstanding, such as in Shell's Brent Spar episode.

Through this process, a broad social perception and hence the *social brand* is created. Ideally, this is a relatively narrow band of meaning, but can easily have a very wide distribution, especially as it reaches across market segments and international cultures. Brands like McDonald's and Coca-Cola try very hard to narrow that spread to a controlled and predictable perception. It is one of the principles at the core of many franchise operations, where the root company's primary concern is consistent brand management through a potentially very diverse group of owner-operators.

Malcolm Gladwell (2000) also points out how 'What we buy increasingly becomes a message of who we are to the people we trust' and 'We base many of our purchasing decisions not on what we know we like, but on what we believe others want us to consume'. We thus use brands socially to construct *ourselves*, putting on not a pair of Nike trainers, but all the images and perceptions that Nike and our friends have colluded to associate with that little swoosh. We dress ourselves not in clothes but the images we want to be.

From intent through enactment to diffusion, the critical effect of the brand is in individuals' minds when they are making decisions. They create their perception from the many inputs they receive, and act accordingly. Let's take a look at this inner process, exploring how our inner systems lead to the hard reality of effective brand perception.

INNER SYSTEMS

As well as the external forces that affect people, we also have our own deep drivers and systems, which move us forward. If brands are to succeed, they must take account of our deep systems of motivation and decision.

Deep needs

Our evolutionary system has left us with deep needs that we constantly strive to satisfy in order to help spread our genes. A simple trilogy that Straker and Rawlinson (2002) derive from Maslow and evolutionary needs, and which is very relevant to questions of brand, is the need for a *sense of control*, the need for a *sense of identity* and the need for *novelty*.

The need for control is closely allied to survival and is supported by the need to predict, for which brands have great relevance. Brand promises are short cuts to trust, which enables prediction. If you break a promise, you are hitting at deep needs, which naturally will cause a strong reaction!

The need for identity is again significant, particularly in the alignment of brand factors such as 'personality' with the sense of identity of its target population. Identity formation happens at the individual level, within groups and within entire companies, with each level of identity affecting all others. These collective identities then effectively become the brand of the company, as brand decisions and the brand-as-enacted reflect the subconscious and conscious beliefs and biases of the driving members of the company. As an example, The HP Way, now very sadly 'retired', was Bill Hewlett and Dave Packard's contribution to one of the best-known management philosophies for a corporate brand. We must all be aware of how fragile our core values can be and how quickly they can change and mutate into those provided by new owners.

The need for novelty drives even the most fulfilled person to keep changing and trying new things. This is both a big lever for brands and a warning never to be complacent about captive markets. The attraction of the new must be used to ensure we keep our brands fresh and stimulating, whilst of course also maintaining the control of a stable core.

Much of what we do is to satisfy our deep needs, although we often do not realize this. If brands, and those responsible for managing them, lack the depth to reach for alignment with these very real drivers of our behaviour, then those brands are effectively disconnected and drifting beyond the people they seek to influence.

Values

To live in tribes, teams and companies, we create and abide by social rules that tell us what is right and wrong, good and bad, important and less important. We then use these rules as judge and jury on one another and ourselves. We will also judge brands (after all, what else are these but 'tribes'?), and reward or punish them accordingly.

One of the greatest crimes a brand can commit is to break a value – and not just a brand value but also a value held by the customers and other stakeholders who judge it. The most common, expected value is for truth and honesty, yet so many companies tell endless lies to their people, shareholders, customers and other stakeholders. Where the values of its executives to 'make money' and satisfy shareholders are in conflict with the values of other stakeholders for truth, then a devastating collision is on the cards, as in the previously mentioned Enron, WorldCom, Andersen and other debacles.

One of the simplest and most powerful values that a company can have is only to promise what they know they can deliver. Yet the desperation to meet targets and to satisfy customers leads salespeople and executives to make blind promises whilst leaving the delivery of these commitments to back-room people who may not have the time, resource, skills or process sophistication to have any real chance of reliable completion.

Measurement

Perhaps this is the point where we should take a brief look at one of the other absolutely critical components of successful business and therefore, by extension, a successful society, we would hope – measurement. Measurement is so misunderstood and badly used. The capability of an organization to deliver on and manage current and desired brand perceptions to all stakeholder groups depends on people, processes, resources and channels. Without an *integrated* measurement system and without a dashboard for our brand performance, it is absolutely guaranteed that no organization will be operating at optimum performance as there will be inbuilt conflicts across the organization. There are just three main reasons to measure:

▐ for understanding (to discover and decide);
▐ to create the right behaviour;
▐ to manage gaps.

With such an understanding, companies can ensure that they build an organization that understands what it is there to do, and is structured and aligned in order to be able to do it – they can therefore deliver *at least* what they promise their stakeholders.

As Peter Fisk (2000) noted, company values and brand values should be congruent and relevant, and have the necessary depth and reach to create effective behaviours and experiences. Trust, once broken, is at risk of never again being repaired and, whilst a partner may allow room to repair a broken trust, you can be sure that, for your business, your customer/stakeholder group will not be half as forgiving (see Chris Macrae's work at www.valuetrue.com). See Figure 9.1.

Breaking of values and trust leads to a sense of betrayal in which our desires for reparative and retributive justice sometimes lead us to extreme acts of revenge. Just consider the hope of 1990s investors, and their terrible

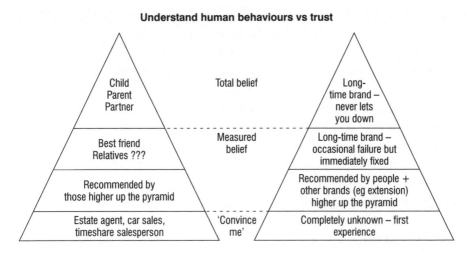

Understand human behaviours vs trust

Figure 9.1 Trust pyramid

punishment in the plunging markets of the early 21st century. Betrayal is one of the most powerful ways there is of changing the brand. 'Enron' now stands for greed, fat cats and outrageous deception – a sickening that has also tainted many other corporates.

Ethics, values and behaviours have to be congruent between all parties to give any relationship any real chance of success. The Russians and Germans attempted to collaborate early in the Second World War, but their divergent idealisms fated this marriage to a short-lived honeymoon before the inevitable divorce.

Emotion

Emotions motivate us, and it is no accident that both words derive from the same Greek roots. We feel love, interest, surprise, fear and hate, based largely around the meaning we infer from our experiences and thoughts. In fact, emotion is singly the most powerful motivational force known to humans – the expression 'crime of passion' exists for a very good reason! Emotion appears from the subconscious mind and it is absolutely the real reason why brands exist, and will always do so. Even in what was believed to be the totally 'emotion-free zone' of purchasers of technology products, in 1997 Interbrand-Schekter in New York published results of a large survey (2,500 respondents) that surprised many. It indicated that the key purchase driver of such products was not price or functionality, both of which had taken turns at being the marketers' arrowhead, but was in fact 'the emotional attributes associated with the brand'. The last few years have seen a significant shift in the way marketing inside technology companies has developed brand positioning and messages (think Orange, think Sony, think Intel). Brands do exist in the mind, but it is fool's gold to believe that they *act* anywhere else than in the heart.

In fact, emotion is at the heart of all companies, and drives people forward together, as Robert Jones (2001) identified when he noted how an idea that creates unity of *feeling* leads to successful companies. Recent work on such approaches as 'emotional intelligence' has legitimized emotion in what has often been an emotionally sterile (at least in conversation) workplace, and we have to manage the fact that emotion appears from the subconscious mind and it is absolutely the real reason why brands exist, and will always do so.

Such powerful subconscious drivers that force us into action may seem like a brand manager's heaven, which, if we understand these anthropological blueprints, they certainly are. It is also a heaven for alarmist journalists, from Vance Packard (1957) to Naomi Klein (2000). The key is about values, ethics and responsibility. Harmful manipulation is clearly wrong, yet persuading people to buy products is as old as the town marketplace.

Mental models

The world is a complex place, yet our conscious mind thinks only in a linear way, processing one thought at a time. We have a simple mechanism to cope with the daily torrent of information, which is to compartmentalize much of what we experience and believe into simplified models. Thus when we see a snake we recall patterns of emotion, values and behaviour that quickly tell us what we should and should not do. Mental models are, of course, gross simplifications and can lead us into inappropriate behaviour, but they are highly pragmatic devices without which we would rapidly become lost.

Mental models become more valuable when they are shared with other people. They then become short cuts for communication, almost like telling just the punchline of a joke as an abbreviation to remind an audience of the whole funny story. Even language and every word is a mental model and each combination of letters is a little package of meaning. Language also highlights the limitations of such shared modelling: we use it every day, yet we constantly misunderstand one another. The map is not the territory, as Korzybski (1933) pointed out, yet we often act as if our internal models are the real article.

Brands are mental models, too. They are containers of emotions, values and promises that offer reliable value in return for allegiance. They help speed decisions and enable people to know and predict what will happen when they act around them. When you buy a bottle of Coke, you not only know what is in the bottle, you also know how it will make you and others feel when you take it out of your bag at lunchtime. Most crucially, brand positioning is founded on a mental model that in reality means you had better make sure your own proposition is clear and your brand is on one of the top three rungs of that mental 'ladder' (Ries and Trout, 2000) – it had also better deliver on the promise your proposition makes, as today's consumers make use of the legs they have if a brand fails.

Inference

When we create meaning we do not accept it blindly – we *infer* it, filtering our outer sensations through a series of internal lenses, each of which colours what we are experiencing and each adding to it.

The initial filters help us recognize and classify what we see, from trees to burger joints. Brands, of course, get in early here, using familiar shapes and colours to get through this stage quickly and easily. Recognition also draws meaning from context, and a fashion model in a slum is not the

How does your organization behave?

Make a promise ... Beat the promise	= Brand excelling	= Customer advocacy/ acquisition
Make a promise ... Keep a promise	= Brand delivery	= Customer retention/ some acquisition
Make a promise ... Miss the promise	= Brand failure	= Customer loss/ agitator

Figure 9.2 Promises

same as on the catwalk (although interesting things have been done with 'slum styles' that perhaps seek to neutralize the guilt of excess in an impoverished world).

After basic recognition we will test what we see against our needs and goals. Will we be harmed? Is what we see what we expected? What does it mean for the future? Brands can threaten as well as promise, as when a fashion becomes 'old hat'. There are many younger people now whose mental models of Levi's, that doyen of 60s freedom, is of stuff their parents wear. As a result, they will actively shun others who are foolish enough to wear the wrong clothes.

We also use our values to create meaning by judging what we perceive against our values. A common value is that the strong should not harm the weak, and even evil dictators can gain surprising global sympathy when larger countries seek to liberate their people. A part of this judgement filter is an assessment as to whether what we are considering can be trusted. There is very different meaning created when considering a brand that is trusted and one where trust is even a little bit uncertain.

We eventually become confused if we cannot easily create meaning, and start thinking more deeply as we seek to infer something useful. This state is often where we are persuaded and where new meaning is created, and as such is why some brands (such as Tango) deliberately use unusual advertisements.

Inference can also have a great effect on (and be affected by) our emotions. If I am feeling angry at the United States, then I will pass McDonald's by on the other side. On the other hand, if I have just seen a feel-good Hollywood movie, then I may well be attracted in for a bite of the real US of A.

OUTER CONSTRUCTION

Given our understanding of the outer evolving world and the deep inner human drivers, we can consequently construct external systems that will optimally lead to desired brand behaviours. Brands can act as facilitating bridges between the outer systems through which we are subject to natural and social forces and the inner systems by which we discover and decide on our responses. Brands can serve both the person and society, shaping individual thoughts and collective behaviour. This anthropological tension is at the heart of human survival and brands may be viewed as anthropological accelerators, operating in myriad ways to shape our personal and social context.

Company systems

Within the company, we can build systems that lead to desired employee thoughts, feelings and hence behaviours. This happens anyway, but with a brand-led view we can construct systems and devices that are more likely to have the desired effect.

Company motivation systems are often perceived as solely those to do with reward and recognition. Although these certainly do have an effect on people, it is often not quite what was expected. Anything we pay attention to signals importance and consequently affects behaviour. As stated earlier, measurement is an incredibly powerful and misunderstood, misused tool.

Taking an anthropological view highlights a wide range of other systems of motivation. A cultural study of a company will highlight many symbolic motivators and behavioural triggers, from the size of the atrium to the positioning of desks. If your brand says 'We love people' yet your call centre is crammed into a dingy backstreet, then you should not be surprised if your employees are somewhat cynical.

Among the most powerful systems of values transmission and behavioural control are the stories that are told within the company. When the district manager tells stories of how the best salesperson made a significant sale, the manager is telling the other salespeople what to think and how to behave. Likewise, when the office gossip tells stories around the coffee machine, messages about behaviour and morals are also being transmitted. Stories use subtle devices such as heroes and villains to tell what is right and wrong. They are an ancient medium whereby we accept and infer meaning often without realizing it.

The formal processes of the company also include many brand-relevant factors. From recruitment to quality management, there are opportunities to err or succeed that can have massive impacts on the brand. Recruit for base character, values and personality because these are what will come through in your brand – you can train for skills. And never, for example, sell on defective products that still carry your brand name and hence all of your values.

Brand systems

As we come towards the final straight of our race back through time, and the impact that our genetic and social heritage demands we understand to enable us both to manage brands today and to build brand systems for the future, we must not forget the most crucial element of all our plans – the customer! At the end of the day, for any commercial organization, *the customer is the only reason you are in business* – however we may choose to try to dress up this most basic of facts!

In the same way that we can act on the inside of companies to build an anthropologically sound internal brand-management system, so too must we work on the aspects of the brand that touch customers and other external stakeholders. In particular, we need to work on the interfaces where misalignment between 'our brand and their brand' can occur.

Understanding the brand of external stakeholders includes investigation of both the brand as espoused and the brand as practised. It also can help a great deal with this understanding if we can better know their inner systems. The ultimate goal of brand management is to align at this deep level, such that we and they feel as if the relationship is like working with a close and long-standing friend, where trust is implicit and transparency is natural. Of course this is a nirvana that cannot easily be approached, yet the potential benefits make the journey well worth while.

Just as stories are created internally we can also create and use stories about our brands. Many brands do this, such as Coca-Cola's stories about how its wholesome nature unites the peoples of the world, or Budweiser's 'heroizing' of the blue-collar workers who build the land of the free.

One way that stories about the brand are created is through philanthropic and other activities of social responsibility. As Michael Porter and Mark Kramer have pointed out (2002), thoughtfully managed corporate philanthropy can serve serious competitive advantage (my co-authors have written more extensively on corporate social responsibility).

The ultimate place for brand stories is in the tales our customers tell one another and our journey to find customer 'advocacy'. Such stories are often based on surprising experiences, where expectations were broken or surpassed. We do have the choice: we can break promises and let their coffee-machine stories revolve around our callous and manipulative ways, or we can meet and exceed promises and become the white knight of their tales. This need not cost much and gold-plating is not necessary, as exceeding expectations by a small way is often enough.

Increasingly, customers and other stakeholders have a critical expectation for transparency in their relationships with the brand. We live in an era where social capital is being eroded and trust is probably at an all-time low. Just as the tragedy of 11 September in New York changed our human world for ever, so the post-Enron world will also never be the same for businesses.

The maturity and success of brands are linked to the maturity of marketers who provide the initial shaping impetus. If they push one way whilst society is going another, then the brand will snap in the larger social storm, hopefully before it does any lasting damage. This is a significant danger of larger brands, such as 'Brand America', which, if it pushes its individualistic culture too far and too hard, may provoke a systemic backlash that leads not to capitalist heaven but ecological breakdown.

Managing a brand is big stuff. It means understanding customers and stakeholders at an extraordinarily deep level. It means understanding the macro-effects in markets and social networks, where ideas diffuse, ebb and flow. It means building companies that constantly and consistently deliver sound values with care and transparent honesty. If you can do this, you will not only have built a great company, you will also have personally contributed real good in a needy world, which is just about the best epitaph that anyone could have.

KEY THOUGHT SUMMARY: ANTHROPOLOGY AND THE BRAND

Anthropology

▐ We are not long out of the trees. We are victims of this recent evolutionary history.
▐ To manage anything to do with people requires a deep understanding of what drives us.

Outer systems

▐ Evolution is a system of inaccurate copying and survival.
▐ This also happens with companies and brands.

∎ Brands must evolve with their targets. Brand death is always around the corner.

Inner systems

∎ We are driven by deep needs, values, emotions and simplistic mental models.
∎ To work with people means working with these systems.

Outer construction

∎ We should build our companies to align our people (and our channels) with the brand.
∎ We can also align the systems that affect customers and other stakeholders.

Customers and other stakeholders

∎ The dynamics of the modern marketplace has made the customer paramount.
∎ Customers are, in fact, the only reason we are in business.
∎ Other stakeholders must not be forgotten, however. Each is a critical part of the brand web.

Brand (reputation)

∎ Goes from intent to enactment to perception, where the real brand is experienced.
∎ Reputation spreads through communication and diffusion through social networks.
∎ Is created, sustained or destroyed from the perception of actual experience of the projected image.

Trust

∎ Is about care and concern, truth and transparency.
∎ Takes time to build, a moment to destroy.
∎ Is multi-layered.

Brand alignment

∎ Your brand and your customers' brands should align for the best long-term relationship.
∎ Delivery of expectations must be enabled throughout the enterprise.

Measurement

▌ Align measurement to drive and manage the brand.
▌ Measurement is always in place but seldom understood.

Measure to discover, understand and decide

▌ Measure customers and other stakeholders to understand needs and target opportunities.
▌ Measure capability to know what you can reliably deliver.
▌ Measure causes of opportunity and performance gaps to focus business improvements.

Measure to create the right behaviour

▌ People tend to act to optimize the measures by which they are judged.
▌ Measurement signals priorities.
▌ A company acts as the sum of its measurements.

Measure to manage gaps

▌ Operationally, companies experience gaps between desired and actual measures.
▌ Operational measures highlight gaps and focus corrective action.

REFERENCES

Argyris, Christopher (1993) *Knowledge for Action*, Jossey Bass
Ashby, W Ross (1956) *An Introduction to Cybernetics*, Chapman & Hall, London
Calvin, William (1997) The six essentials? Minimal requirements for the Darwinian bootstrapping of quality, *Journal of Memetics: Evolutionary models of information transmission*, **1**
Fisk, Peter (2000) Brand magnetics, *Customer Management*, 20 January
Gladwell, Malcolm (2000) *The Tipping Point*, Little, Brown, London
Jones, Robert (2001) *The Big Idea*, HarperCollinsBusiness, New York
Klein, Naomi (2000) *No Logo*, Flamingo, London
Korzybski, Alfred (1933) *Science and Sanity*, Institute of General Semantics
Le Bon, G (1895) *The Crowd: A study of the popular mind*, T Fisher Unwin, London
Moore, Geoffrey A and McKenna, Regis (1999) *Crossing the Chasm: marketing and selling high tech products to mainstream customers*, rev edn, Harper Business, New York
Morris, Desmond (1994) *The Naked Ape*, Vintage, London; first published 1967

Packard, Vance (1957) *The Hidden Persuaders*, Longmans

Porter, Michael and Kramer, Mark (2002) The competitive advantage of corporate philanthropy, *Harvard Business Review*, December

Ries, Al and Trout, Jack (2000) *Positioning: The battle for your mind*, McGraw-Hill, New York

Rogers, Everett (1995) *Diffusion of Innovation*, 4th edn, Free Press, New York

Rosen, Emanuel (2000) *The Anatomy of Buzz: Using invisible networks to spread the word about your product*, HarperCollinsBusiness, New York

Straker, David and Rawlinson, Graham (2002) *How to Invent (Almost) Anything*, Spiro Press, London

10

Transparency, or not: Brand Inside: Brand Outside™ – the most obvious yet overlooked next source for the brand's authentic evolution

Julie Anixter

This chapter looks at the symmetry required to create organizations and teams that authentically engage the human spirit in the design of their organization's brand, identity and future. True symmetry requires that leaders (of companies, institutions, brands, projects, teams) acknowledge the one thing that most brand strategies have historically missed: that individuals cannot be co-opted, but instead can and must be trusted to co-create the brand.

How? By beginning with the acknowledgement that all individuals – employees, stakeholders, CEO, consumers, idle bystanders, audience members – get to play *equally* in the evolution of the brand, and are contributors to the living theatre of the brand's fulfilment through their simple caring about the value exchange the brand represents. Their actions manifest the brand. Their work demonstrates the brand. Their words are a simple litmus test (gets it/lives it, doesn't get it/doesn't live it).

Now for the twist! Through participation in a true value exchange, individuals' talent development, future and opportunities are not only enhanced, but intertwined with the values of the brand. Tight controls are trumped by the individual desire to evolve and to create meaning. This 'intertwining of individual talent and the values of the brand' represents a different future for organizations and brand strategists. It challenges the notion of 'internal branding' to open a bigger opportunity to the natural dance of human desire and energy from outside the orthodoxy of tightly constructed brand strategies that are policed, lock-step 'be the brand' practices, laminated mission statements and all the rest of the hobgoblin of little minds.

We've seen up front what is possible for organizations that want to bring their brands to life with the greatest possible authenticity, using the design principle of symmetry (where the wholeness is created through parts that are balanced). The benefits are many: engaged employees and less costly turnover; delighted customers and less customer churn and bad press; healthier balance sheets that have staying power in volatile economic times.

Symmetry is the primary design principle for bringing your brand to life inside and out. It is a *force majeure* of a design principle. I for one love 'design' as a verb because design is about how to deal with human constraints in an elegant way that meets human needs.

And design you must. Whether you're the CEO, the chief HR person, the town hall or project leader, a pool attendant, campaign manager, the head of housekeeping, a naval officer, or... you. You are designing consciously or unconsciously, awake or asleep, the truthful delivery of your organization's brand promise and your personal brand promise through – what else – your work.

The chapter begins with a 'how to' make that work authentically yours and a representation of the deepest principles of 'brand inside and brand outside' – a phrase that came straight from the PowerPoint bully pulpit of Tom Peters, author of *In Search of Excellence* (Peters and Waterman, 1982) (ISOE in our camp) and globe-orbiting speaker to business audiences for the last 20 years.

It *is* possible to create an authentic Brand Inside:Brand Outside™ organization where the work itself speaks for and channels the brand. That is our passionate message to organizations and to you. Because authentic, transparent, value-creating branding is about your work, it is necessarily then about branding you, authentically, transparently, value-adding-ly or, to say it another way, about consciously creating a reputation that you are proud of years hence and that works for you even as you sleep. You can be 'googled' without apprehension.

This approach will resonate with people who get that brand passion is in fact an unquenchable well to drink from – whether you're Rem Koolhas, Donald Rumsfeld, Carly Fiorina or Mickey Mouse. But it will confound you if you lack appreciation for the power of the brand and wellspring of meaning, value and identity it represents.

Speaking of drinking, I am going to use Alcoholics Anonymous (AA) as *the* exemplary Brand Inside:Brand Outside™ organization, and this chapter will tell you why in more detail. And one caveat: I will address you in the most conversational style that I can transmit on to this page. I love good conversation. I try to model it in my writing, speaking and most importantly in my leadership and consulting practices. Therefore, gentle reader, as Ms Manners – one of my favourite Brand Yous – might call you, I intend to make this a conversation with you. And on this subject of the symmetrically branded work environment, I have 10 things to say, which each start with a question for you to ponder. And if the questions don't exactly cut it, there's a short discussion that opens up and expounds on each idea from a different point of view.

10 QUESTIONS FOR AUTHENTICALLY EVOLVING YOUR BRAND

Here are 10 questions that I will explore with you in this chapter. I will ask you to try to answer each one. There is no test – this is an indicator for you.

And you can use your answers to evaluate your readiness for a symmetrical Brand Inside:Brand Outside™ organization. For each question you have an answer to, give yourself a point. You answer all 10 questions, you get 10 points. You answer one question, you get one point. One point, you're hosed, 10 points, you're enlightened... use your best interpretive powers to decide what it means:

1. It's midnight; do you know where your brand is?
2. Does it, the brand, have any real power for the leader? For you?
3. Does your work reflect the brand? Is your work itself distinctive?
4. Does the talent talk about the brand? Any good stories?
5. Do the leaders walk the brand? Any good stories?
6. Is alignment good, or bad? Why should we care?
7. Do you think execution means a culture of flawless execution, or death?

8. Is there brand passion inside and out?
9. How do you design symmetry into your organization?
10. Why shoot for it and what are the consequences if we don't?

But first a definition

What is Brand Inside:Brand Outside™ and why is it 'the most obvious yet overlooked next source for the brand's authentic evolution'? I'll give you two definitions, informal (yin) and formal (yang).

The informal begins with an experiment I conducted on 22 May 2003. I was staying on the eighth floor of San Francisco's esteemed Palace Hotel. I wanted to get down to the lobby fast around 7 am to meet the people from Deloitte & Touche who were hosting Tom Peters, me and 250 people. I was about as dressed up as I get: high heels, black trousers, green jacket. I took the service lift that was nearer to my room rather than the public lift down to the ground floor – realizing as I descended that it would most likely place me in the kitchen, which it did. And since I had taken the lift to and from my room to the pool the day before and had enjoyed talking to the housekeeping staff *en route*, I was already expecting to have a good experience when I got to the kitchen. On that Thursday morning at 7.03 am when the doors slid open and I said in a loud voice 'Excuse me, I need to find the lobby', approximately seven people within 15 feet perked up, made eye contact and moved to guide me there.

The moral of the lift-to-the-kitchen story – certainly not a new insight but nonetheless still quite valid – is that, when you talk to the front line, the workers, the people in the kitchen or behind the scenes, you really get a sense of whether the brand is authentic or not. I am happy to report that on 22 May 2003 the San Francisco Palace Hotel's distinct brand promise of hospitality was very much alive and helping weary travellers find their way. So perhaps the how to of transparency is to take service lifts. Or perhaps it's my way of seeing the world from an inside-out perspective.

In any event, the formal definition of Brand Inside:Brand Outside™ is 'the systemic development of the organization's brand promise brought to life through the committed action of every employee for every customer experience'.[1]

The reason that we (we being the royal we at the tompeterscompany! and LAGA aka Lipson Alport Glass and Associates) think that a healthy symmetrical balance of Brand Inside to Brand Outside, is the next most obvious yet overlooked source of the brand's evolution is simple: it is the one stupidly simple indicator that tells us what the people delivering the brand promise really think is going on. An equation might look like: brand reality = people's commitment to it.

Do people have a clue, or don't they? Do they know what the ad campaign, service, product, packaging, logo, latest offering or new CEO stands for? Can they articulate it? If they know it and understand it, do they bring the brand promise to life when you talk to them? Do they know what it is? Has anyone bothered to clue them in? If they have been clued in, do they care? If they care, do they think anyone else cares? It's questions like these that get under our skin and keep us up at night as we work with hospitals, banks, hotels, airlines, insurance providers, retailers, manufacturers, schools, military commands and others.

These are only some of the important questions to ask about this subject. If brand inside:brand outside is, as we're positing, the answer to burnt-out brands, why isn't it more widely understood, practised, invested in, measured, sought after and demanded? Why has integrated branding not integrated us? Perhaps the answer is that it's just plain hard. It takes great discipline and consistency of purpose to include people in the story of the brand in a way that makes it theirs, and frankly some of us don't want to be integrated in someone else's story. Or to paraphrase one CEO I know, 'I'm not really interested in the people.' Topped only by 'So don't make me try to be.'

Rich brand inside:brand outside cultures are just the opposite; the CEO, the leader, whether it's Oprah or Carly Fiorina or Marjorie Scardino Charles Schwab or Warren Buffet or three-star Admiral Joe Dyer, can talk to the people – and can ensure that the investments of time, treasure and talent line up to make it so. It's the kind of place that Andy Fastow wouldn't feel comfortable, but Kofi Annan and Steve Jobs would.

The best brand inside:brand outside leaders totally upend and challenge the current notion of 'integrated branding' as mechanistic, linear and unduly flat – powered by brochures and scripts. Working with them is a little like being in what Doris Kearns Goodwin described as FDR's ongoing 'house party' at the White House during World War II, when Winston Churchill, Harry Hopkins and the Queen of Denmark all lived there. Talking about the issues of the day and analysing them long into the night was the entertainment, the way to unwind. As Kearns Goodwin likes to point out, you could never do that today – but that's another story.

A great brand inside:brand outside organization like Schwab or Virgin or FedEx or UPS or Four Seasons or Target points the way to a third path: a practical symmetry with which to create organizations and teams that authentically engage the human spirit and unleash the passion of the brand. We've studied it, watched it happen, been fortunate enough to be part of making it happen, and here's what we've learnt.

Even if you can only get it 'sort of right' you will move closer to the authentic prize that a Brand Inside:Brand Outside™ environment promises:

∎ people confidently and intelligently delivering on promises that satisfy their own longings for mastery;
∎ while satisfying the most demanding customers and stakeholders and, more importantly;
∎ willing to work hard, change, stretch and grow to continue the process of observe–create–delight–respond–observe–create again in the future.

That's the rhythm of symmetry knocking.

The argument for brand symmetry

True brand symmetry is a simple contract between organizations and people that looks like this: the right hand knows what the left hand is doing, and why. There will never be just one hand clapping, because brand inside:brand outside organizations get that the people are the brand. The work they do is the brand, 24/7. It occurs when the organization takes time as Four Seasons Hotels and Resorts has, as AA has, as Southwest Airlines has, as Virgin has, as most Western militaries do, to educate every single member about the purpose and the promise of the organization. Whether it is called a brand is immaterial. The US Marine Corps didn't start out to build a brand, but they have built a powerful brand because of their absolutely distinctive and consistently realized culture. Every AA member, every US marine, every senator, every Four Seasons receptionist, every Southwest Airlines baggage handler, every Virgin HR person knows what the organization stands for and knows that he or she not only belongs to something, but that the something can help him or her realize dreams.

It requires, to use another cliché, a paradigm shift of epic proportions for organizations that view their people as interchangeable moving parts. If, like the CEO I quoted, you don't really care about people but about profits or politics, it's not for you. It wasn't for Andy Fastow and Ken Lay and it's not for you. Speaking of Andy Fastow and Ken Lay, let's get to the questions.

1. IT'S MIDNIGHT; DO YOU KNOW WHERE YOUR BRAND IS?

Midnight. That moment between night and day. Often a private time, when we dream asleep or awake about that which we care about most. Our true selves, unfettered by the day's stimulus (nightclub people, we are not talking to you), can hear ourselves thinking. It's a solitary time, where the endless buzz of stimulus is brought slightly to bay (I can still hear my father's voice yelling at us as kids, 'Keep it down to a dull roar'). So when the e-mails and interruptions cease, we have a little patch of peace and quiet in which to reflect, to see things as they are. Like us, our brands are 24/7. And they ebb and flow. They have more public and private selves. They get interrupted and clarified. And somewhere, someone is always thinking and wondering or dreaming about what could be. There is a watchfulness and a wakefulness and a level of almost biological aspiration that many leaders take for granted.

While they have not been convicted (yet) and the United States is a country of innocent until proven guilty, it's really hard to imagine what the so-called leaders of Enron or Worldcom were thinking at midnight, if in fact they were thinking at all. I cannot help but wonder if they were thinking about the security they were going to rip away, the financial and psychological ruin they were going to unleash on the lives of untold thousands of people, starting with their employees and their employees' families – families who surely wept into the night.

The tragedies of the economic demise of a number of corporations in 2003 are not stand-alone events. Bad judgement and evil behaviour are a fact of history. But I have a perverse hopefulness for our profession that someday we'll come to thank Ken Lay and Andy Fastow and Bernard Ebbers and Dennis Kozlowski and the boards of those fated organizations, and the few small minds at Arthur Andersen, for whatever vigilance they can give us by default, because in the dark of night or the light of day, if you're not wakefully, mindfully watching over the most basic promises you and your organization make, it's clearer than ever that you will be caught – and apparently not sent to the country-club prisons any more.

It's midnight. Do you know where your brand is?

2. DOES IT, THE BRAND, HAVE ANY REAL POWER FOR THE LEADER? FOR YOU?

CEOs and other leaders can be divided into two camps: those who value their brands as precious life-giving assets and those who see them as marketing necessities. Since organizations are inevitably run as power hierarchies, the leader's awareness and personal valuing of brand equity is a make or break. If the brand does not have real power for CEOs, beyond their own personal power (the Ross Perot–Jack Welch–Martha Stewart school of CEO-as-brand is not what we mean here), then give up and go somewhere else because the ground will never be receptive enough to grow a symmetrical organization. Many of the best, well-meaning brand strategists and advocates have been demoralized by CEOs who frankly didn't get it.

Get what? The one thing that most big brands and their strategies have historically missed: that individuals cannot be co-opted or manipulated (for ever or for long) – but instead can and must be trusted to co-create the brand. It is in the process of co-creation that individuals are fully recognized as the unique adults they are – capable of making principled choices that bring value to customers. Before the marketing executives quiver, let's make sure we're operating with the same definition of 'co-create'.

In the most fundamental sense we're here reading this because two people co-created our life. Co-creation means the shared responsibility for generating and producing… something. It's the deeper principle upon which collaboration rests. Applied to our organizational effectiveness it means that we not only can but must encourage and give licence to the people we work with to co-create our brands. This takes some of the power away from the control-freak types but in the end it's not only worth it but a much more interesting and vibrant way to work and live and, yes, customers can feel it (or not).

I've noticed that most weird ideas become identified immediately as empty buzzwords and no doubt 'co-create' is going to get painted in some quarters with that brush. No problem, as the other high concept that brand symmetry requires is what design guru Jerry Hirshberg coined as 'creative abrasion': the concept that ideas and people rub up against each other and create friction: thus providing a source of light, illumination and understanding. So keep rubbing up against this one. Here's what co-creation looks like in action. Think of a cocktail party you've been to. Or a church barbecue. A really good church barbecue cocktail party. Cut to the best conversation you had with someone you didn't know – where the energy was flying and the ideas were interesting, where you were laughing and it just felt good, where possibilities abounded and frankly you wish you'd had more time to keep talking...

The values of the brand get expressed through every employee, for every customer, in every transaction. One of my earliest bosses and mentors, Ray Geraci, taught me this in spades. When work is good, it feels like a cocktail party, barbecue, salon, church social, picnic with the elderly Buddhist monk on the steps of the temple, holiday with friends, life's most satisfying exchange or greatest adventure or both. It can feel very good. And why not: we spend our lives doing it – shouldn't we want it to feel good at least some of the time? So if you're not bringing your best passion to a brand whose values you believe in, why are you there? Your litmus test?

3. DOES YOUR WORK REFLECT THE BRAND? IS YOUR WORK ITSELF DISTINCTIVE?

The greatest discovery that we made at the tompeterscompany! in the past five years is that the notion that 'work matters' is a welcome relief in most organizations. Because it does. Only, with the emphasis on the bottom line, on celebrity CEOs, on quarterly earnings, on a culture of speed, it has been overlooked. Again, work mattering is nothing new. Zen masters and Quakers and jockeys and horse trainers and artisans of all kinds know this in their bones.

Tom has called this the Age of Talent, and at the same time predicted that the white-collar revolution sweeping the globe will destroy 90 per cent of white-collar jobs over a 10-year period that began at the millennium. Speak to him now and he will tell you that he was being far too conservative in his prediction, and others of late from Jeffrey Immelt to Robert

Reich have been much bolder. In 1998 he wrote a cover story for *Fast Company* magazine called 'The brand called you', and *Fast Company* sold more of that cover than any other in history because, as founder Alan Weber said, 'he hit a nerve'.

The nerve is still sensitive and quite broadly experienced in global business culture. It is not, contrary to cynical pundits, the fastest path to individual fame through personalizing the worst of Madison Avenue branding techniques. Instead that nerve at its core is about being recognized for the substance of your work, for the uniqueness of your work and for the passion you bring to your work. Brand You means you and others honour your work, which in turn defines the key touchpoints for the brand. At the tompeterscompany! and LAGA we describe a key touchpoint as 'any product, service, process or transaction that creates a functional and emotional impression of your brand'. When it comes to offering an experience of your brand's essence, that which you stand for, some aspects of your work and some touchpoints are more important than others. At AA, for example, there is real power throughout the process, but somehow it is captured in the consistent introduction: 'Hello, my name is [...] and I'm an alcoholic.' The admission, the repetition, the community experience all communicate volumes and create a culture in which much healing is possible.

The work of AA is, as one member I know and love said, 'to help people deal with alcoholism – it saves people's lives. It is phenomenal.' Everyone who knows AA knows that this is its purpose. Its brand and its purpose are one. They are expressed and made real in the work of their Twelve Step Programme.[2]

At the Four Seasons Hotels and Resorts there are four service values that leadership at each hotel works to imbue in everything. Those values are 'kindness, intelligence, mutual respect and customer delight'. Together, they comprise what Four Seasons Marketing EVP Barbara Talbott calls 'the Four Seasons Experience'.

Four Seasons employees have great freedom to give personalized attention and give it they do. The substance of the Four Seasons organization is so distinct that after 11 September they were one of the few hoteliers not to see their business drop off the charts.

The work of people there, from Isadore Sharp, the founder and chairman, to Amir Malek, a receptionist in their Washington, DC property, is branded. When I was lost *en route* to the Four Seasons in November 2001, during the first 'threat week' in Washington, DC, Amir stayed on the phone with me for 45 minutes – literally guiding me to the hotel in the rush-hour traffic and the rain even though I made many attempts to say that I could find it on my own. The truth is that I wanted the company and he knew it. He insisted and I relented – because in that 45 minutes I experienced a human touch that was akin to nothing short of grace.

Whatever his station, his training and the total environment that surrounded him supported his talent, and I will always be quite grateful to him and to the Four Seasons for defining something so authentic and special for me in a moment of need. Lest you think I'm a snob for luxury let me tell you that I have had equally moving experiences with Southwest Airlines, another organization that doesn't just talk about talent, but reinforces it at every turn.

4. DOES THE TALENT TALK ABOUT THE BRAND? ANY GOOD STORIES?

The story of Amir Malek was told throughout Four Seasons because I sent a passionate e-mail to the general manager of the Washington, DC Four Seasons and, like Seth Godin's notion of an 'idea virus', it spread. But it is only one of tens of thousands of such stories that have flowed through the informal networks of Four Seasons. There's the one about the man in Chicago who showed up for a very special evening at the last minute without a dinner jacket and begged the concierge to find him one – only to have one whisked into his room just in time. When he enquired of the general manager about how it had happened he was told he was wearing the general manager's jacket. True story.

Even though it is a universal phenomenon and as old as the hills, storytelling has only gradually been given respect as a tool inside our organizations. When it comes to talent, we've been trying it seems as a culture in the West to begin a renaissance of appreciation for the value of talent and intellectual capital or knowledge work. 'Be a connoisseur of talent,' Tom Peters has chanted to organizations around the world for years on end – and has then gone on to provide excruciatingly clear examples of how differently Zubin Mehta, James Levine and the great soccer and basketball coaches approach the recruiting, care and feeding of talent compared to the rest of us. There are few ways to understand this shift from personnel to talent other than the visceral experience of seeing the results. Whether it's a retail public-facing organization like Virgin or Jet Blue where we can see and touch the service and experience the difference or the thousand-plus patents generated by NAVAIR, the Naval Air Systems Commands that actually transform the way the US Navy communicates in a joint environment on land and in the challenging environment of aeroplanes at sea.

On a daily basis stories about talent – genuine authentic stories – become the closest thing we have to currency.

Now for the code breaker: through participation in a true value exchange, the individual's talent development, current experience, future and opportunities are not only enhanced, but intertwined. Tight controls are trumped by the individual desire to evolve. When Amir Malek makes a conscious choice to help a stranger he co-creates the Four Seasons brand and in turn it ennobles him.

Amir no doubt was able to make certain choices because of education and the exposure he's received both about the internal commitments of Four Seasons and exposure to its 'outside' perception. He was most likely predisposed and that's why they hired him. And it's a good thing – Amir and the customer are on the same brand continuum. As Denzil Meyers claims in Chapter 2, they're not separate audiences.

This hard truth of reciprocity between the development of the potential of the individual and the development of the brand represents a new future for organizations and brand strategists, and challenges the notion of 'internal branding' to open a bigger window to the natural dance of human desire and energy from 'outside' the orthodoxy of tightly constructed brand strategies and lock-step 'be the brand' practices. When each individual is recognized as not just an advocate but a co-creator there are implications for all aspects of the operation. But our organizations are insanely complex. And it's obvious that, for all the power that comes from unleashing individuals' passion and entwining the DNA of their development with the brand, it cannot happen on an *ad hoc* or random basis.

Finally, it seems these brand inside:brand outside organizations have a much easier time recruiting. There have been a handful of organizations I've worked with at different times – notably IBM, Deloitte, Disney, HP, Cisco, IDEO, Ian Schrager Hotels, Four Seasons Hotels and Resorts, Fast Company, the tompeterscompany! – where if people were lucky enough to be taken on they felt like they had been given keys to a very special kingdom. The brand recruited the talent, and then the talent, if it found that the work environment matched the hype, stayed and gave its best.

This is where leadership's will to lead the creation of a coherent values- or principle-based organization whose very identity people can participate in, even co-create, is the make or break. How can you tell?

5. DO THE LEADERS WALK THE BRAND? ANY GOOD STORIES?

Leadership is the key to a Brand Inside:Brand Outside™ organization. The beauty of leadership is that it has the power to make choices that shape the identity of the entity – who to surround themselves with, what and where to invest, which big ideas to support, and which, to quote Tom Peters quoting Dee Hock, 'we need to get out of our heads' (which is the hardest part).

Leaders have the opportunity every day to demonstrate right-brain, left-brain humanity and business acumen: to demonstrate the values of the brand. And again, they do it consciously or by default. As Boyd Clarke and Ron Crossland have discovered in their research on the 'leader's voice' (2002), leaders communicate and our brains are wired to receive simultaneously on three channels – the factual, the emotional and the symbolic. Leave any one of them out, and it is our nature to fill in the blanks. So, the company proclaims openness but you hear about all major moves second-hand. The hotel wants to be the mecca of gracious living, but employees are screamed at behind the scenes. I recently asked my friend Eunice Azzani, Korn Ferry Managing Director, 'Eunice, what have you been up to?' and she replied without hesitation, 'You mean besides changing the world?' Azzani's factual, emotional and symbolic way of changing the world is to recruit the best possible leaders into leadership positions, and to increase the 'seats at the table' for a myriad of voices – women, minorities, youth and outsiders – because she so deeply, passionately believes in diversity of leadership. And then she talks about it – everywhere. As a result, everyone who knows Eunice knows what she, and as a result Korn Ferry, stands for. It's really not that hard to see the symmetry in action. She does what she believes in, inside and outside of Korn Ferry (although she freely admits that as a leader you have to be willing to be uncomfortable, and to live with ambiguity and learn to let go). I'd take one Eunice Azzani any day over the people we've seen robbing and pillaging their companies. I know what the difference is from experience.

My father is the antithesis of Dennis Kozlowski. When he ran a New York Stock Exchange company with several thousand employees he kept tabs on what was going on in their lives and, when one needed heart surgery that insurance wouldn't fully cover, he and my uncle paid for it. When another employee was abandoned by his wife, who then proceeded to rack up $20,000 worth of credit card bills in two days, they paid the bill. They cared about people and people knew it. Their door was open and, even though some people sometimes took advantage of their generous nature (resulting by the way in jail sentences and firings), they were tough and fair and most of the people who worked in their company respected them tremendously and hung around for decades, practising the brand my father, uncle and Bruce Van Wagner had summed up with 'service is our technology'. Their business had phenomenal growth and success. In the 1960s they said, 'We work for fun and money', and they meant it. They wrote and published a policy manual – 'The Little Blue Book' – that included two blank pages headlined 'Organizational Charts' and 'Job Descriptions', which showed their symbolic hands and shared the core-est of core values – they trusted people to know what to do. The result was a culture in which everyone was a maverick, and yet everyone was aligned with the greatness in the culture, through the years of 30 per cent growth and in the worst of economies. The book was reprinted over 30 times and used with great response in countries around the world to recruit, to train and to lead. It proved that trust is universal.

Leadership of any organization is such a difficult job that many consider it un-doable. And it is if you do it alone. One senior leader said to me that the advice he got upon taking over his job was, 'When you're awake, work.'

But there is one thing we've seen over and over in large and small organizations that balances, symmetrically, the stresses of the job: when leaders are passionate – in their own style (not necessarily the stereotypical cheerleader, but passionately committed) – it is infectious, and we have also seen time and time again that the magic secret is to connect your passion to other people's passion. To paraphrase John Pigott, former and much adored CEO of Anixter: 'You're either the grease or the glue.' When you connect the dots of passion, you're both.

6. IS ALIGNMENT GOOD, OR BAD? WHY SHOULD WE CARE?

In an aligned organization all participants in the brand are equal contributors to the living theatre of its evolution, fulfilling this through their simple caring about the exchange (of value and meaning) the brand itself represents.

When I buy a Volvo, I am really getting safety; when I use FedEx, I will get overnight delivery; when I open a can of Coke, it won't kill me but will refresh me; when I hire Tom Peters, I will be provoked and entertained, maybe even shocked; when I read the *Wall Street Journal*, I'll get factual financial reporting; when I donate money to the Red Cross, it will go to help people in need. As I live and travel through the world, the brands I choose to help me on my journey will not fail me. I believe I can trust them. Delivering this trust requires these brands to align purpose, values and systems and to have people who use the values and systems to deliver on that promise.

As I live my life, I fulfil life's duties and cope with life's many irritations and disappointments and problems, and search for life's little sweetnesses and pleasures. I create meaning and, yes, maybe shockingly I use brands to help me do that. Brands, and the timeless narratives they embody, help me live the life I deem important.

Alignment around the brand's narrative doesn't mean lock-step allegiance to the flag. It means a thoughtfulness about observing what is coherent (and supports rather than undermines the values) and what is not. It means owning your voice to speak up in the line dance of brand delivery if something isn't quite right. It's about alignment to the highest principles, aesthetics and values of the brand. Again, it's not about blind faith. Everyone at AA knows the Twelve Steps of the Twelve Step Programme, but how they embrace them is a personal choice.

To achieve alignment you first have to see the goodness in it. It is easy to see in a thousand of the little things that happen in your business each day. My friend Bob Coble took his twin daughters to Disney World at a tender age, and one got Minnie Mouse's signature in one corner of the park. That night the other sister was beside herself wanting her own special memento of Minnie. The next day they found (another) Minnie Mouse and asked for her autograph. Bob kept his nervousness to himself awaiting the result. Sure enough, it was exactly the same childlike, rolling, cursive signature and Bob sighed a sigh of relief and marvelled at Disney's ability to create the magic that had his daughters believe that there is only the Minnie Mouse they met and that she is real.

Alignment occurs when it's important to people to bring the brand's story to life, and to make choices on behalf of themselves and that story that ring true. To author the story with thoughtfulness is an act of alignment, one that requires knowing and being and doing. Speaking of doing...

7. DO YOU THINK EXECUTION MEANS A CULTURE OF FLAWLESS EXECUTION, OR DEATH?

The opportunity to bring the brand to life authentically through work – to know it, be it and do it – is tested in execution. If the new point-of-sale design doesn't get to the printer in time the launch cannot go on. If the fonts on the business card are not in the client's computer system and they print their own business cards, there will be a serious gap or break in momentum. Without the action of execution everything else is just theory. It's the delivery system without the delivery. The beauty of execution or practice or implementation is that, once you realize the power (and it's not the absolute power, because brands don't have absolute power, but the true navigational power of values), every transaction becomes a stage, a venue to be 'on brand, making authentic choices' at each step in the execution food chain, or not.

Great Brand Inside:Brand Outside™ organizations spend more than average amounts on training, knowledge transfer, workplace enhancements and feedback loops. These range from Six Sigma and the Baldrige Award to nine-month or one-day orientations, from informal lunch discussions to enterprise-wide surveys and focus groups. They are not one-time wonders and they are not discrete events (one CEO I met recently, in response to her team wanting to revisit the values, remarked with great irritation, 'But we gave our people the values six months ago!'). When knowledge transfer works over an extended period of time, values get into 'the water system': then there is water, water everywhere and everyone's thirst for connection, knowledge and meaning can get quenched on demand.

What makes brand inside:brand outside execution truly hard is the whole pre-production and rehearsal phases that need to come before.

While there are many paths to execution, all involve some preconditions without which brand inside:brand outside organizations cannot get out of the starting blocks.

The leadership must care enough about the brand's values to articulate them. They must honour and work hard to identify and communicate those values to the talent, at the same time creating an environment that develops original ideas and talent. Goals and stories must be articulated and the culture must give the time for this to happen. This is really the essence of AA meetings – sharing stories of recovery and redemption. In all likelihood we will never approximate to the power of those revelations in a corporate or institutional setting, but we can and must find venues in which we can communicate more deeply.

When we worked with the US Navy we held a number of information exchanges on naval bases, in hangers and on factory floors in which thousands of people were able to circulate through an interactive town-hall meeting environment and ask questions of their peers about the subject of alignment. It was much like a large-scale open-air trade fair – only there were no vendors pitching products, simply peers sharing ideas they cared strongly about. I will never forget an artisan – a young man in an oil-covered jumpsuit – who worked to repair F-18s saying to me, 'This made me proud to work here. I now understand our future better.' I will never forget the way he said it – with real gratitude and feeling.

Expectations, systems, processes and resources must be shared and communicated before true alignment can really take root. It's great to have employees who are motivated to bring the brand to life but if the tools don't work their efforts can be thwarted. And in the situations where there are scarce resources, such as certain corners of the military or the factory floor where budget cuts have made it hard to get parts, tools or the most basic supplies, it is a small consolation to the workers to be reminded of the fundamental purpose of their work, no matter how challenging the circumstances.

Many of the organizations we've seen up close have taken the time at the front end to listen to people's concerns. Until you understand the issues among your workforce (and there are of course many) you can never understand and address the barriers to alignment. With one client, a lack of understanding about the different parts of their vast organization and how they were connected was the stumbling block that needed attention. Sites were competing with each other, withholding value information and support, when all of their resources were needed to serve their customers fully. We made a 12-minute video documentary that told the story of the whole organization, with the thought that people would give more commitment if they could first see it. We provided basic documentary techniques, while the client and filmmakers co-created the content at each step of the way. Our main client, the CIO, really functioned as the director and producer. The results were mesmerizing. The content: people talking about their work.

In many, many organizations we go into, we find that the brand and all the meaning and values associated with it are locked up tighter than an airport checkpoint by the marketing department, and mere mortals are not invited to participate. The most arrogant corporate marketers shoot themselves repeatedly in their feet when they treat the rest of us as not sophisticated enough to get it. Shockingly, some organizations still penalize Web surfing – even if it's only to surf the organization's own site. This could be perceived in some camps as intelligent behaviour.

All of this is hard to do. Or not.

8. IS THERE BRAND PASSION INSIDE AND OUT?

Punchline number one. It's really not hard when you harness, tap and release people's passion. Peter Senge for years talked about how people always remembered the greatest project they had worked on and the feeling it gave them. It was a feeling and a legacy that lasted well beyond the project. It is very easy to tell if an organization is alive and growing or dead and dying by the quality of its projects. Deloitte's Cathy Benko, in her new book *Connecting the Dots* (Benko and McFarlan, 2003), declares that you can align the whole organization through the management of its project portfolio, and cites mind-boggling statistics about the amount of the GDP that projects comprise.

Projects are a profound unit of passion. You can feel it immediately upon entering meetings, reading the minutes or the e-mails, seeing the deliverables and the documents, and sitting in on the presentations to the clients. As George Simon, the legendary Bay Area transcendentalist philosopher, once said to me, 'It is such a delight to be seen.' It's a delight to witness passion in any form, isn't it?

I have had the privilege of seeing many passionate people work and, as they did, bring their passion to others: Chilean Senator Fernando Flores,

Korn Ferry's Eunice Azzani, Nissan Design International founder Jerry Hirshberg, the Four Seasons' general managers in Washington DC, Atlanta and around the world, the Navy's Susan Keen, author Seth Godin and, of course, Tom Peters. I have watched as they made their passion whole through their work, and changed the world, one person at a time.

It is really very simple to see the passion in people and their projects or in any kind of work for that matter. All you have to do is look. Or not.

9. HOW DO YOU DESIGN SYMMETRY INTO YOUR ORGANIZATION?

There's an expression in AA: 'You can't keep it unless you give it away.' That is the essence of symmetry. It is the essence of generous compassion that the Buddhists and Christians talk about. In a practical sense symmetry means that you can view any step in the life cycle of your organization – inside and out – and see the same conscious communication of core values, 'strategic intent' as tompeterscompany! CEO Boyd Clarke calls it, and the messages that result will be understood by your customers and your employees. This simple act of vigilant sharing can be translated into organizational life in ways that will produce astounding results. It can also save you when you make the inevitable mistakes. New Coke didn't topple Coke. Now it's a case study that underscores their willingness to learn.

Four ideas that can get you to symmetry quickly:

1. Treat your people like customers. When Four Seasons opened an hotel in Atlanta it came with a ready-made workforce. Most employees had worked for the company that managed the hotel before. They had been through stressful times and were apprehensive. The hotel changed hands at midnight, but by 6 a.m. there was a fresh coat of paint at the back of house. The General Manager and his executives served the morning shift breakfast and provided words of encouragement. It was management's way of welcoming the staff and celebrating their work, and it embodied their core values of kindness, intelligence, mutual respect and customer delight.
2. Start an organizational listening project. Have regular secret shoppers/undercover customers or members or your own people whenever possible shop or otherwise engage in the entire 'food chain'

of your organization and report back to a diverse group of leaders. It's sometimes called 'secret shopping', sometimes 'ethnographic research'; there's no substitute for 'being there'. When Jerry Hirshberg's team of designers at Nissan went out to get to know the kind of outdoor enthusiasts they were designing the Xterra for, they discovered that surfers, bikers and campers wanted a vehicle they could slap duct tape on and throw wet equipment into. Jerry's team came away from the listening realizing they needed to build a car that 'felt like blue jeans', and the Xterra was the extremely successful result.

Jerry shared their learnings in a non-punitive way – even though they may have contradicted what some at Nissan 'expected' – and they continued to share them with as many cross-functional groups of people as possible so that people would understand and in fact 'own' the mythos of the vehicle. With that kind of ownership, people who are responsible for the delivery of your product or service throughout the value chain can and will make symmetry of authentic engagement happen.

3. Find outsiders with truly fresh perspectives on how to bring the outside in and the inside out, culturally speaking. Find a few 'freaks', as Tom has been admonishing us to do for years. Those freaks can be customers, your children, your employees' children, architects, designers, thinkers, changes agents, retired generals, board members, journalists, almost anyone who's honest will do. The real brand strategists gain their power from their ability to listen deeply, to read the world and to co-create their brands with the people who deliver the brand and/or use it. This stuff is hard, it takes more than 10 seconds and you need magicians or at the least world-class observers to help you. The magicians/observers can come from anywhere: inside your company or outside. The key is to find a couple you trust and make them part of your team.

4. This one's simply diabolical. Merge HR and marketing. Merge budgets, departments, functions, physical spaces. If they don't kill each other something really fabulous – even symmetrical – could happen. The messages to your customers and to your people will not only match, but will be the same.

10. WHY SHOOT FOR IT AND WHAT ARE THE CONSEQUENCES IF WE DON'T?

AA saves lives and makes them whole again. Each one is a recovering alcoholic – and the significance of the present tense 'recovering' is, to quote a recovering alcoholic, 'enormous', because it means arrested and not fully cured. It means always vigilant and awake to the possibilities of helping another drinker in need. It's one of the Twelve Steps.

Authenticity literally saves organizations. Each person who practises telling their truth about what the organization stands for, and connecting the dots between that 'flame' and their work, honours the work and the people who do it. It's the ultimate adventure minute by minute, project by project, year by year. Choice abounds: healthy or toxic; up or down; in or out; here tomorrow or gone today; Enron or engage. While it is a nearly meaningless cliché to say in 2003 that every organization is a system, it is painfully clear that every system requires conscious design, conscious healing, conscious help or, left to its own impulses, it will unconsciously morph to the path of least resistance.

Dr Fernando Flores, educator, philosopher, inventor of groupware, calls that state 'the drift'. He and his fellow Chileans, some of whom were political prisoners and taken in front of firing squads regularly as a form of psychological torture, refused, once out of prison, during Pinochet's regime to let their relationship with their beloved country, even in exile, drift. Instead, he continued to invent educational, technological and financial solutions from afar. Today he has returned to become a senator there, bringing his life and work full circle.

From where we sit you have two options on this adventure: 1) lead the way *up, in, here* (the World Wide Web, Rumsfeld's military, Nokia, Four Seasons, Starbucks); or 2) find your organization *down, out, gone* (Arthur Andersen, Tyco, Enron, Saddam Hussein's government). The design challenge is exhilarating and excruciating: the truth or fiction, mastery or mediocrity, up or down the evolutionary food chain, into – or out of – existence. Here today, but practically speaking always living with the possibility of being gone, of falling off the wagon, tomorrow.

What does it mean then consciously to design a system that is at once fundamentally human, transparent and also intentionally fabricated, automated and adaptive in its complexity? Each person and organization's answer is obviously unique. The brand, if shared, if articulated, if co-created, is a powerful flame that can illuminate the process and help everyone make principled choices.

We who work with brands have it so wrong. We've been too focused on the 'out there' of the almighty customer and the almighty dollar/euro/yen. We forgot that we best reach them in here, where we live – and that economic rewards then follow. It's a truly democratic approach to brand evolution, and democracy comes with a heavy price and one that you must pay over and over again: trust.

But thanks to this century's follies, foibles and failures – of a few people who then toppled Arthur Andersen, of a few people who created the brutality in regimes like Saddam Hussein's, of a few people who failed to protect pensions at Worldcom and Enron – we now have a moment of greater global awareness and demand that all our systems – people, financial, legal, brand – be transparent. I say, let them also be beautifully, powerfully symmetrical. Let us co-create.

REFERENCES

Benko, Cathleen and McFarlan, F Warren (2003) *Connecting the Dots: Aligning projects with objectives in unpredictable times*, Harvard Business School Press, Boston, MA

Clarke, Boyd and Crossland, Ron (2002) *The Leader's Voice: How communications can inspire action and get results*, SelectBooks

Peters, Thomas J and Waterman, Jr, Robert H (1982) *In Search of Excellence: Lessons from America's best-run companies*, Harper & Row, New York

NOTES

1   See www.tompeters.com.
2   Twelve Steps and Twelve Traditions.

11

Leadership branding

Thomas Gad

We must become the change we wish to see.

(Mahatma Gandhi)

In the beginning of all human achievements is the entrepreneurial spirit: the will to do something different, to stand for something you believe in and to want to communicate that to a number of different people. In larger corporations, the distance or the gap between that initial entrepreneurial spirit and daily operative business is usually vast. This is the reason why we need new tools to bridge that gap – branding is such a tool.

When I started to research branding for an earlier book, I began by studying some 15 of what I believed to be the most successful brands. I wanted to map out exactly how they had become so successful. One of the first things that struck me was that there was nearly always an individual behind each of these branding successes. In some cases this was obvious, like Ingvar Kamprad at IKEA (his initials are even in the brand name). In some cases the link was even more evident – the name of the entrepreneur being the name of the company. But in a lot of cases it took some research to find out who that person was.

Branding in my mind has since then always been about re-creating the entrepreneurial spirit in a company and enabling it to transfer that to all its stakeholders: employees, buyers and users of goods or services, investors, suppliers and other publics. That's why branding for me has a really strong link to leadership.

Also, branding generally answers the most important question that I have as a stakeholder: 'What do you stand for?' And the question to every leader is basically the same: 'What do *you* stand for as a person?' The problem in today's business world is that these answers are usually very unclear and full of contradictions.

Especially contradictory is the relationship between what the company stands for and what its leaders stand for. A lot of companies officially commit themselves to serve all their stakeholders well, by creating customer benefits and shareholder value. But the reality is that leaders' actions in many cases are quite the opposite; they are cynical about customer value – trying to make customers believe they are getting value even when they are not; taking big bonuses and compensation, even if their companies are suffering and are near liquidation; lacking solidarity with their employees, even if it says in the corporate strategy how important employees are to the company's business. And last but not least they rob their companies by cheating their investors of value.

Coherence between a company idea and its leaders is simply the essence of leadership branding: 'This is what our company stands for and this is what I stand for as one of the leaders of this company. As you can see, it's linked together and proven by action.'

What could modern branding teach us? What role exactly can the brand play in leadership? How could branding become a management tool, not just a marketing label on a product or service?

The brand actually almost always becomes the manifestation of the qualities of leadership of a company. But it also works the other way. The brand can help leaders to become those good, modern leaders that business needs. My intention with this chapter is to show this. It will connect in various ways with much of the content of my fellow writers.

Another discovery of my branding research was that the anatomy of a successful, strong and respected brand is four-dimensional. I explored this idea in my book, *4-D Branding* (Gad, 2001), where I tried to create a systematic approach on how to build a successful and sustainable brand. The four-dimensional model is very simple and it serves as a tool for the practitioner, in building a dynamic brand.

The catalyst for 'beyond branding' is that we now live in a different and much more networked and transparent world with more critical, often cynical, and demanding consumers. It's an entirely new and different situation from that of the early days of marketing and branding. It's also a world with dramatic problems and a need for more leadership responsibility, politically as well as commercially.

THERE ARE MORE DIMENSIONS TO A BRAND

The old and classical view of the brand has been very one-dimensioned – what I call the 'functional dimension': delivering benefits for the customer or user and delivering profit to the producer or manufacturer. In our world, this is simply not enough. Advertising of this functional dimension of traditional international brands is preoccupied, narcissistically, with exaggerating differences in the product or service behaviour. Even though consumers have real everyday problems in their lives, the self-centred brand adopts a stance of overweening importance.

Today, the transparent nature of our world means a brand has to do more than operate at the functional level. As Figure 11.1 shows, there are other important dimensions. In its social dimension the brand serves an identification role as a centre for a community of customers, users and employees. Brands have taken a place in our lives that supports our own identity, which was previously defined by heritage, family name, our place

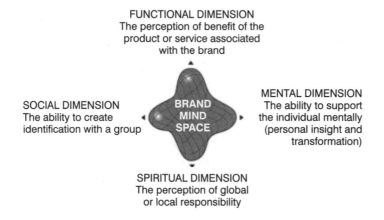

Figure 11.1 Brand Mind Space™

of origin or a well-defined profession, like being a carpenter or saddle maker. Not even the schools we went to serve to identify us in a social context. Brands are taking over that role. Brands are for many people the answer to the question: 'What do you do for a living?' The answer is usually of the kind: 'I work for H&M.' This is also the reason why some strongly branded companies can get away with paying low wages and still having, and attracting, very competent people who stay with the company for a long time. Are these people unusually stupid? By definition they are not. They stay because a company with a strong brand satisfies their need for identification better than anything else.

The mental dimension is about the mentoring and coaching aspects of a brand's delivery: how the brand can become an inspiration and a change agent for people. When Nike says 'Just do it', something happens in our minds; we are reminded about the wisdom that action simply is the core of most achievements.

Brands, like celebrities, very easily become role models in our lives (to compensate for the lack of real role models, such as members of a traditional large family). The success of a brand in a market inspires a potential success for me as a person.

The fourth dimension – the spiritual dimension of a modern brand – acknowledges the fact that the brand is not isolated, but a part of the universe and has a responsible role in that universe. The brand can serve the purpose of, or provide a model for, answering the really important human existential question: 'What's my purpose in life?' A lot of people feel a great lack of purpose – and so do many brands. But some brands show the entrepreneurial spirit and at least partly answer that question – by showing insight and pointing at something that is making the world a little better.

This spiritual dimension does not have to be as grand as many brand builders may aspire to, but it can still be significant. It might be to make a contribution to change the world immediately around the brand through business ethics or the definitions of the business. For example, Anita Roddick, the founder of cosmetics chain The Body Shop, initially took up the contentious cause of animal testing in the cosmetics business, which she later extended into the much more ambitious concern for developing world ethics.

This dimension of responsibility has become something of a business trend, but I maintain the belief that this dimension has always been important for branding entrepreneurs. For example, Ray Kroc's 'spiritual' idea with McDonald's was to give parents (mothers particularly) a possibility to take the whole family, with children, out for dinner.

The four-dimensional system is a way to remind the brand builder always to stretch out what I call the 'Brand Mind Space' in the minds of the audience; it's much like stretching one of those 'slimes' that children have to play with: unless you keep on stretching your brand it will implode and eventually vanish in people's minds.

BRANDING IS ALL ABOUT COMMUNICATION

The most important aspect of branding is that it is all about communication, and communication is always about what is received at the other end. Branding is what happens in the mind of the audience.

A lot of focus in branding has always been on the strategy, sometimes far too much. A strategy that is beautiful in the brand strategist's mind may not be at all beautiful in a stressed and very pragmatic consumer's mind.

A brand does not exist in the patent office like a trade mark. It's not concealed in a design manual. A brand is only a brand when it is in somebody else's mind.

This is also the biggest issue and problem with leadership – it's not what's said and thought in a company by its leaders that is important; it's what's received, understood and emotionally accepted by the people in that company.

So a branding approach to leadership has to be extremely aware of what happens in people's minds and very attentive to how things should be communicated to have strong influence on other people's thinking.

THE MANAGEMENT COMMUNICATION GAP

The problem of management is seldom lack of ideas or strategies. The problem in most companies is that the people out there in the company, who are supposed to perform numerous processes, internally as well as externally, including interaction with other stakeholders such as customers, investors and suppliers, have only vague ideas as to what the strategy is. Maybe they shouldn't know all of its content, because some of it might be cynical to their daily work – like increasing the efficiency of the workforce. But they do need to know most of the essentials of the business strategy, not least because they will be controlled and judged by how well they perform, based on the objectives in the business plan.

Some Scandinavian research shows that top management in larger international companies use significant amounts of their time to command and control the business strategy so that it is performed as planned. The reason for spending so much time on control is mostly that the idea of the company – the brand – is poorly communicated to the employees.

My observation (like many others) is that if a company is brand driven and if the ideas of 'what the company stands for', including a strong sense of issue, are well communicated within a company, the efficiency of the whole company is dramatically increased. Top management can spend more of their time on future development issues and less on commanding and controlling. Also the company is perceived by people on the outside as more open, more sympathetic, easier to deal with and more modern.

To bridge the management communication gap the brand is needed as a tool. The first step is to try to establish the *issue* of the company or its driving force. This is more than a strict business mission; it's the overall *raison d'être* for all the stakeholders of a company. It involves what the company is best at, as well as the core of the logics of the business. It's where the passion of the company is found. It is 'Connecting People' at Nokia, and 'Revolutionary and Entertaining' at Virgin.

The next step is to build a brand platform, including the four-dimensional Brand Mind Space, a Brand Code with a Brand Motto, which quite often is the same as the issue statement. Based on the brand platform, the organization integrates brand storytelling, usually by picking up the existing stories in the company that support the brand platform.

SOLVING PROBLEMS ON A HIGHER LEVEL THAN THEY OCCUR

Many problems in business management are solved at the same level or a lower level than where they occur. When something needs to be changed in a company it's usually done by changing the organization, by exchanging people or sacking people. In many cases change can be done by communication instead. Branding and communication are still tools far

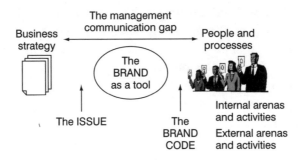

Using the ISSUE to fill the BRAND with meaning, to make the BRAND the tool for change and increased efficiency

Figure 11.2 The brand as a tool approach

too little used in everyday management, and the reason for this is that far too few leaders are communicators. Business leaders are either specialists or administrators who have become leaders as a part of their career. This career can be developed with usually very little communication practice. Then suddenly, when they get the leadership role, there is no time or opportunity for training in communication skills; leadership has to be exercised immediately.

Let's take an example of how communication can be used to solve an organizational problem. The case of Sony is typical and interesting. In 1998 the Sony conglomerate was a company in disarray with over 49 different product divisions and R&D labs spread over three different continents. The challenge was to get a greater degree of cohesion within the company creating a 'one company–one team' feel. Several ideas were discussed: setting up electronic cafés where Sony employees from around the globe could talk to each other and share ideas; or breaking the company up into different divisions with new brands; or moving everyone to one place, probably Japan.

But instead of reorganizing its operation and creating new divisions, which would have been the traditional solution, Sony did it another way. The problem at a lower level was a lack of integration and cooperation. But on a higher level it was one of identification and sense of idea. Sony decided to solve the problem on a higher level – a communicating level. The way they did it was pure leadership branding. They asked the key question: what do we really stand for? What is the issue of Sony? The answer came naturally. Creativity! Creativity is the heart of Sony.

An initiative was set up to get everyone to align their product in a creative context: Walkman, computers, PlayStation etc. New products were created to facilitate alignment. The most interesting among them was The Memory Stick™ – it became a tangible symbol for unifying the different gadgets produced by Sony. The Memory Stick™ is used to transfer information between cameras and personal computers and mobile phones.

Internally, a creativity contest was set up under the slogan: 'Work with other divisions and do something creative.' Sony employees were encouraged to make contact with Sony colleagues elsewhere – to travel and visit them and to stay with them in their homes. A most amazing action plan came out of the idea of creativity.

Internally all this was done like any branding campaign for consumers. The brand of the initiative became: 'Go create!' But hey, haven't we seen this in ads for Sony? It can't be *that* internal. The truth was that it all started just like described, as internal branding – but when the advertising people heard about it they found it could work equally well for consumers. And, of course, this is key. In a transparent world nothing is better from a communicative point of view than to have one message – one company – externally and internally.

LET'S ROLE-MODEL ON SUCCESSFUL ENTREPRENEURS

The communicative entrepreneur is my role model in branding and certainly in leadership branding. These leaders are 'living the brand', as the title of Nicholas Ind's (2001) book says, in a way that can be inspirational to all of us.

As a Swede, I might ask whether Swedish leaders are better than other nationalities at leadership branding. Probably not. But there are at least two well-known Swedish-based company examples that come to mind: Ingvar Kamprad for IKEA and Erling Persson (now succeeded by his son Stefan Persson) for H&M. Both these companies are international retail operations, working in product areas with constant change (furniture and fashion) and employing a lot of their workforce on a short-term basis. In other words, they are interesting examples of businesses that are difficult to manage and lead consistently.

The most interesting common theme with these successful business leaders is strong alignment between the companies and themselves as leaders. You probably would argue that since these people own their business there should naturally be alignment between the owners and the business. But that is not always the case; some owners never even appear in their companies. Furthermore there are many cases of very communicatively skilled leaders who have come in later and have changed or saved companies without being the owner. One who comes to mind is Lou Gerstner, who turned IBM around using communication as his main instrument; he created the communication concept of 'e-business', which gave IBM a focus and a new role in the marketplace and the employees an idea to work for, not just a very well-known dominant company.

Later in this chapter I will suggest a technique actually to copy these entrepreneurial skills in the corporate environment of a large corporation with a team of professional managers. But let's first study how the talented communicative entrepreneur does it.

CREATING YOUR OWN MYTH

If you role-model on the most successful brand builders, you will notice that there are a lot of good stories about them. These stories are filled with symbols and rituals that these people enact to create a place in people's minds, quite often intuitively. A good example of myths that drive the brand of a whole worldwide organization are the stories told about Ingvar Kamprad, founder of IKEA; some of them are probably true, but some are apocryphal, of course. It doesn't matter; they are great pieces of personal marketing as well as an excellent way of communicating company values:

▮ *Story 1*
 When he visits any of his stores worldwide he performs certain rituals. For example, he might pick up a piece of furniture that has been thrown out (maybe by himself just beforehand) and tell the staff that he doesn't want to see such waste: the 'damaged' goods could be sold off cheaply instead.

▮ *Story 2*
 He asks customers at the counter about their perception of the value of a product they have just bought. 'Is it really worth its price?' is an example of the sort of question he might ask. He persists until the

customer says 'No' or repeats his or her 'Yes' frequently enough for him to be satisfied. Then he knows if the price is right.

▎ *Story 3*

This is one of many stories about his extreme cost-consciousness: when inaugurating a statue of himself in his home town of Älmhult, he wouldn't cut the ribbon, but instead untied it and gave it back to the mayor, saying 'You can use it again.'

The communicatively talented entrepreneur knows the value of creating symbols and rituals; it's simply a way to dramatize the difference encapsulated in the company brand. And the leader makes him or herself lead actor in this script. But the act starts with a strong idea of 'what to stand for' and very importantly there should be a strong sense of issue in that idea. Then the entrepreneur elaborates on that issue in a way that appears (and quite often is) spontaneous.

The founder of H&M, Erling Persson, is also the subject of many stories. One of them is about him attending the opening of a new store. The crowd of customers waiting to pay for their merchandise were causing chaos. Instead of just standing there and watching, Erling Persson quickly emptied the cigar box that he carried in his briefcase and, using it as a till, started to work as an additional cashier. His son Stefan Persson now carries on with the family traditions and is known for being very straightforward and practical in his leadership style.

Storytelling is a very important part of leadership branding, and the whole business of branding for the entrepreneur is an economical way to 'reproduce' oneself – an efficient and simpler way to lead.

YOU HAVE TO STAND FOR SOMETHING OF YOUR OWN!

Thinking about how to apply the entrepreneurial role model in your own situation, maybe in a larger corporate organizational environment, may lead you to assume that you yourself have to align with the company you work for and not the other way around. That's also the traditional way to look at leadership branding of professionals – the leader becoming a spokesman or spokeswoman of the company.

I believe that open modern management requires something more than that – the leaders of today have to have strong personalities of their own to act as role models. If you don't know what you stand for, or if you try to hide behind your role as a leader, you will be confusing and even threatening. It will simply never work in the end.

Work life used to be separate, but today it is likely to be far more integrated with your personal life. In both areas people demand to know who you are. The relationship we all want to have with other people is built on knowing, liking and accepting what they are in certain ways. It's when we don't know with whom we are dealing that we get uncomfortable and we begin to make our own hypotheses of who that person might be. The uncertainty makes us unsure and suspicious. Just as we don't like corporations that we can't trust because we don't know exactly what they stand for, the same applies to individuals. There are equally good reasons for human beings and corporations to stand for something. Being authentic is very important in the transparent world in which we now live (see Chapter 7).

INTRODUCING PERSONAL BRANDING

When working with branding for companies I sometimes became a little frustrated. I was able to initiate and get acceptance for the change process of the corporate brand, but I stumbled on the personalities of some of the leaders. Sometimes leaders with whom we made great progress with a new brand platform would come to me frustrated about themselves: 'Since the company is now so brand driven, I feel I have to be different as a leader.'

After several cases of handling a personal change process *ad hoc*, I felt I had to work out a systematic approach to personal branding for leaders in brand-driven companies. This was the outset for the 'Brand Me' method and thinking, which was very much in sync with my earlier four-dimensional branding ideas and was later published as a book with co-author Anette Rosencreutz (Gad and Rosencreutz, 2002).

The basic approach of Brand Me is to treat your own personal development as a brand development and decide what you want to stand for in the same way as a company does. Then you communicate it into the minds of other people, basically in the same way you would communicate a corporate brand. We use the same models as we do for the corporate, slightly adjusted, including the four-dimensional analysis of what you want to become in other people's minds, and the spider-looking Brand Me Code (Brand Code for companies) format, which has the Brand Me Motto in the centre.

WHAT IF 'WHAT I STAND FOR' IS NOT THE SAME AS 'WHAT THE COMPANY STANDS FOR'?

We usually say that the Brand Me Code is for your personality as the DNA code is for your body. It's your differentiation code: it will constantly remind you, in a personal way, how you are different from other people. The Brand Me Code has six 'inputs' – benefit, positioning, style, mission, vision and values – and all these are crystallized into your own personal Motto, something to keep in mind as a personal 'mantra' to associate to and above all to base your personal decisions on.

This is all very well, but how do you coordinate your own personal brand with the brand of the company you work for? If the company you work for doesn't fit you, you'd probably like to know. It's in your own interest, as much as your employer's, to understand how well you match your company.

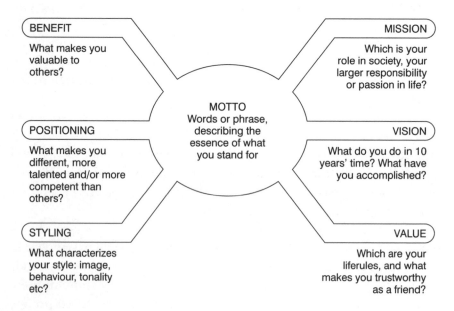

Figure 11.3 The Brand Me Code

In today's recruitment market these are very important matters. To get the right kind of talent, to attract people and to match people to your business are top management issues. It's not so different from making an acquisition of another company. In both cases you have to know what the other part stands for.

There are several good reasons for wanting a good brand fit between employee and employer:

▪ The brand is the core of the corporation; it's there for everybody to see.
▪ The same questions that define the brand can easily be used to define a person.
▪ People are one of the greatest assets in a modern business, and also the single most important asset in building a brand.

So, to have one transparent value system for both the company as a whole and the individuals working for that company is as close to the entrepreneurial ideal of a brand as possible.

The brand is the differentiation code of the company as well as the personal brand of the individual – not that this means the individual should be exactly the same as the company (that is, unless you want an army of soldiers in uniform). The talents of individuals should complement the company, within the framework of the company brand. This is a common problem for every company when hiring talent: if individuals are outside the company framework, it doesn't matter how talented they are! The perfect tool to match your own brand with the brand of the company you work for, or are about to work for, is the Brand Code (or Brand Me Code for individuals). To use the Brand Code from a personal branding perspective, you start with the Brand Code of your company.

If your company doesn't have one, you will have to construct one. To do that you need to read its Web sites, annual reports, corporate presentations and recruitment ads. You can also ask responsible people in the company specific questions in order to be able to fill in the six inputs: product, positioning, style, mission, vision and values. You might have to guess or estimate. You might also find an expression that could serve as the Brand Code Core Message (the Motto of the company).

THE PERSONAL ISSUE MANAGEMENT TEAM METHOD

In order to recreate the entrepreneurial spirit in the management team of a larger company it's necessary to connect the personal agendas of the members of the management team with the corporate issues of the company. But is it really possible to make professional managers of a large company as involved and personally dedicated to the company as would be an entrepreneur?

With the leadership branding method that I outline here and have practised with a few clients, it will come as close as possible to that entrepreneurial experience of total dedication and focus. The basic idea of the method is to let each member of the management team 'own' one issue that is important in the company.

Step one is to analyse the brand of the company and map the issues that are building the corporate brand (using the four-dimensional model as a structuring tool).

Let's say that we have an investment bank and the functional dimension of the bank includes a certain fund management idea that makes investors more involved in the investments than usual. This could become one issue that has to be communicated.

The social dimension of the brand includes an issue to create a meeting place for investors of different kinds who want to be involved in the business that they invest in and to discuss and cross-fertilize ideas. This

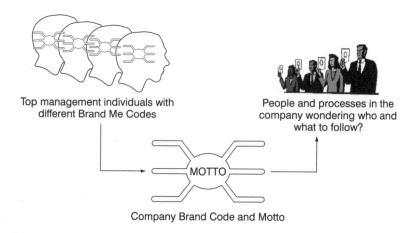

Top management individuals with
different Brand Me Codes

People and processes in the
company wondering who and
what to follow?

Company Brand Code and Motto

Figure 11.4　The leadership dilemma

becomes another important issue. You go on in the same way with the mental and the spiritual dimensions.

Step two is to analyse the stakeholders' present perception of the corporate brand. The result is presented in three categories: not communicated issues, correctly perceived issues and misunderstood issues.

Step three is for each member of the management team to create a personal branding code and motto. The issues of the company (from step one) are distributed among the management team members according to how well they match each member's personal brand code. The point is that each key corporate issue should belong to an individual team member or two or three members who can share an issue and divide the responsibility between them.

Step four is to make sure that each of these issues is owned passionately by one or more top executives; to make it a project equipped with sufficient support in terms of funding and resources, such as researchers, communicators and public relations experts. Several of the key issues of a company are usually internal and of course they should get the same professional communication attention as the external ones.

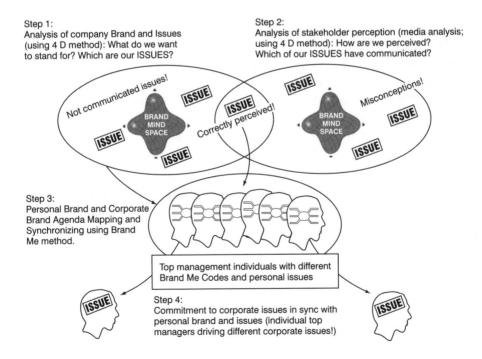

Figure 11.5 The personal issue management method

SUMMARY

In this chapter on leadership branding I have based my thinking on the idea that branding is entrepreneurial and thus well connected with leadership. Branding is an economical way to 'reproduce' oneself, as an entrepreneur and also as a leader – an efficient and simpler way to lead.

The problem of leadership today is that there is usually a great divide between the corporate intentions and the corporate brand and individual leader personalities and personal brands.

I have also underlined the fact that branding is communication and that it deals with what happens in other people's minds. To bridge the management communication gap between business strategies initiated by top management and people and processes in the organization, branding can be used as a highly efficient tool. Branding proves to be a powerful management toolbox with tools like: issue, Brand Code and Brand Motto; and brand storytelling.

Personal branding and the Brand Me method is a way to learn to know yourself better as a leader and establish what you stand for – all this in order to become a more authentic leader, a person for your people to respect and like.

You can integrate your own personal brand with the brand of your company, analyse the match or mismatch and make a decision to stay or leave the company before it's too late. If you find a strong match it strengthens your motivation and personal satisfaction.

Furthermore, I have introduced a way to map the branding issues of a company, and distribute these issues among the top executives of a company, synchronized with their personal brand.

A final conclusion is that branding still offers unique possibilities for leadership in a transparent world with high demands on integrity, and that it is, with many companies and organizations, still an underestimated toolbox for leadership.

REFERENCES

Gad, Thomas (2001) 4-D Branding, Financial Times/Prentice Hall, London
Gad, Thomas and Rosencreutz, Anette (2002) Managing Brand Me: How to build your personal brand, Pearson-Momentum, London
Ind, Nicholas (2001) Living the Brand, Kogan Page, London

12

The brand manifesto: why brands must act now or alienate the future's primary consumer group

Jack Yan

Every year this century, brand experts have been gathering at Medinge, Sweden, making the two- to three-hour drive west from Stockholm. These brand experts, some of whom are authors of this title, have grown increasingly disappointed and frustrated by the way many brands are managed. When they assembled in June 2002, they were confronted by problems connected to globalization and corporate responsibility. By 2003, there was the spectacle of corporate dishonesty writ large. The fear of 'another Enron' through which people could lose millions prompted the group to take action.

The reality is: brands are in trouble. They were designed to act as a shorthand for sometimes complex ideas and to build trust among buyers. They still do the former but, increasingly, trust is failing. People are more demanding and more cynical. They no longer accept the language of marketing as entirely credible. And as the example of Enron shows, there is no strong reason to trust the language of finance either.

But branding itself is not the villain here. Put simply, its context has shifted. Brands are being traded so rapidly that Calvin Klein is Dutch-owned and Jaguar is in US hands but both play out their respective Americanness and Britishness whenever possible.

That contextual shift coincides with others in society. We can't expect our neighbours to have the same values as we do. We can't expect our politicians to be flawless with strong values. We can't even expect it from religious institutions. Yet as human beings, we seek affirmation of who we are. As Mathews and Wacker (2002: 204) put it, 'Offering value alone is no longer a sustaining platform for brand loyalty. While the greatest generation sought out tangible value (defined in the relationship between product feature, function, endurance and price), its children and grandchildren assume transactional value exists and are looking for a deeper sense of values.'

The younger Generation Y members – born between 1979 and 1994, if you follow one definition – are less brand loyal, because they have been brought up on a diet of hype and fluff. It hasn't got better: today's child sees over 20,000 commercials annually.[1] These facts, plus the increasing segmentation of markets and the resulting variety of products, have given them what one commentator called a 'built-in BS meter' (Khermouch, 2002).

It's easy to imagine how the BS meter was developed, through the shared experiences that Generation Y has. It takes it little effort to go to a Web site to find out more. And if those Web sites include places like CorpWatch.org, the moderate San Francisco-based group that monitors corporate misbehaviours, or nologo.org (identified by its prominent No Logo logo), then marketing claims tend to play second fiddle.

Therefore, to prevent the BS meter from going off, companies need to be authentic, genuine, real and responsible. If they fail to be so, they risk losing what will likely be the largest consumer group in the coming decade. And if they fail to start now, they risk becoming yesterday's news, mere nullities when Gen Yers come of age and begin running society.

ACT NOW OR FOREVER HOLD OFF PEACE

At a glance, today's youth can't be readily understood. Every middle-aged establishment marketer finds the youth market hard to define. Occasionally, it gets lucky, such as when Lee Iacocca and his Ford colleagues realized that the baby-boomers were about to enter the marketplace with demands for styling, performance and price, and that the company was getting a high number of letters asking that it produce a new, two-seat Thunderbird – a car that, a few years before, had not sold well. The Mustang was, effectively, born (Iacocca and Novak, 1984: 68–69). And when this author began in business, the rage was on defining Generation X. Then the focus shifted to Generation Y. And already, research is emerging about today's children.

The non-Gen Yers looking in might have some valid questions. To use one example quoted by Brooks (2001): how can they work for Merrill Lynch and Save the Children and not see a contradiction? Another study indicates they are skilful consumers who pay their bills (Ministry of Education, 2001). When they rebel, it is less against the values that the institutions perceive they have, and more against the way those values are practised (or not practised). It's difficult to say that all anti-globalists despise a unified world; without the globalization of media they would never have had the information at hand that allowed them to rebel or advance arguments.

But we learnt a lot about Gen Y immediately after the events of 11 September 2001. Viral e-mails about peace were sent out and a casual count indicates they outnumbered those about vengeance. This group has ideals and, according to Jennifer Corriero of TakingITGlobal (www.takingit-global.org), an organization encouraging young people worldwide to effect positive change through networking, its members are more idealistic than their parents.

Corriero, who herself is in her 20s, said, 'They are not institutionalized and are, therefore, more idealistic, and in a better position to be able to think and learn about the world's problems from an idealistic perspective. They are seeing the repercussions of the problems that past generations have created and are more connected to each other globally, which has increased their likelihood of [having] an impact.'

She and her fellow TakingITGlobal co-founder Mike Furdyk live these ideals. They believe that 'young people have more power and potential to create change [through the] internet' and believe in the leadership capacity of young people. 'They need to unite with their peers and other stakeholders in order to develop and implement programmes,' said Corriero.

But the change is happening more subtly. Rather than adopt a uniform that marks them out as being rebellious, some of the change is happening from the inside. There's so much fashion out there now, it's probably an insult to one's individuality to adopt a uniform anyway.

If Corriero is right and young people have been good observers at previous generations' efforts, they might have also caught on to the success of the gay movement, which took place inside institutions. It found itself inside the power structure – something that the women's movement didn't find as simple initially. While she does not believe that anyone should ask youth to conform to a culture in order to have a voice, she recognizes that some of TakingITGlobal's activists are 'on the inside' and notes that, 'in attending global conferences and events, youth representatives are very knowledgeable, passionate and diplomatic'.

This is not taking place in a vacuum. In the background is an emerging awareness of an international community. While young people are divided over whether borders truly exist, they are not afraid to look beyond their own to generate action. Corriero's identification of leadership being key is notable: the previous big youth movement in the 1960s, for the most part, lacked it.[2]

Regardless of how they dress or look, they desire action. Amongst US Gen Yers, they have witnessed leaders who do more talking than acting. It's no surprise to find that they have a greater trust of NGOs than political groups. In New Zealand, considerably more 19- and 20-year-olds voted for the Green Party than the established National and Labour, largely thanks to the Greens' Internet marketing and visible activism. Green MPs even joined anti-globalization protests in other countries, showing that their political status didn't take the radical out of them. In corporations, Enron had policies on everything from climate change to anti-corruption (Waddock, 2002). It's less likely they'll be drawn to companies like that or Andersen today, and there's some anecdotal evidence – not least at the author's firm – to show that the smaller company that acts on its claims is where Gen Y has its eye (Byrne, 2002).

It is, however, still not easy to determine how close perception and reality are. But organizations should be concerned about the different sources of information that audiences have and creating programmes to live the brand remains the best way to ensure that every channel is largely consistent. Corriero believes that today's audiences' judgement is formed by 'a mix of determining both the current negative impact that they are having and the positive social or environmental development that they do'.

The Greens are a perfect example of an organization that not only talks of its policies, but acts on them. When the public sees MPs going to other countries to protest world trade, then that suggests a link, whether registered consciously or subconsciously. It is an example of not only authenticity – ensuring that one's actions are consistent with one's word – but a belief in an ideal and the willingness to act upon it. Their actions are covered not through Green Party press releases, but by independent media.

TakingITGlobal believes that people can see through its actions largely through transparency. It involves its stakeholders and does more than send out a regular newsletter to its 13,000 members. Its Web site is structured in such a way that members can witness the dialogues and interventions, while Corriero adds that it attempts to 'learn from others'.

In addition, TakingITGlobal insists on 'remaining self-sufficient. If we become too reliant on funding sources, it might become difficult to remain individual.' This independence contributes to the image that TakingITGlobal cannot be compromised. A similar lesson for those organizations that depend on outside funding is being transparent – not just to consumers, but to investors and employees.

Typical comments cited by this author in a paper for the *Journal of Brand Management* (Yan, 2003a) include:

> Philip Morris can spout about its good works and funding given to a certain organization all it wants, but I think consumers ultimately write it off as rhetoric. The company pushes products that have damaged the quality of life of so many people, sending out a press release about a new campaign to raise money for children's music programmes just seems like an empty effort.

It is, said another Gen Yer, a case of guilty till proven innocent: marketing claims are taken with a pinch (if not a whole kilogram) of salt until the organization demonstrates it means it.

TakingITGlobal walks its talk 'through key partnerships at conferences and events, [eg] at the youth employment summit where TIG was recognized,' recalled Corriero, not to mention the group's attendance at international conferences. Coupled with the Web site's forums, its ideals and willingness to act upon them are visible.

Conscious of this, Brad Batory, a fashion designer in Dunedin, Florida, is a young entrepreneur who understands that brands have to make people happy. His solution: ensure that proceeds from his première Indashio fashion show, staged in March 2003 when he was 19, go to the National Foundation for Teenage Pregnancy Prevention and the Candie's Foundation (see Yan, 2003b).

While some companies may pick the environment because of current fashion, Batory's choice revolved around personal experience with teenage mothers: 'Many of my friends are teen mothers, my grandmother was a teen mom, my cousin was a teen mom. I've seen what they go through on a daily basis... I feel for them and I wanted to do something to show them that I do understand their daily struggles.'

He doesn't have a glowing report for the establishment. 'I'm giving all I have and busting my ass to do something good and when [I] contacted numerous corporations for their support, I get none,' he said. 'It's definitely very discouraging.' Therefore, it isn't a surprise that Batory buys from like-minded organizations. He cites Candie's but abhors companies that prevent customers from being themselves.

Gen Y doesn't forgive easily – while Gen X and previous demographics were happy to (because brands act as a useful short cut) (Baker and Sterenberg, 2003), this group knows there are more brands round the corner. 'As any honest brand marketer will tell you, brand loyalty is no longer an inheritance', wrote Mathews and Wacker (2002: 232). 'It has to be re-earned every day.'

As capital movements become more free, then the ability for new brands to reach fruition is increased. Even during a recession, there has not been great change on this front.

So while previous generations sought value in brands, Gen Y demands what might be termed the activist brand (Yan, 2003b), one that combines basic ideas of walking the talk, the need for moral and ethical business dealings and a possible awareness that a virtual United Nations made up of netizens may succeed better than the physical one. To this group, activism feeds directly into recall, awareness and brand equity.

Therefore, as a starting point, an organization could, for instance, tally up its negatives and positives – a SWOT analysis for the 21st century. Instead of analysing old-economy strategic imperatives, it could analyse aspects relating to transparency, how well internal and external audiences view its ideals and how well it carries them out, and what positive social and environmental consequences it has realized.

THE BRAND MANIFESTO

When asked what an organization needs to capture the hearts and minds of the modern public, Jennifer Corriero had two suggestions: 'Deliver on what you say that you are going to do' and 'Engage people in as many ways as possible.' They are a good prelude to the brand manifesto's eight points, which, when applied, can address the concerns that tomorrow's consumers have. Authored by those assembled at Medinge, they additionally help restate what branding is meant to do.[3]

1. Branding unites people's passions

Brands may unite people better than organizational edicts or mission statements. In the ideal branding situation, a vision is formed by top management, but only with the assistance of the rest of the organization. This unity, summarized in a brand that is then communicated to internal staff and then external audiences, is tighter than mere staff-directed advertising.

The second part of this manifesto entry is that people do not necessarily understand numbers. Those without accounting training or awareness will find balance sheets and financials in annual reports to be less than useful. Brands are a more suitable interface between the organization and its audiences.

Unsurprisingly to branding experts, when accounting firm KPMG published its 'What makes a good annual report' as part of its New Zealand site,[4] headings included 'Talk straight' (do not use euphemisms) and 'Stay branded', with the first paragraph reading:

> Annual reports are more than just statements of disclosure; they say a lot about your brand and your culture. One of the most interesting developments in recent years has been the decision by many companies to treat their annual report as a marketing communication rather than simply as a compliance document. As a result, increasing numbers of annual reports are doubling as corporate profiles, helping prospective customers to better understand the finances and structure of the organisation they intend doing business with.

Annual reports, in other words, are branded communications. They should represent the organization and, therefore, must represent that organization's unity.

Today's online brands have a good chance at creating unity around people's passions. TakingITGlobal, for instance, has not narrowly defined its mission. New programmes are often suggested by members, dealing not only with environmental issues. On the (dynamically generated and, thus, constantly changing) home page at the time of writing, there were links to action groups on employment, peace, rehabilitation for criminals and innovation. The young women's site nzgirl (www.nzgirl.co.nz) attempts to be its users' 'best friend' to unite their passions (see Yan, 2001). Online brands, with which Gen Y is familiar and future generations will find second-nature, can sometimes be so loosely defined (Yan, 2001) that they are better summarized as an 'attitude' (see Yan, 2000c) – a precursor, possibly, to brands in the future being measured by a sense of passion, not their revenue or intellectual property worth.

Measuring by passion is not totally new. Sandra Fekete, for example, developed a tool based on psychological research to gauge the personality types of organizations. In a corporate sphere, passion might include measures of:

▌ how strong the correlation between vision and the elements of brand equity are (eg the association between what the organization's *raison d'être* is and what the audiences, including staff, believe it stands for);
▌ how often 'legends' or stories are shared within the organization and how well they are modelled as part of getting team members to live the brand;
▌ how well ethical standards are maintained (and, logically, how many employees do not feel compromised to breach them and the vision);
▌ whether behaviour in line with vision and ethical standards is incorporated in the review of staff performance;
▌ employee satisfaction and employee impression of how well they are valued.

2. Brands must have focus to be relevant

Too many organizations go through the motions of a branding exercise without living them. But a true brand is something that penetrates the entire organization.

Nicholas Ind's *Living the Brand* (2001) is aimed toward getting companies to bring brands to life through employees' knowledge and actions and is one of a line of books that stresses that everything about an organization must reflect a set vision. There must not be false claims about helping the planet. And yet, the vision must be focused and real enough to have meaning to people.

The author attended a 'branding presentation' for a well-known fashion label in Wellington, New Zealand in early 2003, but when the CEO and his staff were quizzed privately on what their brand stood for, none of them could respond. The CEO said that his company had a vision but not necessarily his brand. The staff were even more poorly informed. This makes living the brand practically impossible for the label, with the likely consequence being a waste of money in trialling different marketing strategies until it finds one that comes across as authentic to its audiences.

A similar lack of brand focus plagued Mazda Cars in the 1990s when the company sailed into red ink. Was it a volume company or a multi-brand one? Quirky or mainstream? In fact, what did its logo look like? (The cars had a badge but it was seldom in any of its marketing materials.) In 10 years, it lost half the market share it had in Europe in 1990, thanks to an obsession with finance and a corresponding lack of passion in its brand (Johnson, 2001).

A constant change of where Rover stood within the BMW organization would be more to blame for that company's woes than anything that it did wrong – under BMW, Rover Cars lacked vision, as shown by its frequently changing positioning (Yan, 2000b). The more frequent its changes, the more it suggested to consumers that it lacked relevance – leading up to its billion-dollar loss in 1998 (Miller, 1999).

Across the Atlantic, Chrysler spent several years in the same boat under DaimlerChrysler, wondering how to coincide the brand's formerly luxury positioning (with cars such as the LHS, New Yorker and the Town & Country minivan), which potentially cannibalized fellow brand Mercedes-Benz, with one that was more volume and downmarket (accommodating the vehicles from the price-leading Plymouth brand when that was retired in 2000). Unfocused branding came first; the image in consumers' minds became confused; poor financial performance followed suit.[5]

3. Branding is about delivering what you promise

In a previous article I summarized the Medinge view as: the strongest brands are promise-keeping ones. Failing to keep those promises leads to an embarrassing exposé. Good branding leads to sincerity while failure to use branding principles leads to collapse (Yan, based on Gad *et al*, 2002). This may seem obvious, but it is surprising how often brands ignore these principles.

There are older examples, such as that of Talbot, the brand that succeeded Chrysler in Europe in 1980. At the time, Talbot's claim was that it would create youthful, fun cars although very few fitted that mould. While Talbot launched the Samba Cabriolet, a small convertible, in 1982, the rest of its range was made up of humdrum cars, including what was once the Hillman Avenger – a car that was once exported to the United States as the Plymouth Cricket for 1972 and withdrawn after that model year. By 1985, Talbot had all but disappeared as a brand.

Yahoo!, for example, has been subject to criticism in the latter part of 2002. The brand went from cool – it marked one of the great IPO moments in the 1990s – to drab in a short space of time. Yahoo!'s story has been covered many times: two Stanford postgrads put together a links' list to keep track of the sites they liked. Eventually, it grew rapidly and became (and at the moment remains) the number-one visited site on the Web. However, the discontent is rising.

Berlin-born, Bangalore-based Atul Chitnis, Chief Technology Officer of Exocore Consulting, is better placed to comment on computer issues than most people. His experience with Yahoo! was so poor he was forced to go public with it after failing to make headway with the company in solving his problems. In a diary entry in 2002, Chitnis attacked Yahoo!'s Mail, Messenger and Groups services, and added: 'This is a nightmare, and no one in Yahoo seems to care, or be able to do anything about it. "More advertisements" is the focus for these people, not "better and reliable services".'

The problem lies deep inside Yahoo! It is a problem often seen when a company becomes top heavy, when the people at the middle and operational levels don't really care any more or lose touch with reality.

His lament was that Yahoo! promised certain services and failed to deliver. A check of his claims holds true. For example, Yahoo! Groups help is unable to deal with anything but routine enquiries. A support address advertised on the site elicits an autoresponse. Its help pages, for example, are very basic, and if there are additional questions, Yahoo! Groups asks users to fill in a form. However, the response the author received to a query was, 'For assistance with this matter, please visit the Yahoo! Groups help pages at: http://help.yahoo.com/help/groups/' – referring one back to the page from which one came.

Yahoo!'s Full Coverage pages used to link independent sites – today, they largely reflect the media establishment with headlines from the *New York Times*, the *San Francisco Chronicle*, Reuters and the *Guardian*.

It is cold comfort to those who believe that the Yahoo! brand is about community and its users – which is what its image suggests.

Before long, Chitnis wasn't alone. The following month, *Business 2.0* questioned whether Yahoo! CEO Terry Semel was the right man for the job, pointing to staff members leaving before 5 o'clock and saying sources claimed that people within the firm were demoralized:

> Many employees say his aloof, bureaucratic style has demoralized key personnel. He has been unable to pull off any grand Hollywood linkup or other dramatic strategic initiative. 'He showed a lot of faith at first, made us think that he was really going to turn the thing around,' says Kal Syed, an engineer who left Yahoo in August 2001. 'But there is an increasing feeling of frustration, and too many unmet promises.'
>
> (King, 2002)

Writer Ralph King said that, if Yahoo! didn't shape up, there would be a possibility of Microsoft or News Corp taking it over.

The days of Yahoo!'s exuberance were over and, while Semel's order might be a good thing as opposed to anarchy, the brand still suggests the 1990s entrepreneurial drive of two Stanford postgrads. Usage may be up, but Yahoo! may have lost its loving feeling.

4. Good brands should make people happy

Whatever a brand has to offer to consumers (whether purely functional, emotional, associative or empathetic), it must make people happy to part with their hard-earned money and feel satisfied in the process. Today, there is evidence that, to make people happy, companies need to be involved in real social responsibility. Given the earlier part about Gen Yers, the trend is set to continue – and, indeed, may give many developing-country brands an entry point by taking over the gaps left by brands that have been tarnished by recent scandals.

In a consumer economy, people may look for validation about themselves through the brands they purchase. In other words, they and their brands must have some affinity. If tomorrow's primary Gen Y consumer group is determined to have activist brands, then good brands need to respond.

Without hopping off into the future, the public perception of corporations is already determined more by their corporate citizenship than other brand characteristics, according to research cited by Unisys's Ian Ryder in the *Journal of Brand Management* (see Macrae *et al*, 2003). Marketers should be asking themselves, 'What socially responsible programme can my firm bring to the table that is in line with our brand attitude?'

It is not just external consumers that should be happy with the organization but also employees. Some people have lamented the lack of loyalty of modern employees, with their insistence on flexible working and temporary allegiances to the organization. But how many people have questioned whether they are geared – spiritually, infrastructurally or however – to offer their employees a catalyst to achieve their 'highest selves'.

The trend is, for example, toward recognizing the freedom of the employee. With Internet access commonplace in the Western workplace, people have been able to manage work and play for the most part. While there are uncommon stories of, for example, Mr Justice Robert Fisher who surfed porn sites while at work (*Ananova*, 2002), most behave themselves. Meanwhile, people bring work home and access the office via the Internet. This may lead, longer-term, to people indulging in their hobbies as work, and Jennifer Corriero agrees that the lines are being blurred. They may, for instance, economically survive by working on their passions from their computers. Car nuts write motoring columns. Plenty of geeks contribute their thoughts on computer usage and software reviews. Any visit to Amazon.com and the Internet Movie Database reveals how there are hundreds of thousands, if not millions, of amateur book and movie reviewers – all without monetary reward.

Their workplace's brand needs to accommodate the new reality if it is to survive this change in the context of 'work'. Banning Hotmail access – as at the Prudential in High Holborn, London have done – seems out of step in an era when people need to build breaks into their day through Internet shopping, chatting, exercising or picking their children up from school. SAS Institute, Inc has nutrition counselling and day care in-house, and a kindergarten was planned at the time Diane Brady (2002) examined the private software company in Cary, North Carolina. 'It's all about trusting employees,' SAS's HR director Jeff Chambers told Brady. Trust makes people happy, too.

5. Finance is broken

One of the author's earlier studies showed that, if a company gets its brand right, it can win consumer support and raise its brand equity, and this would lead to improved business performance, defined either strategically or financially (Yan, 2000a). Outside the financial community, it makes considerably more sense to say that consumers will find affinity with a brand and drive the company's performance than to say that they will find affinity with the financial results first.

Jonathan Lebed, the New Jersey teenager who attracted the scrutiny of the US Securities and Exchange Commission, made hundreds of thousands of dollars understanding this. He told author Michael Lewis that Qualcomm's share price in December was 'being driven, not by fundamentals, but simply by the fact that a high price target was issued and many people were trading it… Nobody makes investment decisions based on reading financial filings. Whether a company is making millions or losing millions, it has no impact on the price of the stock' (Lewis, 2001: 52–53).

But their brands might.

Public perception about Martha Stewart – herself a brand with a cult following – influenced the share price of her company. Stewart was caught up in a scandal, with suspicions cast about possible insider trading of ImClone shares. She was a friend of ImClone CEO Sam Waksal, who had been arrested on that very charge.

Between 6 June 2002, when the first report of a congressional investigation emerged, and 9 July 2002, the share price of her company, Martha Stewart Living Omnimedia, Inc, had fallen by a half (Webster, 2002). By 31 October 2002, it reported a 42 per cent drop in third-quarter earnings, and the next magazine it planned uncharacteristically lacked the Martha Stewart moniker – unlike its sister titles. Adam Feuerstein (2002) wrote in his tech stocks column, 'Of course, Stewart's personal image is... what drives the fortunes of Martha Stewart Living, so if she gets dragged into the Waksal scandal, her company, and its investors, will suffer right along with her.' Another way to put it is that her brand – image being a consequence of it – drives her finances.

Many other brands fall short. Some might go through the motions of setting a vision, performing research and expressing the brand but, if they focus too deeply on the financial side and do not live each stage of the branding process, then they will fail to unite their audiences. Financial figures – share prices, accounting statements – are not a good way to instil this unity.

Those with accounting training might still find that balance sheets reflect poorly on reality. For example, as Marjorie Kelly pointed out in *The Divine Right of Capital* (2001: 22–26), employees are listed as liabilities. When the company tries to maximize its return to shareholders, it's not uncommon for staff to be cut. This puts any claim of 'looking after our team' into grave doubt, even when employee productivity has risen dramatically in the modern era.

'In accounting terms, employees have no value', wrote Kelly. 'They appear on the income statement as an expense – and expenses are aimed always at a singular goal: to be reduced' (Kelly, 2001: 24). A similar worldview of the environment is in financial statements, says Kelly, so, traditionally, companies' financial statements regard the need to pay for environmental abuse as a cost. The consequences are disregarded: 'This allows the corporate worldview to maintain the myth that social issues are soft (not businesslike, not important), while financial issues alone are hard... Translated into human terms, this means that what affects stockholders is important; what affects everyone else is not important' (Kelly, 2001: 27).

But given what consumers demand today of 'THEM' – Transparency, Honesty, Ethics and Morality – the growing sense of dissatisfaction toward financial reporting and the Wall Street mentality should be noted. It is not a matter of disclosure, but one of revamping this finance-first worldview – something that rocks the existing establishment. But without change, finance becomes less relevant, while brands retain their interface between organization and consumer.

The change is one that Gen Y and tomorrow's consumers are likely to push for as they insist on a new definition of 'THEM and us'.

6. Brands are not advertisements

Branding and promotion are two different things. Good brands act, not just speak or sell. There remains a prevailing thought amongst many businesspeople that slapping on a logo and boosting sales is 'branding'. A lot of branding's bad rap has come from misuse of the term.

General Motors, for example, removed what it called its brand structure, but it was really a thinly veiled sales structure, since during that period brands never really drove product development. Today, Bob Lutz, as one of its vice-presidents, is driving product development with the same passion he brought to BMW, Ford and Chrysler. He has managed to find the soul of each GM brand and push it through each division. In fact, General Motors, with extravagant show cars such as the Cadillac Sixteen and new products such as the Opel Signum, a luxury hatchback, illustrate not only the company's renaissance but the divisions' rediscovery of their sense of purpose. Cadillac has a vision to be the best in automotive luxury, Opel to be an innovative mass-market producer. Under Lutz, GM's Saab and affiliate Subaru are cooperating on a subcompact car while the former is going to use branding to help differentiate its other products, despite using Opel platforms (Engeseth, 2003).

Advertising can be a necessity for some products. However, it is no substitute: the American Advertising Federation (AAF) acknowledges it is a tool for branding with its campaign tagline 'Advertising. The way great brands get to be great brands.' It can create sales and value for brands, but it is not the be-all-and-end-all. After all, Ford's failed Edsel was supported by a huge advertising campaign in its first year.

Some of the best brands do not even need advertising. Linux, for example, is one of the computer world's most enduring brands. Being open-source, it never required any above-the-line promotions. Its success depended on individuals spreading the word – yet it is one of the most powerful brands in the operating system market, rivalling Windows. It has the trappings of any brand and the individual elements of brand equity, right down to trade mark ownership, assigned to its creator Linus Torvalds in 1997 after a lengthy lawsuit. Torvalds gave away his creation, possibly starting the whole open-source movement.

7. Brands bring humanity to the organization

According to the Medinge group: 'Brands are the rallying-point for the positive empowerment of all connected with the organization' (Yan, based on Gad *et al*, 2002). Many examples are covered above, but there is additional, academic evidence for this.

The organization needs a strong human element for success. Academics such as Narver and Slater (see, for example, Dau and Thirkell, 1996: 369–86) identified the need for management commitment, facilitative management and interdepartmental connectedness – fancy ways of saying that bosses need to work with their people and their people need to work with one another. Hence, there are companies that spend plenty to find out what is at their 'soul', just so they can get their employees working in a unified way. Employees can then identify with their company through its brand.

The goal is to create workplaces where people want to go to work and feel they are part of the organization – but, as mentioned earlier, this doesn't happen often enough if employees are counted as liabilities. Nor does it really happen through bonuses alone – a sense of humanity cannot be bought.

It's through brands that organizations become more than vehicles to maximize shareholder return. No employee can feel tied to numbers, but one can feel tied to a brand that represents the ideals and the visions of an organization – provided that there has been proper employee input into them.

New Zealander Stephen Tindall's the Warehouse has grown to become a trans-Tasman chain from humble beginnings in 1984. He has publicly disagreed with the notion that the company's primary duty is to maximize its returns to its shareholders and talks of the 'Warehouse way'. His company is now part-owned by his charity. Tindall himself serves on the New Zealand Business Council for Sustainable Development and various other councils, all of which enhance his brand's socially responsible image. In 2001, *Unlimited* magazine estimated that he invested NZ $100 million (*c* US $50 million) of his own money into what might be termed 'New

Zealand, Inc', to promote the country's innovation and growth (Rotherham, 2001). And while there are detractors saying that he clamps down on supplier costs, generally Tindall and the Warehouse enjoy, internally and externally, a rosy image.

It makes sense to run companies this way, if winning future consumers is important. Those inside the organization have to experience the vision if they are to sell it to external audiences.

Saturn once enjoyed being the anti-establishment GM division, proclaiming 'A different kind of company. A different kind of car.' That image still holds, even if the vehicles are less original – the L-series is a previous-generation Opel Vectra and the Ion's underpinnings are shared with other GM compacts.

Saturn was able to live the brand at dealer level, too. When it started, it offered a money-back guarantee on its cars within the first 30 days or 1,500 miles, whichever came first. In 1994, it organized its famous 'homecoming' for over 40,000 Saturn owners who brought their cars back to the plant for a social event – a literal case of rallying around the brand. It was one of the first with a Web site where visitors could configure a Saturn car. Today, there's still a SaturnFans.com Web site and the official site at http://www.saturn.com continues to run regular stories written by satisfied Saturn owners. Through this, an external audience is empowered, feeling they have a better relationship with their brand than the commodity approach that some automakers employ: making sales through incentives and then providing no after-sales contact.

The next hot brand might be Volkswagen. In this era where corporate responsibility is more valuable, Volkswagen's creation of a workers' charter in June 2002 could be a useful means of communicating what the company stands for. Volkswagen said that, under the charter, all 320,000 employees would have the same social rights. Therefore, a VW worker in Mexico and one in Germany would have the same rights. While presently the company is in need of new models, focusing on the charter may not only give employees a reason to rally around the brand, but create new meaning for customers when purchasing their cars. Customers might feel empowered because they are doing their bit for workers' rights.

Positive empowerment might even include having workers own a share of equity in the brands they build. What made many of the 1990s dotcoms exciting places to work at was the chance to possess just that. Simon Anholt, in his book *Brand New Justice: The upside of global branding* (2003), gives one example of the Wild Coffee Project. The brand is marketed in the United States and elsewhere, and its income funds community development and conservation programmes in the Kibale National Park in Uganda, from where the coffee comes. 'The point about the Wild Coffee Project', wrote Anholt, 'is not primarily to sell wild coffee, but to manage the natural ecosystem by encouraging the harvesting of wild coffee only within scientifically derived controls and limits, and to save wild coffee through a cause-related brand' (2003: 158).

8. Brands create community

The Saturn case leads nicely into what Gen Yers do seek and are used to getting through the Web – but they are not alone. People can find validation for their choices in groups. Knowing they are part of a community, as opposed to a customer list, is the final duty of brands under the manifesto.

Brands are not created by a handful of bosses, but by everyone in a system. The allure of the Napster brand – if we could overlook the legalities for a moment – was its ability to create a community of users, all of whom were interested in sharing their tastes. It has become the archetypal brand for file-sharing services, even if it no longer operates in its original form. Seventy million people were drawn to Napster on the strength of what its brand represented and what it ultimately delivered. It's the same community that Corriero and Furdyk have created at TakingITGlobal.

Swedish management consultant Stefan Engeseth wrote:

> Some companies have more customers than the population of small countries. Letting the customer into the company is a way of utilizing this power. In a changing world, where both literal and figurative borders are constantly changing, a new world order is slowly taking form... Today, customers sometimes know more than the company representatives that serve them. Why not use this know-how and enthusiasm to teach employees to follow rather than lead[?]
>
> (Engeseth, 2001: 82)

The principle behind this is that it is all right for a company to be more transparent and to give up some of its power, so that consumers can provide feedback and new-product ideas. This creates affinity and a stronger bond with them – particularly if the organization has useful feedback loops and is willing to credit those consumers.

It is not dissimilar to how a government might work. In the ideal democracy, citizens may create referenda or use their representatives to propose ideas for new laws. Parliaments then pass them. Companies are beginning to adopt some of the same ideas as their 'customer bases' become their 'communities' – especially when the communities are becoming as fascinated about the organization and its leaders as they are, if not more so, about certain countries and their cabinets.[6]

These arguments can be taken further. If commercial organizations are taking on the trappings of political ones, while countries now talk of nation branding, then it may be the brand's duty to cover some of the ground left by retreating state institutions. If we do not take things that far, brands do have a duty to educate and reinforce positive behaviours.

One example could be that a brand being manufactured in Third World countries could charge a small premium and use that money to help educate its workers and their children. Countless more were proposed by Anholt in his book, as he seeks to use branding principles to advance more equitable wealth distribution. He cites Paul Weatherly's Shared Equity model, of which the Wild Coffee Project is an example, where farmers or other commodity producers own a share of equity in the brands that market their commodities. He further and rightly believes that ethical purpose and corporate self-interest can be reconciled: for example, Hewlett-Packard is working with governments and NGOs to improve access to water, food and other necessities – because this will ultimately lead to improved lives that create consumers for its products (Anholt, 2003: 160–01).

This is as good as any example on which to conclude this chapter. Following the eight points should guarantee a safe position for the brands of tomorrow. As Gen Yers seek responsible brands, companies can tell themselves – especially those trapped in the cycle of maximizing share-holder returns – that it can be for long-term self-interest. As was pointed out earlier, the largest, most influential market of tomorrow is more fickle, less brand loyal and harder to fool than previous generations.

There's every sign that the generation after – currently termed by marketers as 'tweens' – continues the trend. Martin Lindstrom, author of Brandchild (2003), which looked at the 8- to 14-year-old market, said in an interview:

Tweens don't complain of 'information overload'... they can see instantly if the advertisers are being less than honest. So brands today and in the future must be true to their promises. This has enormous implications for the marketing community – many brands are shallow and cosmetic. If tweens don't have confidence in a brand, they won't buy it. And they're very unforgiving. If a brand fails to come up to expectations, they'll drop it. If they're kept waiting at a call centre, they'll call off and boycott the brand. They're the most critical customers we have ever seen.

Research shows that, for example, more than half of this age group say they will not support brands that are not environmentally friendly – a healthy sign which indicates their exposure to so many brands has not been all negative. These attitudes are promoting improvements in products and services. To satisfy kids' demanding requirements, brands will have to be interactive 24 hours a day, 7 days a week so that companies can respond instantly to calls demonstrating their commitment to the consumer. If marketeers fail to communicate adequately with and respond to tweens, they will pay the price. A quarter of all kids communicate internationally every week via the Internet, so a rumour of a brand failing to deliver will spread like wildfire.

(Powell, 2003)

The activist brand is something companies need to build today. From an early 21st-century perspective, the brand manifesto makes understanding the components of the brand of the future easier.

It is more than that, however. All organizations – indeed, all gatherings of people – can be regarded as catalysts for individuals achieving their greatest goals. Further, they can be regarded as a mirror or validation for those individuals on the premise that like attracts like. Since tomorrow's consumers are unlike today's – or, rather, they are a sophisticated evolution of today's – then organizations need to reinvent themselves so that they can attract what will be the largest and most influential group: the ethical, socially aware, information-rich Gen Yer. Doing so requires plenty of attention on the brand: understanding and forming a true vision, expressing it accurately and living every ethical promise it makes.

REFERENCES

Ananova (2002) Judge apologises for accessing porn on work computer, 17 February, http://www.ananova.com/news/story/sm_523188.html?menu=news.quirkies

Anholt, S (2003) *Brand New Justice: The upside of global branding*, Butterworth-Heinemann, Oxford

Baker, M and Sterenberg, G (2003) Global brands at the crossroads, *Research International*, 14 January, http://www.research-int.com/library/library.asp?id=324

Brady, D (2002) Rethinking the rat race, *Business Week*, 26 August, pp 88–89

Brooks, D (2001) The organization kid, *Atlantic Monthly*, **287** (4), April, pp 40–54, at p 49

Byrne, JA (2002) After Enron: the ideal corporation, *Business Week*, 19 August, pp 40–43

Chitnis, A (2002) What's wrong with Yahoo?, Atulchitnis.net, diary entry, 9 September, http://atulchitnis.net/diary/showentry/111

Dau, R and Thirkell, P (1996) The relationship between marketing orientation and export performance: further empirical evidence, *Proceedings of the 1996 Australia–New Zealand Marketing Educators' Conference*, Wellington

Engeseth, S (2001) *Detective Marketing: Creating common sense in business*, Stefan Engeseth Publishing, Stockholm

Engeseth, S (2003) Saab needs to go outside the car box, *CAP Online*, 24 January, http://www.jyanet.com/cap/2003/0124fe0.shtml

Feuerstein, A (2002) Martha Stewart's image, share price hammered, TheStreet.com, 12 June, http://www.thestreet.com/tech/adamfeuerstein/10026875.html

Gad, Thomas *et al* (2002) The brand manifesto, *CAP Online*, 9 September, http://www.jyanet.com/cap/2002/0909fe0.shtml

Iacocca, L and Novak, W (1984) *Iacocca: An autobiography*, Bantam Books, New York

Ind, N (2001) *Living the Brand*, Kogan Page, London

Johnson, R (2001) Mazda got discipline, but lost its passion, *Automotive News Europe*, 16 July, http://europe.autonews.com/article.cms?articleId=41918

Kelly, M (2001) *The Divine Right of Capital: Dethroning the corporate aristocracy*, pp 22–26, Berrett-Koehler, San Francisco

Khermouch, G (2002) Didja C that kewl ad?, *Business Week*, 26 August, pp 100–01

King, R (2002) Is Yahoo!'s CEO the right guy for the job?, *Business 2.0*, October, http://www.business2.com/articles/mag/0,1640,43535,00.html

Lewis, M (2001) *Next: The future just happened*, WW Norton, New York

Lindstrom, M (2003) *Brandchild: Remarkable insights into the minds of today's global kids and their relationships with brands*, Kogan Page, London

Macrae, Chris *et al* (2003) Editorial, *Journal of Brand Management*, **10** (4–5)

Mathews, R and Wacker, W (2002) *The Deviant's Advantage: How fringe ideas create mass markets*, Crown Business, New York

Miller, K Lowry (1999) How not to buy a car company, *Business Week*, 5 July

Ministry of Education (2001) *Composite News Bulletin*, November, Ministry of Education, Helsinki

Powell, S (2003) Spotlight on Martin Lindstrom, *Emerald Now*, 3 April, http://rudolfo.emeraldinsight.com/vl=3392562/cl=32/nw=1/rpsv/now/spot-light.htm

Rotherham, F (2001) The patriot, *Unlimited*, October, http://www.sharechat.co.nz/features/unlimited/article.php/a7d41adf

Waddock, S (2002) Fluff is not enough: managing responsibility for corporate citizenship, *Ethical Corporation*, February, http://www.ethicalcorp.com/NewsTemplate.asp?IDNum=178

Webster, K Kirby (2002) Martha Stewart: still living, MarketingProfs.com, 9 July, http://www.marketingprofs.com/2/kwebster4.asp

Yan, J (2000a) The business of identity, *CAP*, **4** (3), Spring, pp 4–10, 22

Yan, J (2000b) How John Towers can save Rover, *CAP Online*, 10 May, http://jyanet.com/cap/2000/0510ob0.shtml

Yan, J (2000c) The attitude of identity, *Desktop*, October, pp 26–31

Yan, J (2001) Online branding: an antipodean experience, in *Human Society and the Internet*, ed W Kim *et al*, pp 185–202, Springer, Berlin

Yan, J (2003a) Corporate responsibility and the brands of tomorrow, *Journal of Brand Management*, **10** (4–5)

Yan, J (2003b) The humanitarian designer, *Lucire*, 21 February, http://www.lucire.com/2003a/0221fe0.htm

NOTES

1 See American Academy of Pediatrics, Television and the family, http://www.aap.org/family/tv1.htm.

2 'Barbara Epstein, who teaches at the University of California at Santa Cruz, has studied the 1960s movements and attributes their loss of energy largely to "structural and ideological rigidities associated with insistence on consensus decision-making and reluctance to acknowledge the existence of leadership within the movement".' In J Hari (2002) Whatever happened to *No Logo?*, *New Statesman*, 11 November, pp 20–22, at p 22.

3 For information about the brand manifesto's authoring, see Rydergren, T (2002) Go logo! Brand-soldaterna slår tillbaka, *Résumé*, 34, 22 August, pp 22–23.

4 See http://www.kpmgmodels.co.nz/diverse/ann/gar/gar_02.html.

5 Consequently, today's Chrysler is planning cars based around Mercedes-Benz and Mitsubishi engineering, and will build 600,000 of a certain motor

that will also come out of Mitsubishi and Hyundai plants. R Kranz and M Connelly (2003) Chrysler alters product plans, *Automotive News*, 17 March.

6 Cf W Olins (1999) *Trading Identities: Why countries and companies are taking on each other's roles*, Foreign Policy Centre, London. It is a logical development of those that Olins spoke of, namely with companies and countries swapping places in people's minds.

Postscript

Malcolm Allan

AND NOW TO ACTION... CAN YOU GO BEYOND BRAND?

It's time for you to think about what you have read and its relevance to what you do, to your enterprise, your organization and the communities in which you live and work.

Now it's your turn to go beyond branding, to go beyond your current thinking and its constraints, to find value in the application of the thinking in the preceding chapters.

As stated in the Preface, this book has grown out of the frustration of a group of people who feel that for too long branding and branders have had a particularly narrow view of the world, one that is short-termist, shareholder focused, narcissistic and communications led. If, having read the book, you are in agreement with the contributing authors' analyses and conclusions, you can take action to further this cause. Some ideas on what you might do, a primer for action, are set out below. But before considering and deciding how you might further this cause, let's just draw together the many strands of thought contained in this book. They can be summarized under the three themes of:

▊ new models for the conduct of business beyond brand;
▊ valuing authenticity in belief and behaviour as the basis for business;
▊ putting true value into business, brands and places.

An encapsulation of the 'cause'

A conclusion of the authors' arguments is that if branding is to have continued relevance it needs to have a wider social and economic perspective beyond the needs of individual companies and their products and services. It needs to be based on trust, value, openness and integrity. It needs to meet and fulfil the needs, wants and aspirations of people and organizations. It needs to do what it says on its tin and be completely transparent about how it is achieved. To do so the businesses, organizations and governments that create and promote brands need to operate in a new way, based on transparency of operation, the creation of trust and authenticity of purpose and delivery.

NEW MODELS FOR THE CONDUCT OF BUSINESS BEYOND BRAND

The contributing authors argue for new models of business based on openness and transparency of operations, of honest declaration of values and for authentic responsibility for social, economic and environmental impact.

They see the need for business and organizations to become more agile, to learn to adapt culture and processes to the short-term fluctuations in the world, while sustaining a steady evolutionary purpose towards a clear and transparently declared set of objectives that take into account the needs of stakeholders and the world around them. They argue for the adaptability, sensitivity, fit and relevance of business and organizations, and for systemic collaboration that encapsulates the ability constantly to alter and develop the nature of organizations' interrelationships with stakeholders and the environment.

They believe that organizational agility is not confined to operations but also defines the brand's ability to adapt constantly the ways in which it delivers value to the changing needs of its stakeholders.

In summary, the continued existence of brands requires organizations to:

▌ create and construct shared mental models of how they should operate with all stakeholders: employees, suppliers, partners, investors, regulators and the media;

▌ create effective means of sensing change in their operating environments, workplaces, customers' workplaces, chosen markets, others' markets and the communities in which they live and work;

▌ promise stakeholders a product or service that really means something of value: something they have articulated a need, want or aspiration for, in a value-adding and wholly transparent way, and that indicates that the organization cares about customers and is passionate (and compassionate) about meeting their needs;

▌ ensure that the values that drive their brand are those that unite stakeholders and are relevant to their lives;

▌ create true value through transparent relationships with all stakeholders;

▌ have a human perspective on what they do and the way in which they operate so that it benefits employees and external stakeholders;

▌ recognize accountability not only to shareholders, but also to all audiences and to society as a whole;

▌ recognize that greater value will result from creating more and open and trusting relationships with stakeholders, and that transparent value exchange leads to more relevant marketing and branding through which they can play a positive, value-adding role in communities;

▌ incorporate into their brands this broader definition of stakeholders and adopt measurement systems that focus on benefiting them;

▌ recognize that the brand's value stands or falls on its ability to foster positive exchanges of value between all of its stakeholders;

▌ endeavour to find opportunities to account to the full array of stakeholders for what they do by constructing and introducing measures for intangible values that have been identified in this book;

▌ get closer to customers, and to influencers and decision makers, to build better relationships and respond to their expectations, needs, wants and aspirations;

▌ create new leadership teams that increase the transparency of business strategy and operating objectives;

▌ create a commonly shared purpose and objective in the enterprise, which can dramatically increase the likelihood of success in the development and delivery of response to change;

▌ accept that corporate governance issues will increasingly dominate agendas, with corporate and social responsibility objectives rapidly rising up the list.

A dizzying array of action or a clear list that you could begin to do something about now? Can you reconstruct or build your business in this way? Can you champion this approach in your business or organization? What, if anything, is stopping you doing so? What's to stop you thinking through the relevance of these actions to your enterprise but your own commitment to thought and contemplation? What's to stop you discussing the relevance to your enterprise but your own commitment to questioning how you currently operate? Go on, accept the challenge. Go beyond branding.

VALUING AUTHENTICITY IN BELIEF AND BEHAVIOUR AS THE BASIS FOR BUSINESS

The authors argue that authenticity needs to lie at the heart of what business and organizations do, their transactions with others, the value they add to people's lives and the ways in which they help meet their needs.

People want services and products they can rely on and that deliver what they promise. People also want to know that this is an authentic offer, that manufacturers or providers actually care about what they do and how they do it and that they do not abuse people or the environment in doing so. Similarly, the loyalty of employees can no longer be taken for granted. The most common reason why employees become negative and cynical about the way they are managed is because the business articulates one set of values and manages by a completely different set. So what is said and what is done are different. The business is not authentic, does not create trust and lacks transparency. Recognize it? Too close to home? Uncomfortable? What can you do about it?

The answer to the last question is a great deal.

When you put all of the ideas on authenticity in this book together (all of which you could take action on today), your business or organization needs to:

▌ be willing to speak the truth about what it does, makes or provides, and to behave in ways that are consistent with its beliefs;

▌ be honest about defects, instead of trying to live up to impossible ideals;

▌ base marketing and brand activity on real human needs, wants and aspiration, established through open conversations and value-adding relationships;

▮ recognize the difference between creating value for stakeholders and just making a profit in traditional accounting terms;

▮ encourage people to express themselves more freely: with that ability, you can work to challenge and adjust whatever bureaucratic or ideological framework happens to be in vogue, so that the organization remains responsive to the needs of its stakeholders;

▮ adopt or develop a style of operation that's based on facilitation rather than dictation, a style that relies on improving the quality of human contact to allow people to access more of their innate resources for connecting with stakeholders.

Is this too much to ask of people, business, organizations and government? Could you make a small personal start on the assault of the citadel of 'inauthenticity'? Why not start with yourself? Ask yourself what you truly believe in, what you really want to do: how you do things, how you treat others, how you provide services to your customers and what you truly think of them. How does this fit with your image of you, your brand, at a personal and corporate level? Now, what are you going to do about the realizations you have had and the conclusions you have reached? Going beyond branding cannot wait for others to take action. You need to take action yourself. Make the commitment. Go beyond brand.

In addition, if you lead a business or organization and you want its brand to be truly engaging, you will have to encourage and support your people and provide a creative and innovative environment in which they can release and unleash their potential. If that's not what your working environment feels like, ask yourself what is stopping you from creating it. Are the barriers in your mind or are they institutional? If you are the leader, then you may have the inner power as well as the institutional power to change things. Go on, go beyond brand.

Also, ask yourself what are the lessons you have learnt from this book that you can act upon without waiting. Who do you need to influence and what are the arguments you will use?

PUTTING TRUE VALUE INTO BUSINESS, BRANDS AND PLACES

The authors have demonstrated from a variety of standpoints that branding can really add value to people, business and the places they operate in and live in, providing that it is based on trust. Their arguments can be summed up as:

▌ When a business or organization manages its brand or brands in an open and transparent way it can balance stakeholder demands and meet or exceed expectations. In doing so, people benefit.

▌ True value is created when a brand offers people something worth their while and they are persuaded to provide something in return, eg their time, money, attention, allegiance, brainpower and so on.

▌ Value is thus an intangible substance made up of qualities like trust, reassurance, excitement, efficiency and so forth. Value creation is not the same thing as making money, but making money is often the result of creating value and a prerequisite for sustaining an organization's value-creation activities.

The authors also connect the arguments for creating new and more transparent models of business and the benefits of business based on authenticity with the conclusion that brand building is a vital technique for companies and governments to learn if they wish to use the forces of globalization to their advantage rather than remain perennially its victims, especially those in the developing world.

The beneficial effects of more open business models and transparent and responsible branding, which can create inclusive and effective communities of employees within companies, as well as inclusive communities within societies, are worth building on at the level of the nation as well. The key arguments are that:

▌ The knowledge of the process for creating open, transparent and value-adding brands can and should be transferred to less developed nations in order to improve the lives of their populations.

▌ If organizations in these countries apply brand thinking to their activities, they will be better able to provide their stakeholders with what they want.

▌ It is time for a positive initiative to help organizations – whether they are companies, governments, NGOs or community initiatives – to learn how to take advantage of the benefits of branding while staying fully aware of the ensuing responsibilities. This transfer of skills and knowledge should be aimed at improving the lives of the stakeholders of these organizations through value creation that is aimed at providing them with the means of emancipation.

▎ There are a number of ways in which branding skills and knowledge
can be transferred to less developed nations:
- sending branding and marketing experts to Third World and former
  communist countries as volunteers to aid local organizations in their
  brand-building and marketing activities;
- encouraging multinational companies to transfer their brand-
  building knowledge to local organizations;
- aiding national, regional or local governments to brand themselves
  by helping them to understand the strengths and weaknesses of
  their territories in terms of natural and human resources, and determining how best these can be applied to tourism, export branding,
  inward investment, foreign relations and representing culture.

If you care about the world that you live in, if you care about the way that
the business or organization that you run or work for operates, if you care
about the impact it has on the communities in which it operates, then you
need to go beyond branding as you have known it and take action to
correct the imbalances and imperfections that you observe. You cannot
just leave it to others. You and those like you need to take responsibility for
your beliefs and the realization that all is not right with the way business
operates and the way that brands can distort and create negative values.
You must decide. What, precisely, are *you* going to do?

Index